THE GOOD HOUSEKEEPING

NEEDLECRAFT

ENCYCLOPEDIA

THE   GOOD   HOUSEKEEPING

Needlecraft Encyclopedia

EDITED BY

Alice Carroll

DIRECTOR,
GOOD HOUSEKEEPING
NEEDLEWORK ROOM

STAMFORD   HOUSE

NEW YORK, NEW YORK

PREFACE

➤➤➤Tʜɪs book is for the beginner as well as for the experienced needle-woman. For the beginner it is a step by step picture-instruction book of every popular phase of needlecrafts. For the experienced woman it is a refresher course, with many suggested ideas for designing.

To Jean Sage, a very special note of gratitude is due for her coopera-tion; to Catherine Scholz of W. H. Lackie Company for clear-cut illustra-tions; to Hans Van Nes for the photographs taken at B. Altman Com-pany, New York; and to the following companies for their gracious assistance: The American Crayon Company, The American Thread Company, Emile Bernat and Sons Company, Donar Products, Singer Sewing Machine Company, The Spool Cotton Company and Stark Brothers Ribbon Company.

Alice Carroll

CONTENTS

CHAPTER 1

SIMPLE SEWING

SIMPLE SEWING

→>>Women will always be interested in needlework. From time immemorial women have done handiwork, first through necessity, then to express their love of the beautiful in exquisite stitchery, and now because education has given us an appreciation of beauty and art, combined with an eye for the practical.

As the artist must first sketch the outline of his subject in bold, simple lines before he can give expression to his canvas with fine strokes and shadings, so must the needlewoman learn the a, b, c's of sewing before she can undertake with assurance the more technical phase of tailoring.

A knowledge of plain sewing is essential before one can learn to master the more intricate stitches of simple and advanced embroidery; and indirectly, if not directly, for an intelligent and clever application of the principles of knitting, crocheting, weaving, etc.

It is most gratifying to design, but before one can play with stitches, needles, and threads, the professional-to-be must know and understand thoroughly a few elementary steps and the importance of a few indispensable tools to make the exploration of this old, yet ever-new field, both pleasant and profitable.

Instructions for Sewing Basket (Color Plate A, see pg. 14).

Design your own from color plate A

With a bit of ingenuity, you can design from a sewing basket.

A. ***From Side Front Piece of basket lining*** *(Ak, pg. 16)* ***make:***
1. Utility apron for gardening, sewing, knitting or housekeeping equipment (Aa).
   For example, cut fabric 26″ x 13″, making 4 pockets. Gather and join to a 2-inch band, desired length to tie a bow at center back.
2. Door-rack for slippers, socks, handkerchiefs, etc. Bind and tack to inside of closet door. Double length, if required.
3. Drawstring bag for sewing, knitting or shopping.
   Join 2 pieces for the lining of the bag. Join this lining to the outside fabric of the bag. One-half inch from the top, run 2 rows of stitching, one-half inch apart, for drawstring-casing.

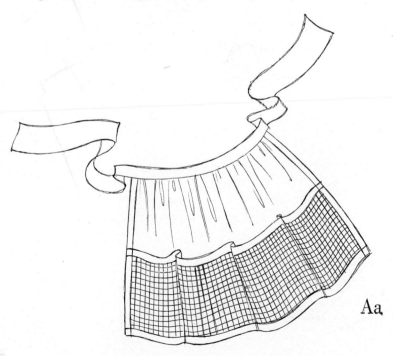

Aa

B. From Side Back Piece of basket lining (*Aj, pg. 16*) make:
   1. Handy-hubby apron, in which tools may be put in pockets (Ab).
   2. Silver, needlepoint, knitting or crochet roll (Ag).

C. From Quilted Top Piece of basket lining (*Al and Chapter 5*) make:
   1. Place Mats and Napkin (Ac).
   2. Clothes pin Bag (Ad).
   3. Potholders—Half all measurements (Ae).
   4. Pillow (Af and Chapter 13).

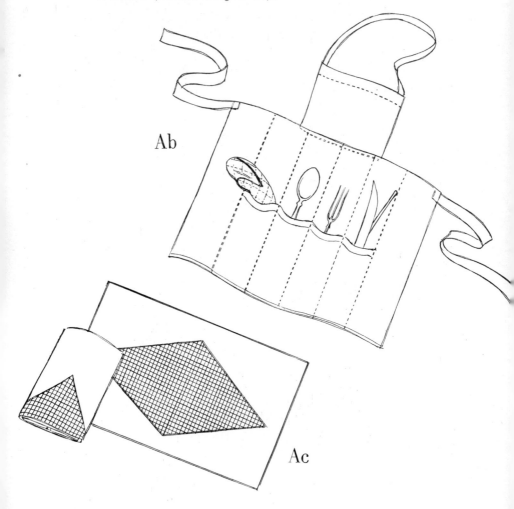

Ab

Ac

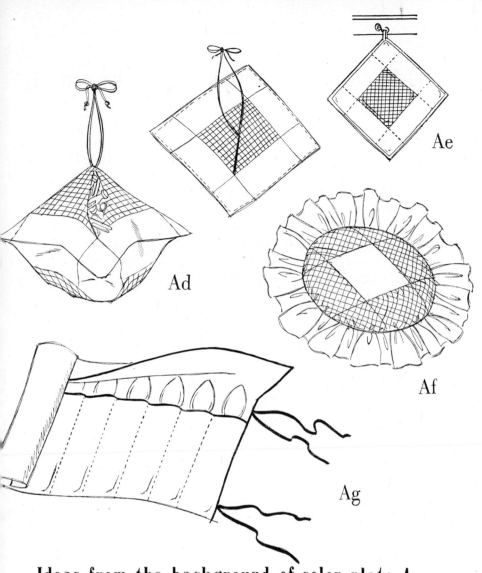

Ae

Ad

Af

Ag

Ideas from the background of color plate A

For helpful hints, turn the pages.
1. For instructions on ruffles and flounces (pgs. 32 and 33), as shown in curtains and pillow (Chapter 13).
2. Instructions for braided rugs may be found in Chapter 11.
3. Instructions for socks (Chapter 6, pg. 227).

13

Instructions for sewing basket (color plate A)

Materials Required For Sewing Basket 19½" x 12" x 12":
2½ yards 36" cotton fabric; ½ yard cotton batting; 1 spool of sewing cotton; 7" diamond of felt.

1. For cutting instructions, follow layout chart (Ah).
2. Seam allowance ½". Each square equals 1 inch.
3. Turn and stitch ½" hem on all pocket pieces.
4. Place pocket piece H on end piece A, two inches from top edge (Ai). Pin and baste along sides, lower edge and center of pocket piece H. Stitch across lower edge. Make two rows of stitching ½" apart through the center (Ai).
5. Place pocket piece I on end piece A, one inch from bottom edge. Join as explained for pocket piece H (Step 4).
6. Join pocket pieces J and K to end-piece B in same manner as pocket pieces H and I (Steps 4 and 5).
7. Cut a 20" strip; lay across side back-piece C, 4" from top edge and stitch at each end. Double stitch at 2" intervals to form holders for scissors, darner, etc. (Aj)
8. Using pocket-piece L, fold three 1" inverted pleats (A 60) at 3" intervals and one side pleat (A 58a) at each end. Place pleated piece 2" from top edge of side front piece D. Pin and baste along sides and lower edge. Double stitch through center of each pleat (Ak).
9. Place pocket piece M on side front piece D, 1" from bottom edge. Make one inverted pleat (A 60) at center and one side pleat (A 58a) at each end. Join in same manner as pocket piece L (Step 8).
10. Pin, baste and stitch in proper order A to C, to B, to D, and D to A.
11. Join bias strips (A 67 a and b). Fold 2" bias strip twice, forming a ½" strip. Stitch to upper edge of basket lining and join ends.
12. Join bottom piece G to completed piece.
13. Place lining in basket. Staple or use upholstery tacks to fasten to basket.
14. Cut cotton batting same size as top E. Place cotton batting between top E and top F. Forming a 6½" diamond at center (Al), quilt as explained in Chapter 5 (pg. 141).

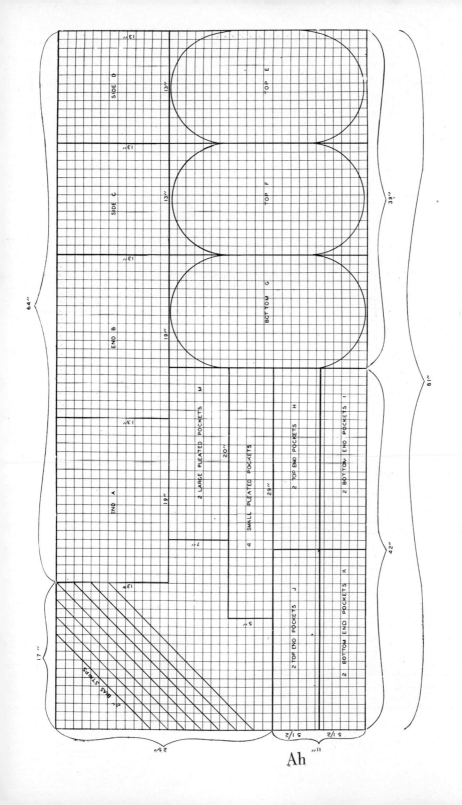

Ah

15. Cut a 61″ bias strip. Pin, baste and stitch folded bias to top F and E.
16. Appliqué 7″ felt diamond over 6½″ quilted diamond, leaving an opening at one end. Pad as shown in E 8c.
17. Cut two strips 20″ x 2″. Stitch. Insert one strip between lining and staple to basket. Leaving sufficient length for desired opening, draw through slot of cover from inside; bring diagonally across basket cover to slot on opposite side. Insert at this point between lining and basket-cover; staple to basket cover. Join second strip in same manner on opposite side.

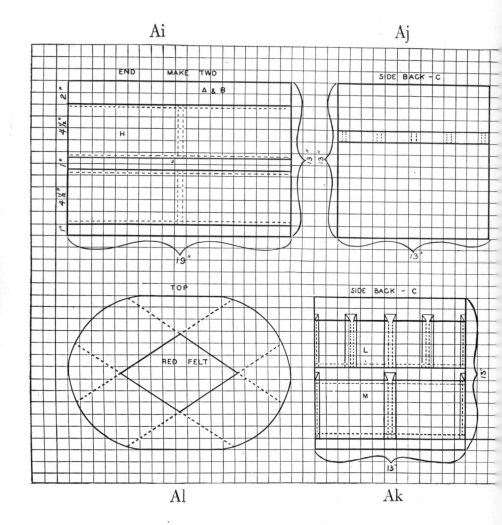

Ai   Aj

Al   Ak

The equipment you need

Needles: The kind and size to use depend on the weight of the fabric and the type of sewing being done. Never sew with a crooked needle as it makes ugly and irregular stitches. The needle should always be a little thicker than the thread in order to make an easy opening in the material for the thread. Hold the needle between the thumb and the forefinger so that the eye is near the thimble finger and the point is poised in the direction of the work.

Thimble: A thimble is a "must," and is usually worn on the middle finger of the right hand. Always be certain that the small round grooves or millings are deep enough to hold the needle and that they extend down the sides.

Scissors: Scissors are another important accessory. There should be two pairs in every work-basket, a pair of large ones for cutting out, with a rounded and a sharp point (the latter to be placed above the material while cutting) and a small pair for cutting threads and removing excess materials.

Thread: Sewing and embroidery thread should be selected according to the use you plan to make of it. Except for tacking, a needleful of thread should never be more than 18 inches long. When threading a needle, always pass the end broken from the reel, through the eye as the other end is more apt to unravel. It is preferable not to make knots and for the ends to be concealed in the stitches on the wrong side of the work.

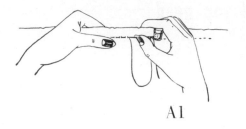

A1

Position of the Hands: In simple sewing, grasp work with left hand with thumb on top and use the left thumb and forefinger as a guide. (A 1). One may also hold the material between the thumb and forefinger, allowing the material to fall easily over the other fingers. If the material needs to be slightly stretched, hold it between the third and fourth fingers to prevent the work from becoming puckered or dragged. For embroidery, use a frame or hoop whenever possible.

Stitches

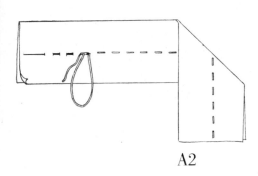

A2

Running Stitch: This is the first and simplest stitch made by passing the needle in and out of the material in an horizontal line; usually several stitches are taken on the needle before it is pulled through (A 2).

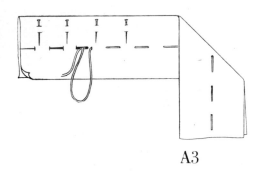

A3

Even Basting: The process by which ½-inch long running stitches are used to hold two pieces of cloth together while they are permanently sewed (A 3). Always pin before basting.

Uneven Basting: A long stitch followed by a short stitch so that both stitches are taken on the needle at once (A 4). This stitch is used in seams where there is no strain or as a guide line for stitching.

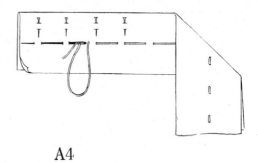

A4

Diagonal Basting: Used for holding together two or more thicknesses of material. This is a slant stitch on the top side of the material and a straight up-and-down stitch on the under thickness (A 5).

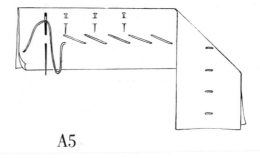

A5

Slip Basting: Used in matching stripes or plaids or when the fitting is done on the right side. Take the right side of one piece, fold under the indicated allowance and still keeping the stripes exactly in line, slip needle along in fold of upper layer, draw it through and then take the short stitch in under layer (A 6).

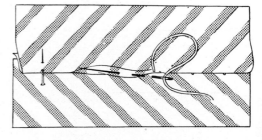

A6

19

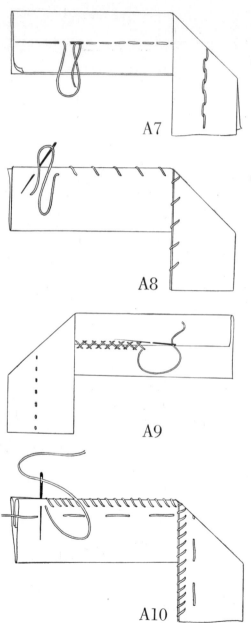

Back-Stitch: Take a small running stitch, pass needle back over running stitch to wrong side and over twice as much space as original stitch; bring needle to right side and down to wrong side at end of running stitch (A 7). Repeat.

A7

Overcast Stitch: Trim edges and make diagonal stitches over raw edges (A 8). Always keep the stitches twice as far apart as they are deep and never draw stitches tightly.

A8

Catch-Stitch: Fold raw edge over. Working from left to right, take a tiny stitch in the hem or seam and then in the material with the needle pointing to the left (A 9). Repeat, keeping an even slant between stitches.

A9

Overhand: Fold edges of material; and baste together. With needle at right angles to fabric edge, slant stitches on wrong side and take straight stitches on right side (A 10).

A10

20

Hemming or felling

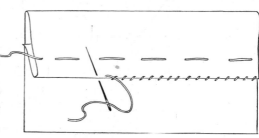

Hemming or Felling: Fold edges and baste. Conceal thread under fold. Using a small slanting stitch, take up a thread or two in the cloth and in the fold (A 11).

A11

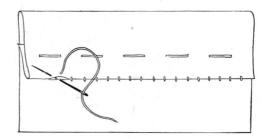

Vertical Hemming: The stitch is taken perpendicularly (A 12).

A12

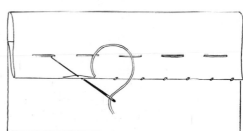

Blind Hemming: Take up a thread on under side, then a few threads in the fold (A 13). The stitches should not show on right side of work.

A13

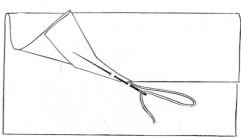

Slip-Stitch: Using a running stitch about ¼ inch long, take only a portion of the thread in the cloth and a few threads in the fold to make the sewing invisible on both sides of the work (A 14).

A14

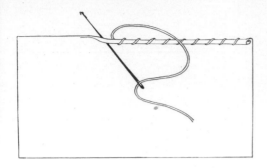

A15

Whipping: With wrong side facing, turn edge slightly and roll only an inch or two at a time. Use the plain hemming or overcast stitch, passing the needle under the roll and not through it (A 15).

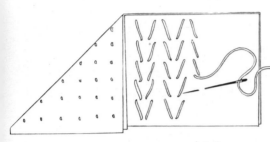

A16

Padding Stitch: Take a long diagonal stitch on the inside and a short stitch barely catching the fabric on the outside (A 16). Do not pull the stitches tightly. This stitch is used to hold a second piece of material in place.

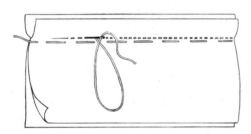

A17

Seams

Plain Seam: With the edges even, place right sides of two pieces of material together and baste. Join by a simple running stitch or by machine (A 17). Press seams open or turn seams to one side of stitching.

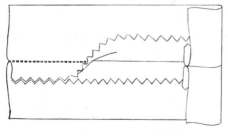

A18

Pinked Seam: Before pressing, pink edges by snipping small pointed pieces with cutting shears, pinking shears or with pinking attachment for the sewing machine (A 18).

Overcast Seam: Stitch and press the seam open, then overcast each side (A 19). Always work from right to left and do not draw the stitches tightly. This is a very durable seam for medium-weight fabrics.

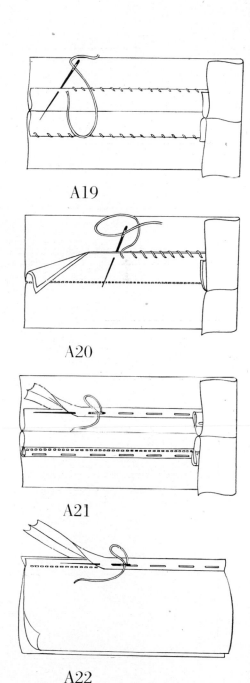

A19

Double or Closed Overcast Seam: Overcast the seam edges together and then press to one side. (A 20).

A20

Bound Seam: Stitch and press open seams; then bind each edge with bias binding and baste. Stitch on the inside of your basting (A 21). This seam is used for unlined garments.

A21

Double-Bound Seam: Insert seam edges in binding, baste and stitch (A 22).

A22

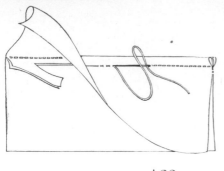

French Seam: A seam within a seam. Make a plain seam half the depth of seam allowance on outside of garment. Trim close to stitching. Turn and make a second seam deep enough to take up remainder of seam allowance and to cover raw edges on inside (A 23). Press on inside.

A23

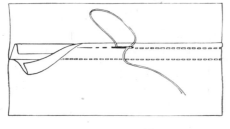

A24

Simulated French Seam: Make a plain seam; turn edges in toward each other, then stitch edges together (A 24).

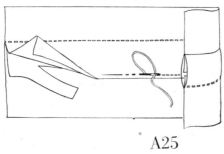

A25

French or Flat Fell Seam: Make plain seam; trim one side to within ⅛ inch from stitching; fold other edge over to line of stitching. Topstitch close to turned edge (A 25). This seam is sometimes called a false French seam.

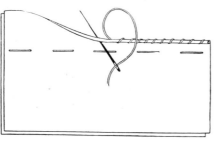

A26

Rolled Seam: Roll edges together very carefully to avoid "puckers;" hem while rolling, putting the needle under the rolled edges when hemming (A 26).

Welt Seam: Make plain seam. Trim under side of seam narrower than top side to reduce thickness. Fold, then baste wider seam over narrower seam. Stitch on outside about ¼ inch from seam line. The broader seam may be left unfolded and overcast (A 27).

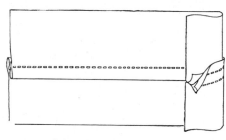

A27

Curved Seams: Edges should be clipped and raw edges overcast or pinked, then pressed open or together. Where one edge is slightly longer than the other, as at the top of the sleeve, the longer edge must be eased in. Hold the side to be eased toward you, pin at frequent intervals. Baste, then stitch (A 28).

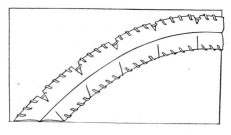

A28

Crossed Seams: Stitch and press first seam. Stitch second seam which crosses first seam. Trim first seams at corners to reduce thickness and press. Overcast each edge (A 29).

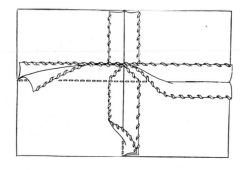

Decorative seams

A29

Piped and Corded Seams: Baste bias strip or cording in place on seam line. To make a cording (A 30a), cover cable cord with bias strips.

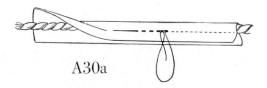

A30a

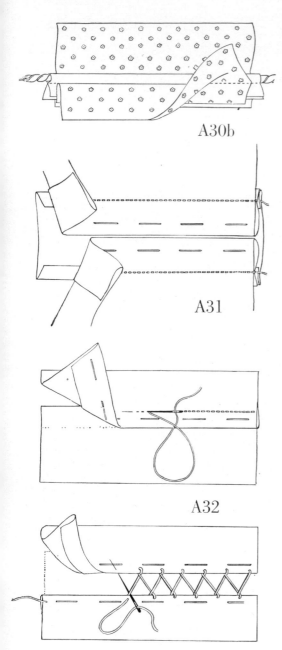

A30b

Apply the second piece of material as for a regular seam. Using basting line as a guide, stitch very closely and firmly (A 30b). To reenforce, as well as to make a tailored finish, add a line of stitching on the right side, close to the edge.

A31

Slot Seam: Cut a straight strip of fabric equal in length to the seam. The width must include both the seam allowance and whatever amount of fabric you wish to show, if any. Run basting down center of strip. Turn under seam allowance on both sides of seams and on strip. Baste and stitch to strip, allowing ¼ to ½ inch of contrasting fabric to show. Stitch firmly any desired distance from folded edges (A 31). Remove bastings. The folded edges of the fabric may be made to touch when not using a contrasting fabric.

A32

Tucked or Lapped Seam: A top-sewn seam used for yokes, parts of sleeves and panels in skirts. When basting, keep folded edge of upper piece for tuck directly on marked line of under piece (A 32). Stitch desired distance from edge of seam.

Fagoted Seam: Fold back the edges of the seams about ¼ of the distance the edges are to be apart when finished. Baste to strips of

A33

paper and fagot them (see embroidery stitches) or use the fagoter attachment for the machine (A 33).

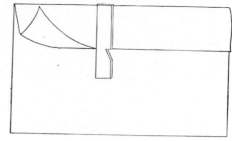

A34a

Hems

Hem: This is the finish of a piece and should be uniform in depth. The first step in making a hem is to mark it evenly with a ruler or a cardboard gauge with a notch. The straight edge of notch will indicate the depth of hem (A 34a). Trim hem evenly and proceed with a suitable finish. If a hemming attachment is used on the machine, the fabric is turned and stitched in one operation (A 34b).

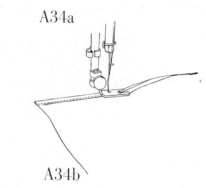

A34b

Slip-Stitched Hem: Turn under and baste hem in place. Slip the needle through the edge of the hem. Pick up several threads of the fabric and slip the needle back in and along the edge of the hem, thus making an invisible stitch (A 35). Do not pull the stitches tightly. Take a backstitch in the edge of the hem every few inches.

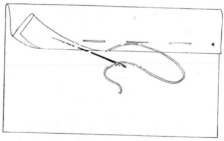

A35

Catch-Stitched Hem: Fold hem over and catch-stitch (A 9). It is used to hold in place the hems of fabrics which do not fray (A 36).

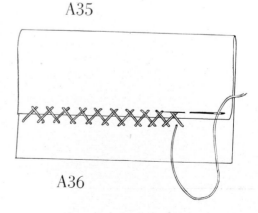

A36

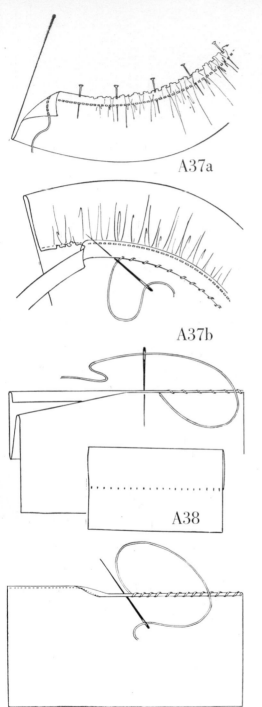

Circular Hem: Mark hem in usual manner, gather the edge by using a running stitch or a long stitch on the machine (A 37a).

A37a

Draw up gathers to fit and fasten thread. Stitch bias binding over gathers and sew hem in place. (A 37b).

A37b

Damask or Napery Hem: Fold a narrow hem; turn it to the wrong side of fabric. Overhand the two folds. (A 38). Open the hem and press flat. As the name implies, it is used for table linens, napkins, towels, etc.

A38

Rolled and Whipped Hem: Overcast or machine-stitch close to cut edge to keep edges from stretching. Roll hem toward you a little at a time and catch roll in place with slipping or whipping stitches. (A 39).

A39

Shell Hem: Fold hem and baste. Make running stitches on edge of hem, then at equal intervals take two stitches over edge, drawing thread tightly. Slip needle under hem to next point. Repeat two stitches (A 40). Remove basting.

Hems with Corners: See page 47.

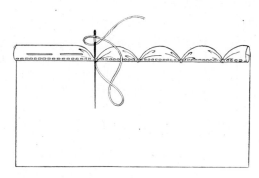

A40

Tucks

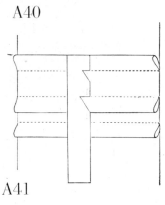

A41

Tucks: Folds used in various sizes and combinations to hold fullness in place or for decorative purposes. Tucks may be made in lengthwise, crosswise, bias or curved lines and sewed by machine or by hand with a running stitch. Mark with a cardboard gauge having both the width of the tuck and space between indicated by notches (A 41).

Parallel Tucks: Tucks made easily and accurately in parallel lines by hand or with the machine tucker (A 42).

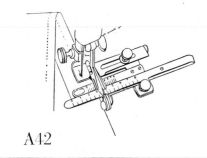

A42

Pin Tucks: Mark the lines for tucking by creasing or pressing. Taking only a thread or two for depth of each tuck, stitch close to crease (A 43).

A43

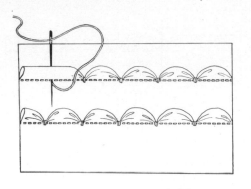

Shell or Scalloped Tucks: After creasing the tuck, mark equal distances for shell or scallop. Sew tucks with tiny running stitches (A 44). Finish in same manner as for a shell hem (A 40). The length of the shell or scallop is usually twice the depth of the tuck itself.

A44

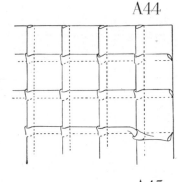

Cross Tucks: Measure and make all tucks running in one direction. Then measure and make identical tucks crossing the first set at right angles (A 45).

A45

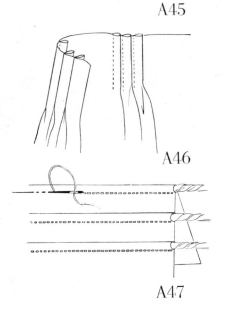

Cluster Tucks: Arrange tucks in groups as desired (A 46).

A46

Corded Tucks: Measure for tucks. Encase cord at the line of marking and stitch on right side close to the cord (A 47). In machine stitching use the cording foot.

A47

Trimming Tucks: Mark placement of tucks. Taking just a few
threads of fabric with each stitch,
overhand along marked line (A 48).

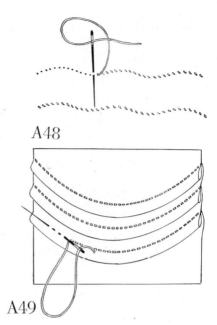

A48

Circular Tucks: Mark as usual.
When stitching, be sure to pull in
the under or broader part of the
material (A 49).

Gathering and shirring

A49

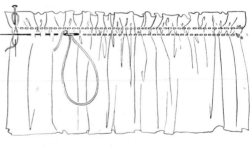

Gathering: The drawing together
of extra material. For hand-gather-
ing, knot the thread, draw thread up
from wrong side and reenforce with
backstitches. Take short, even running stitches, pushing material off
needle as it becomes full. If a great
amount of material is to be gathered
into a small space, take a long stitch
on right side and a short stitch on
wrong side. Draw fullness up to desired size and wind excess thread
over pin (A 50). Secure with small
overhand stitches or cut a piece of
material required size, turn under
raw edge and hem against gathers
on wrong side (A 51).

A50

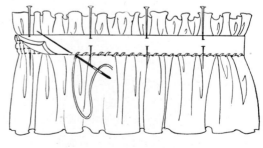

A51

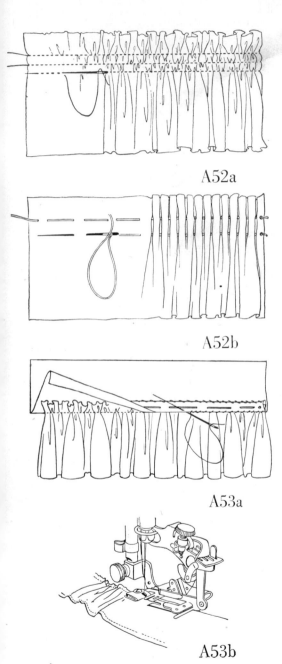

Machine-Gathering: If the regular presser foot is used, loosen the tension and lengthen the stitch. Fasten threads at one end and draw up under thread. If the gathering foot is used, use a long stitch and a tight tension. To increase the fullness, lengthen the stitch.

A52a

A52b

Shirring: Parallel rows of gathering where the stitches on each row must be directly in line with the stitches on the row above (A 52a and b). The gathering foot attachment shirrs as you sew on the machine. In shirring, always reenforce with a stay piece as explained for gathers.

A53a

Ruffles and flounces

Ruffles and flounces may be shallow or deep, full or scant, straight or circular, gathered or pleated, and attached in various ways. Finish lower edge of flounce, baste, then stitch in place. Bias binding may be used to finish edge. Ruffles may be joined to a hem (A 53a) or to a collar, set

A53b

under a tuck or in a seam, or may be hemstitched to a garment. The ruffler attachment makes ruffles of any desired fullness; and by a simple adjustment the ruffles may be changed into small pleats (A 53b).

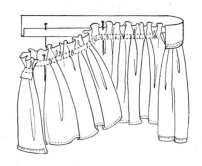

A54

Ruffle or Flounce with Gathered Heading: Turn edge the width for desired heading, plus seam allowance. Make two rows of gathers. Baste flounce or ruffle to position, spacing all gathers evenly (A 54). Then, stitch in place.

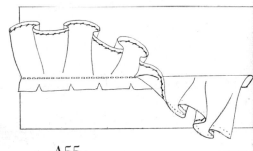

A55

Circular Ruffle: Finish lower edge of ruffle first. Mark placement of ruffle on garment. With right sides together, baste and stitch ruffle in place (A 55).

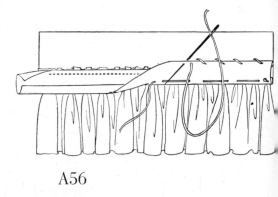

Ruffle with Bias Strip: Baste gathered edge of ruffle between right side of fabric and bias. Stitch, trim, then turn bias over these edges and hem to material (A 56).

A56

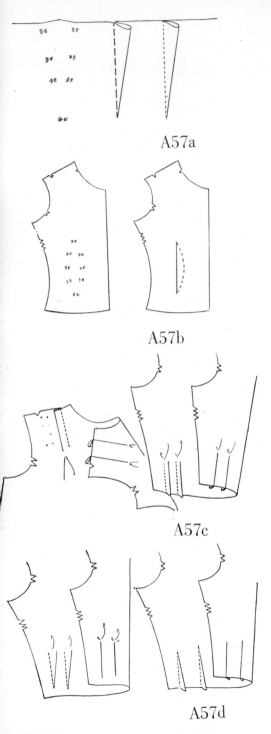

A57a

A57b

A57c

A57d

Darts

Darts: Used to direct fullness to the proper parts of the figure, to form effects holding fullness where needed, and to lend design interest. To make darts, mark placement of dart, baste and then stitch, graduating to nothing at point. Finish dart with a square knot (E 7b and c). If dart is over ⅜ inch in depth, slash through dart, trim and press open unless other directions are specified. A 57a shows how to make a graded shoulder or under arm dart; A 57b, the graded waistline dart for a blouse or jacket; A 57c, the straight dart or tuck for shoulder or waistline; and A 57d, two versions of the graded waistline dart or tuck.

Pleats

Pleats: Equal amounts of fabric held in folds to give fullness to certain parts of the article. To assure a pleat hanging straight, always stitch from the bottom up. To prevent strain from opening stitches, tie thread ends securely on wrong side, using a square knot (E 7b and c).

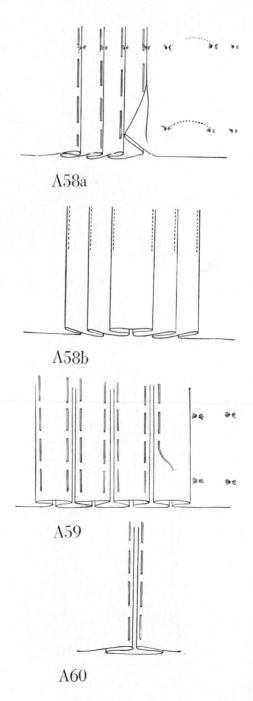

A58a

A58b

A59

A60

Side Pleats: Groups of single pleats turning in one direction. Match marked lines, baste and stitch close to edge on right side (A 58a and b). This is the basic pleat from which a variety of pleats is formed.

Box Pleat: Formed by two side pleats turned in opposite directions (A 59).

Inverted Pleats: The same in appearance as the wrong side of a box pleat. They are box pleats in reverse (A 60).

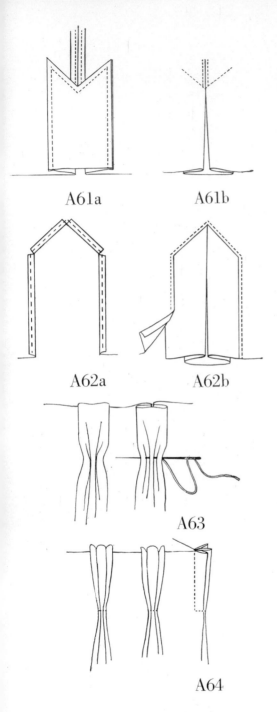

A61a   A61b

A62a   A62b

A63

A64

Set-in Inverted Pleat at Seam:
Stitch seam above pleat and press
open. Stitch underlay to pleated
section (A 61a). Top-stitch seam
and across top of underlay (A 61b).

Set-in Inverted Box Pleat: Clip
corners and press seam edges. Place
pleated section in opening. Baste
(A 62a). Top-stitch close to edges
(A 62b).

Note: The following pleats are used
mainly for curtains and draperies
and are usually reenforced on wrong
side with buckram.

French Pleats: Make a large box
pleat, then at lower edge of heading,
divide this large pleat into three
smaller pleats. Run needle through
three pleats, draw up thread and
fasten securely (A 63).

Pinch Pleat: Make a large pleat.
Evenly divide pleat into three small
pleats and press firmly. Stitch across
lower edge of heading and along side
to top edge (A 64).

Cartridge Pleats: Merely small
round pleats left loose and filled

with a roll of cotton or heavy cord (A 65).

Pipe Organ Pleats: Enlarged cartridge pleats which can be filled with self material rolled and inserted, or a large roll of cotton (A 66).

Binding

To cut a True Bias: Fold the material so the warp (lengthwise) threads are parallel to the woof (crosswise) threads (A 67a), then cut through the diagonal fold. Measure the depth needed for the strips from this fold and cut as many strips as desired. Bias edges are always at right angles to each other. In joining strips, lay the two diagonal ends together, right sides together and stitch (A 67b). Press and trim extended corners.

Single Binding: Cut bias strips twice the width of the finished binding plus seam allowance. Stretch bias strips slightly while pinning it to material. With right sides together, stitch along edge of right side, turn binding over the seam to wrong side, turn raw edges under and hem (A 68).

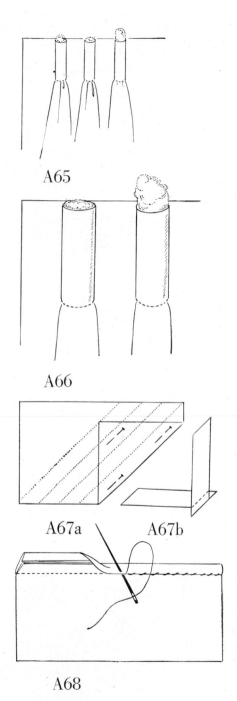

A65

A66

A67a   A67b

A68

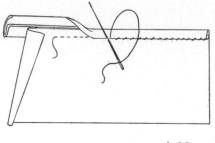

A69

Double Binding: Cut strips six times the finished width, fold binding through the center with the right side out and press lightly. Pin to fabric without stitching; baste and stitch. Turn binding over seam to wrong side and whip by hand or hem folded edge along machine-stitching (A 69).

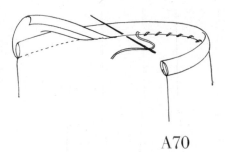

A70

False Binding: About 1½ inches from edge, make a tuck on the inside; bring edge over the tuck, fold in seam and slip-stitch on wrong side (A 70).

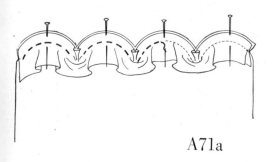

A71a

Binding Scallops: With right sides together, ease the binding slightly along curved edge and stretch tightly at the corner as you pin. Baste, stitch along edge and

A71b

trim (A 71a). Remove basting, turn binding over edge to wrong side. Mitre binding at corners as you hem folded edge on wrong side (A 71b).

Binding Corners: With right sides together, stretch bias at corner as you pin (A 72a and c). Remove basting. Turn binding over edge to wrong side. Mitre corner as you hem folded edge on wrong side. Always hem along machine or first stitching (A 72b and d). When turning a corner in machine-stitching, keep the needle in the fabric, raise the presser footer, turn corner, then continue stitching.

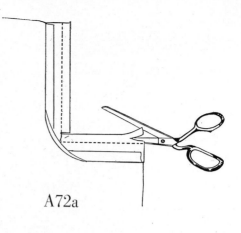

A72a

Corners: See Chapter 2, pg 47

Cordings, Fringe, Tassels, etc; See Chapter 14, pg 443

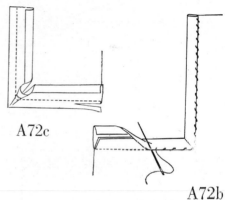

A72c

A72b

Piping

Pipings and Cordings: Cut bias strips and join (A 67). For corded pipings, cut and join bias strips. Then cover cord, allowing for seams. Baste and stitch close to cord. The sewing machine binder attachment holds the binding so that it does not have to be basted. One row of stitching will do (A 73).

A72d

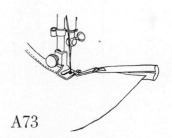

A73

39

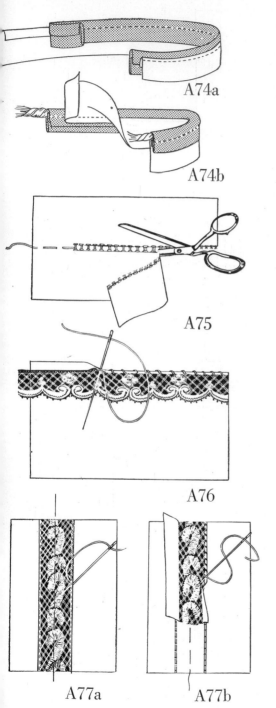

A74a

A74b

A75

A76

A77a

A77b

Piping and Facing in One or Edge-Stitched Piping: Fold bias strip making the turn on the lower side twice as deep as the upper fold. Turn in edge of garment. With wrong side of fabric facing folded edges of the piping, baste piping so that it extends beyond the edge. Stitch in place, then slip-stitch lower edge (A 74a). For a corded piping, first encase cord in bias strips, then follow above instructions (A 74b).

Edgings and laces

Picot Edge: Mark the line of hem-stitching with self color; hemstitch and cut directly through hemstitch-ing (A 75). In machine-stitching, the hemstitching attachment is a great time-saver.

Lace Edge: Using very fine thread and with right sides facing, over-hand very closely (A 76). In ma-chine-stitching, the zigzagger at-tachment simulates the hand-stitch-ing in applying lace appliqué, monogramming and many decora-tive stitches.

Lace Insertion: Baste insertion through center to material; hem with fine stitches on right side (A 77a). Leaving a very narrow edge, trim on wrong side, roll and whip carefully (A 77b).

Joining Lace: Match design perfectly; join with hemming stitch interspersed with buttonhole stitch. Trim on both sides (A 78).

To Gather Lace: Whip over edge with fine thread and long stitches, then draw up whipping thread. If thread of lace is loose, draw up thread in lace to gather (A 79).

To join Lace and Entre-deux: Since both edges are finished, simply overhand with fine thread (A 80).

Gathered Lace at Corner: When lace edge is joined to fabric, draw up thread in edge of lace, gather and whip lace to fabric. When lace edge is joined to insertion, mitre corner of insertion and gather edge as described above (A 81).

Lace Medallions: Place medallion in position on right side of fabric and fasten around edges with running stitch. Turn to wrong side; trim fabric to within ⅛ inch of stitching; roll edge and whip, catching lace with each stitch (A 82).

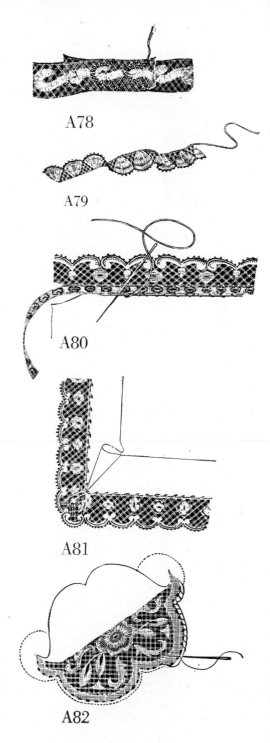

A78

A79

A80

A81

A82

A83

Lace Flat at Corner: Match design perfectly, overlapping the edges so that the corners lay flat. Trim around pattern and join (A 83).

Mending Lace: See Chapter 14, pg 439

Making Hairpin Lace and Net: See Chapter 8, pg 276

CHAPTER 2

ADVANCED SEWING AND TAILORING

ADVANCED SEWING AND TAILORING

→≫ LEARNING the elementary steps of any subject is only a fore-ʲ taste of the satisfaction to follow from a deeper and better understanding of the art itself. Similarly, when the needlewoman has gained the knowledge of the basic steps in sewing, she desires to become proficient, and in time, master of its many angles. Hence, this chapter is for the particular woman who *has* mastered the fundamental steps of sewing and wishes to become more professional in technique. In making a tailored suit as in Color Plate B, her goal is to achieve the professional look of a skilled tailor, by the simplest methods. A pattern will be necessary at first, but eventually the pattern may be eliminated.

In using a pattern, always give particular attention to the "straight of the material" instructions printed on each pattern piece. This insures the proper draping and line of the finished garment. Draping, which is the expression you give to fabric results directly from an understanding of the term, "straight of the material." This knowledge clarifies the terms used consistently in sewing instructions. For example: 1. "Cut on the fold," means to fold the fabric following a true cross thread (selvedge to selvedge); or a true lengthwise thread, commonly referred to as "straight of the material." 2. "Cut on the bias," means to determine the diagonal line that cuts the cross and lengthwise threads of the fabric at a 45° angle or half a right angle. 3. "Materials required," means to use the kind of fabric suggested, deviating from this suggestion only when you are certain that your substitute will produce the professional look of the experienced tailor to your finished garment. A great help in achieving the professional look is to understand your sewing machine, its uses, its adjustments (tension and stitch gauge) and its attachments.

Ba

Bb

Design your own from color plate B

With a bit of ingenuity, you can design from a tailored jacket.

NOTE: In lining garment, note that garment has a wide self facing at closing and a narrower self facing at neck and sleeves. Adjustment for any variation in size of lining pattern is made at these points. For a beginner, it is advisable to cut lining same size as garment, to fold back and trim excess lining material as required for perfect fit.

1. For bolero jacket: Cut at waistline, omit collar and pockets and shorten sleeve, if desired (Ba).
2. For blazer jacket: Pipe collar (pg 40) and 4 flap pockets (B 49a and b) in contrasting color. Make 2 button closings. (Bb and pg 65).
3. For vest: Make pointed finish at bottom edge; omit sleeves and collar; make 4 welt pockets (B 48a, b, c and d) and 6 small buttonholes (Bc, B 35 and B 36).

Bc

Bd

Be

Bf

4. For sport jacket: Omit collar, pockets and buttonholes (Bd).
5. For cardigan jacket: Omit collar and pockets, button to neckline and double stitch if desired (Be).
6. For sleeveless jacket: Omit sleeves; make 2 diagonal welt pockets (pg 71); and shape bottom edge (Bf).

Ideas from the background of color plate B

For helpful hints, turn the pages.
1. For instructions on draperies (Chapter 13).
2. For instructions on textile painting as shown on scarf (Chapter 14).

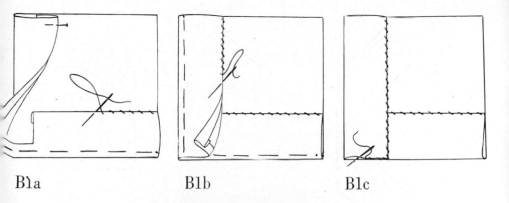

B1a   B1b   B1c

Corners and facings

In making corners, keep turn of a corner true with the grain of the fabric. Avoid unnecessary thickness by trimming overlapping edges.

Straight or Square Corner: This is sometimes referred to as a Corner with Hem Overlapping. Measure hemline and crease it; cut away fabric of overlapping edge to within seam width, turn in and baste (B 1a). Hem turned edge down and slip-stitch edge (B 1b and c). In machine-stitching, do not extend stitching to outer edge at corner but leave the needle in the fabric at corner; turn and continue stitching. When finished, slip-stitch hem from corner to outer edge.

Mitred Corner: 1. Turn hem desired width to right side, pin out fulness at the corner; baste and stitch. Trim away fulness (B 2a) and press seam open (B 2b). Turn hem to wrong side and sew hem (B 2c).

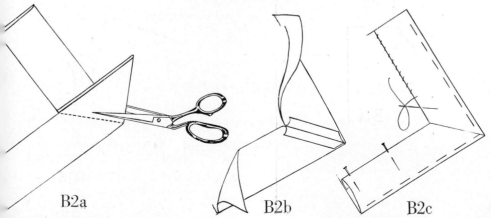

B2a   B2b   B2c

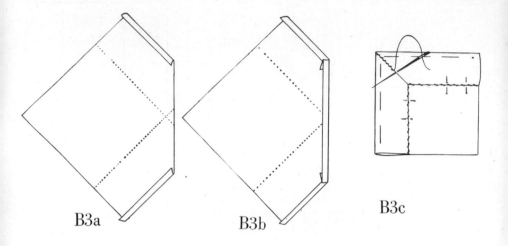

B3a

B3b

B3c

2. Turn edges and crease at hem's width. Cut diagonally across corner to within ¼ inch of crease (B 3a). Turn edge under (B 3b), fold at creased line and stitch. Slip-stitch edges of corner together (B 3c).

Corner with Bias Trim: Cut diagonally into corner the desired width (B 4a). Fold hem to wrong side (B 4b). Stitch bias edge of triangular piece diagonally across corner (B 4c). Trim, turn raw edges in and hem in place (B 4d).

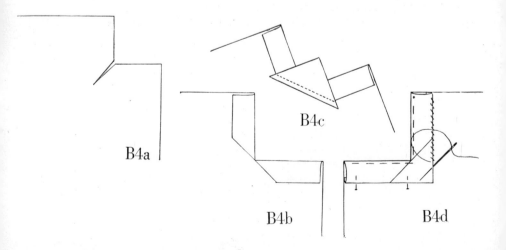

B4a

B4b

B4c

B4d

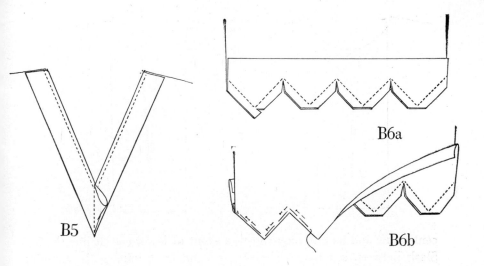

B5

B6a

B6b

Corner with Straight Facing: Cut facing same grain and as deep as desired; with right sides together, baste facing to corner. Stitch, trim and press open mitred corner. Turn facing to inside and turn in raw edges, pin, baste and slip-stitch (B 5). Apply a bias facing in same manner, allowing a sufficient bias at corner to mitre.

Facing for Saw-Tooth Edge: With right sides together, baste facing in place and stitch. Trim seams, cut away outer points, slash inner points and turn facing to right side (B 6a). Pull out points, pin and baste along pointed edges; then, stitch straight edge of facing in place (B 6b).

Necklines

Collars

Cuffs

Facing for Slash Opening: Cut material on same grain as part to be faced and at least ½ inch longer than opening. Stitch outer edge of facing. With right sides facing, baste to garment, stitch on each side of

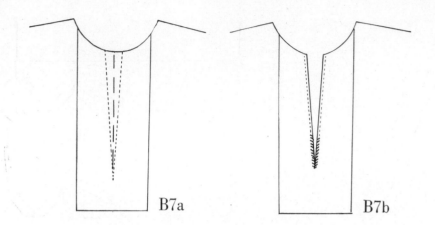

B7a

B7b

center line and let stitching run to a point at lower end of line (B 7a). Slash between stitching and reenforce end of opening with whipping stitches, press and stitch around neck edge if desired (B 7b).

Facing for Square Neck: With right sides together, baste straight or bias facing to garment. Shape corners of facing to correspond with neckline of garment and stitch (B 8a). Trim, slash corners and turn to wrong side of garment. Press and stitch around neck edges if desired (B 8b). If outer edges are not stitched, turn under raw edges and slip-stitch.

Facing for Round Neck: Cut material same grain and contour as part to be faced. With right sides together, baste facing to garment. Stitch, clip curved parts of seam, trim and turn to wrong side of garment (B 9). Crease folded edge, turn in edge of facing and baste with running stitches to itself. Tack, blind-hem or machine-stitch to garment.

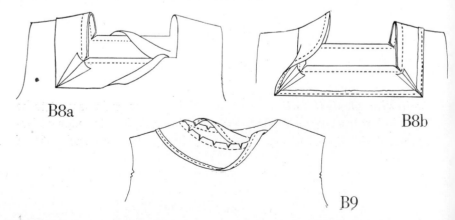

B8a

B8b

B9

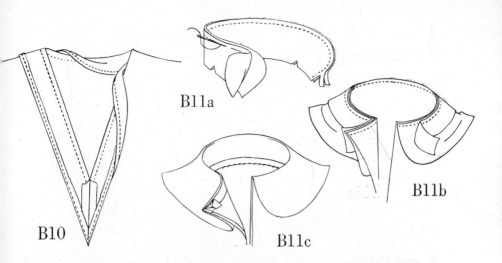

B11a

B11b

B10

B11c

Facing for V-Neck: With right sides together, baste facing to garment allowing sufficient material to mitre at point. Pin out fulness at point, stitch, trim and press open seam at point. Stitch close to edge around entire neckline. Slash corners and turn facing to wrong side of garment (B 10). Tack, blind-hem or machine-stitch to garment.

Attached collars: These are usually cut double. With right sides together, stitch outer edges together (B 11a). Trim seam and turn inside out and attach as shown (B 11b and c).

Detachable Collars: Usually finished with a narrow bias facing or seam binding (B 12a). The opening and the neckline of the garment should be bound, faced or finished with a continuous folding (B 12b). For a continuous fold, cut a strip four times the width of the required finish. Stitch to opening, turn to wrong side and blind-hem (B 12c).

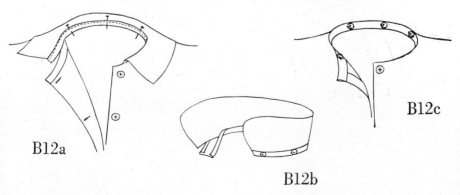

B12a

B12b

B12c

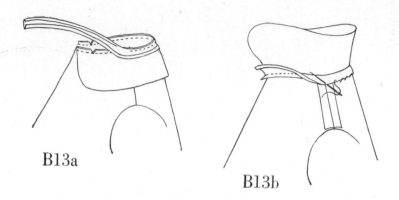

B13a

B13b

Round Collar with Bias Strip: With right sides together, pin and baste collar to neckline. Be sure to match identical notches if a pattern is used. Cut a bias strip about 1½ inches wide; baste and stitch folded bias binding to collar and neckline of garment (B 13a). Remove bastings, turn collar and binding; baste turned-in edge to stitching and blind-hem in place (B 13b). Press collar to right side.

Curved Collar with Bias Binding: With right sides together, stitch outer edges, trim seams at corners, turn and press. Pin and baste under-edge of collar to neckline. Hold neckline a trifle snug to prevent buckling. Baste bias binding along upper edge of collar and stitch (B 14a). Turn, baste and blind-hem binding to wrong side of garment (B 14b).

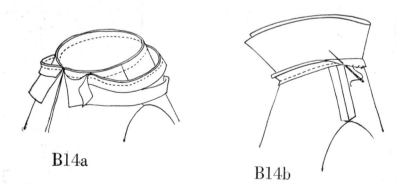

B14a

B14b

B15a

B15b

Tailored or Notched Collar: The same principle as in the curved collar is applied, allowing for the extended edges of the revers (B 15a). Also clip garment seam at shoulder and front of collar (B 15b).

Straight Standing Collar with a Faced Front Opening: Stitch collar at each end; clip raw edges at each end; trim corners and press. With right sides together, stitch facing to front of garment (B 16a). Pin seam of collar to seam at front opening; baste and stitch inner edge of collar to neckline of garment (B 16b). Clip seam; press and turn collar and facing right side out (B 16c). Baste turned edges; press and blind-hem collar to stitching of neckline at back. Turn inner edge of facing; stitch to garment.

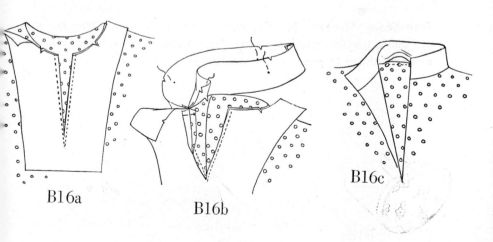

B16a

B16b

B16c

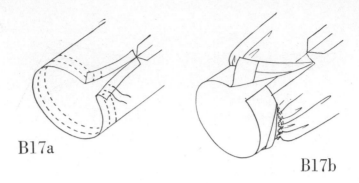

B17a

B17b

The method of making cuffs is same as preceding method described for collars. If an interlining is used to give cuff more body, baste interlining to under-piece of cuff on wrong side, and baste other section of cuff to this double piece. Consider interlining as part of under part of cuff.

Straight Cuff: If sleeve is full, run 2 rows of gathers within seam allowance of sleeve (B 17a). Pin, baste cuff to right side of sleeve. Stitch; turn free edge of cuff under, cover seam. Blind-hem or stitch (B 17b).

Turned-Back Cuff with No Opening: Place seam of cuff to wrong side of sleeve seam, baste and stitch (B 18a). Turn free edge under, cover seam and blind-hem or stitch (B 18b). Press and fold up cuff (B 18c). Stitch a single or double row all around edge of cuff to reenforce.

One-Seam Sleeve: Match notches and with right sides together, pin seams together placing pins at right angles to seam (B 19a). Gather or dart fulness to give freedom at elbow; gather, dart or pleat fulness

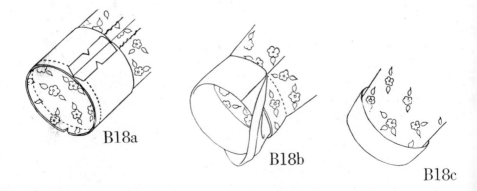

B18a

B18b

B18c

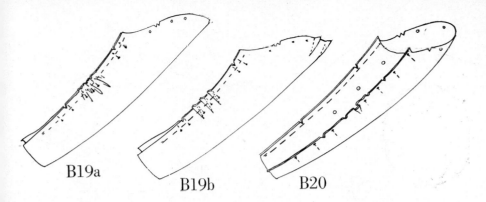

B19a

B19b

B20

at top of sleeve (B 19b). Stitch; press seams; pink or overcast edges.

Two-Seam Sleeves: Pin and baste front seams first. Then, pin upper section of sleeve to under section being sure to pin from top of sleeve to elbow or upper notch, and from bottom of sleeve to lower notch. Gather or dart fulness at the elbow. Baste and stitch seams, leaving back seam open three inches from hand (B 20). Press seams on sleeve board; and pleats or darts on tailor's cushion.

Kimono Sleeve: In a simple kimono sleeve, merely clip as needed at the armpit. If the kimono is closely fitted, a gusset is often placed in the sleeve for freedom and to protect the sleeve from tearing out under the arm. To insert the gusset, cut a slash about 3 inches in length at right angles to the seam at the top of the under arm (B 21a). Overcast around opening. Insert a diamond-shaped bias piece in this opening. Pin and baste in place (B 21b). Sew in place tapering corners and press (B 21c). If desired, cut a second gusset and use it as a facing.

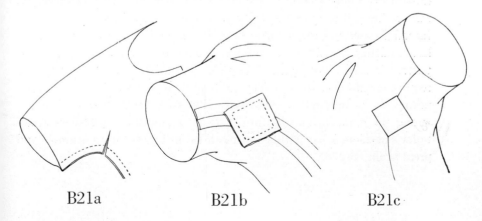

B21a

B21b

B21c

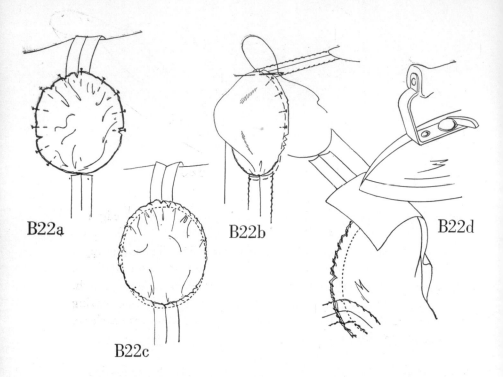

B22a

B22b

B22c

B22d

Setting-In a Sleeve: The lengthwise thread of the sleeve should fall
straight from the top of the shoulder and down over the top of the
shoulder or else the sleeve will draw. Turn finished sleeve to right side
and garment to wrong side. Holding wrong side of waist toward you,
draw upper part of sleeve into armhole, pin to armhole seam being sure
to match the notches of sleeve with those of the garment (B 22a and b).
If there is a diagonal wrinkle across the top, either drop top of sleeve or
raise sleeve under the arm. Always note position of elbow fulness and
raise or lower it as required. If loose at wrist, baste a new line with long
thread. Loosen basting to take off sleeve; draw up again and mark new
line. In fitting the sleeve cap, pin sleeve in armhole matching notches if a
pattern is used. Draw gathers to place and fasten (B 22c). All sleeves
require shrinking at the top. Try garment on to see if sleeves are correct,
noting the pitfalls mentioned above. Remove sleeves and with sleeve
wrong side out, shrink out fulness over end of sleeve board or small
tailor's cushion. Press with a wet cloth to shrink. Stitch to armhole and
press again (B 22d).

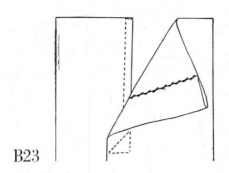

B23

Plackets

A placket, commonly speaking, is the facing of both sides of a slash opening so that there is an overlap and an underlap. A Simple Placket is a hem on each side of an opening and reenforced at the bottom to prevent tearing down as in a shoulder placket or a simple skirt placket (B 23).

Continuous Placket: Cut a strip of material twice the length of opening plus 1 inch, and at least 2 inches in width. Baste and with right sides together, stitch around outside of opening (B 24a). Trim, then turn in free edge of facing to enclose seams and to form a lap on each side (B 24b). Hem to original stitching. Join ends of placket (B 24c).

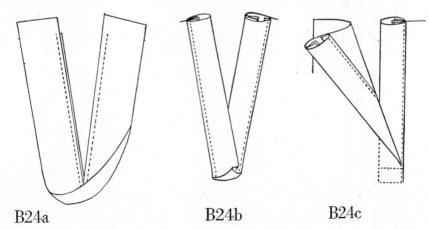

B24a   B24b   B24c

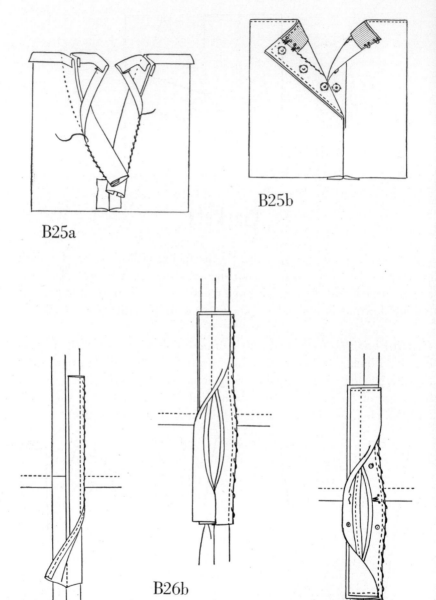

B25a

B25b

B26a

B26b

B26c

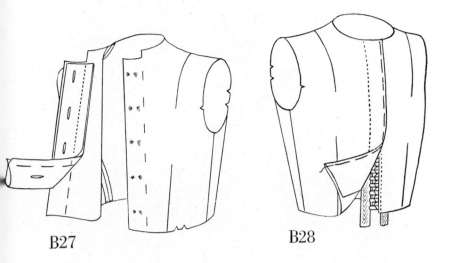

B27

B28

Two Piece Placket for Skirt: Cut a bias strip 1¼ to 1½ inches wide for front facing and a strip 2 to 3 inches wide for extension on back. Cut both pieces ½ to 1 inch longer than opening. Turn edge of front facing under ¼ inch and stitch. With right sides together, stitch facing to front edge just in back of seam line and place over folded extension and top-stitch to skirt (B 25a). Press both sides, placing placket with facing overlapping the extension. Stitch end of placket together. Stitch waistband to top of skirt. Sew snaps on placket and hooks and eyes on waistband (B 25b).

Two Piece Placket for Dress: Cut bias strips and apply in same manner as for skirt (B 26a). Sew ends of placket together (B 26b). Fasten placket with snap and a hook and eye at the waistline (B 26c).

Buttoned Fly Front Closing: Stitch the top end of fly, turn, baste and work buttonholes (pg 64). Baste fly under front overlap. Stitch the four layers together (B 27). Finish neck.

Slide-Fastened Fly Front: Stitch the left front of blouse below the jog, over the fastener tape. Stitch the turned and basted front overlap over the other side of fastener (B 28).

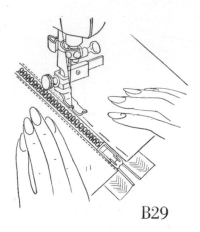

B29

Slide Fastener or Zipper Closing: Mark all openings ½ inch longer than zipper. Cut zipper tape ends to ¾ of an inch and keep zipper closed when applying. Stitch close to metal, easing fabric to tape so metal will lie flat (B 29). Press all seams, folds and edges before advancing to next step. In machine-stitching, the cording foot is an excellent aid in applying zippers.

Visible Zipper Closing in Slash Opening: With right sides together, baste a 2-inch square to lower part of opening with center of square directly over end of marked line for opening. Stitch along each side of center including lower part of square. Clip diagonally at corners (B 30a). Turn facing to inside, baste and press (B 30b). Pin and baste edges of opening to tape. Turn in ends of tape and stitch close to edge of fastener (B 30c).

Visible Zipper Closing for Jacket: Note: Sew zipper between the jacket and the facing. Turn under ⅛ inch more than regular seam allowance on front edges of jacket. Baste folded edge close to metal teeth of zipper. On right side, stitch close to edge (B 31a). Turn a seam on front edge of front facing; baste to wrong side close to metal teeth. Concealing ends of tape in seam, stitch facing to tape (B 31b).

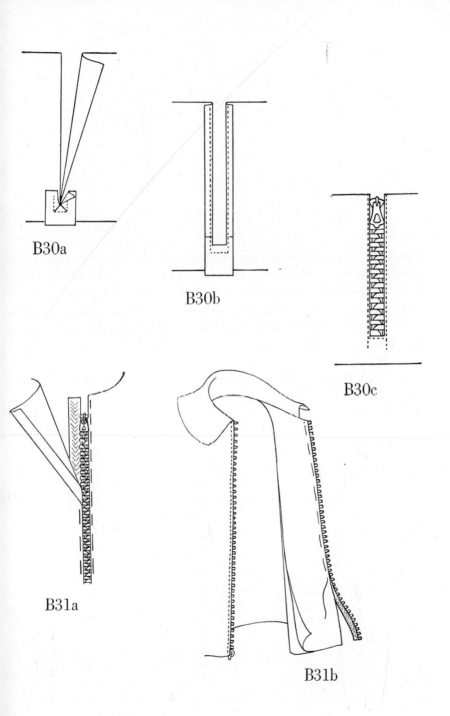

B30a

B30b

B30c

B31a

B31b

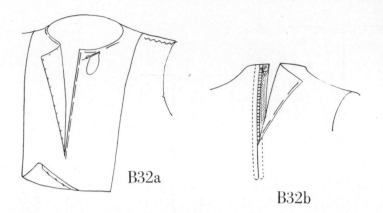

B32a

B32b

Concealed Zipper Closing in Slash Opening: Stitch a strip of material for facing on right side. Reenforce at point. Slash opening. Turn facing to inside, baste and press. Baste edges of slash together (B 32a). Pin zipper with right side down over temporary closing. Baste zipper in place concealing metal (B 32b). Stitch; trim facing even with edge of tape and overcast edges.

Concealed Zipper in Dress Placket: With right sides together, stitch a bias facing 1¼ inches wide and 1 inch longer than opening, to front edge of opening along seam line (B 33a). Trim seam; turn facing to in-

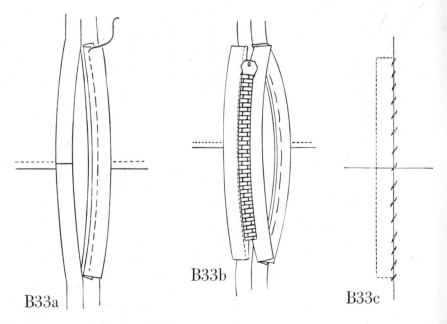

B33a

B33b

B33c

side; baste edge and press. Turn under one half of seam allowance of back edge about ⅛ inch outside of seam line. Baste folded edge to tape of zipper close to metal and stitch (B 33b). Extend stitching beyond opening at both ends of tape. At ends of tape, clip back seam allowance, being careful not to cut stitches of seam. Overlap front on back concealing zipper with seam lines meeting. On right side, baste front edge of placket to seam line. Making an allowance for the extra width of the metal slide, stitch front of placket to tape at that width (B 33c).

Concealed Zipper in Skirt Placket: Leave opening at seam ¼ inch longer than zipper. For heavy fabrics, stitch bias facing 1½ inches wide and ½ inch longer than opening to front ⅛ inch back of seam line; trim and turn facing to inside on seam line; baste edge and press (B 34a). For light fabrics, merely turn in front seam allowance, baste and press. At back opening, turn seam edge under ⅛ inch away from seam line, pin; baste folded edge to zipper and stitch (B 34b). At bottom end of tape, clip back seam allowance in seam, being careful not to cut stitches of seam. Overlap front on back concealing zipper with seam lines meeting on right side. Baste front edge of placket to seam line. Making an allowance for the extra width of the metal slide, stitch front of placket to tape at that width (B 34c).

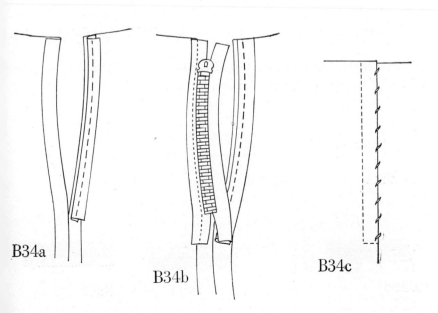

B34a

B34b

B34c

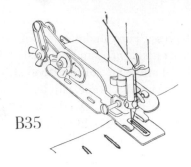

B35

Buttonholes

The size and shape of the button determines the size of the buttonhole. Ordinarily, the allowance for a buttonhole is ⅛ inch longer than the width of your button; however, ball and ornate buttons require a larger buttonhole than flat buttons to allow for their height or thickness. It is advisable to determine size needed by cutting a test buttonhole in a piece of waste fabric. The distance from the edge of the garment is ordinarily one half the width of the button to be used. Measure accurately for placing of buttonholes. Mark position and length of buttonhole by line of running stitches or with tailor's chalk. If buttonhole is to be worked through two or more layers of material, baste layers together before cutting buttonholes. In machine-stitching, the buttonhole attachment makes buttonholes in less time than required for handwork (B 35).

Worked Buttonholes: Mark position exactly on thread of material. Stitch twice, preferably by machine, around marking (B 36a). Cut on

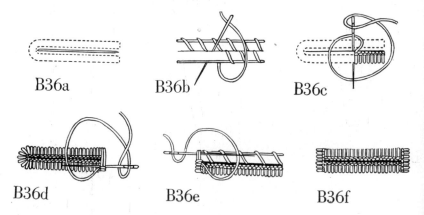

B36a   B36b   B36c

B36d   B36e   B36f

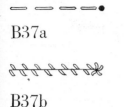

B37a

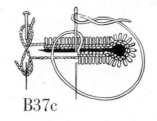

B37d

B37b

B37c

marked line, then overcast edges (B 36b). Begin at lower right hand
corner and buttonhole-stitch as shown (B 36c). Work bar at one end as
you turn to upper side (B 36d). Make two stitches across the inside end of
buttonhole, blanket-stitch over end stitches and through material to
complete bar (B 36e). Buttonholes may also be made with a bar at each
end (B 36f).

Tailored Buttonhole: Punch one end with a stiletto (B 37a); cut on
marked line and overcast both edges and around punched hole (B 37b).
For a cord edge, work buttonhole over a strand of heavy thread or twist
held taut with a pin (B 37c). Work a bar at square end (B 37d).

Bound Buttonhole: For a single buttonhole, cut a piece of material
true to grain, 2 inches wide and ¾ inch longer than the buttonhole is to
be made. For a group of buttonholes, cut a strip of sufficient length to
cover all. Placing right sides together, mark position for buttonhole.
Stitch ⅛ inch each side of marking and across ends (B 38a). Slash
through center between stitchings and clip diagonally to corners. Turn
strip through slash to wrong side (B 38b). Turn seam away from slash.
Make inverted pleat at ends forming a piping on outside with edges at

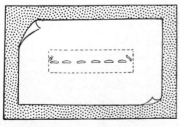

B38a

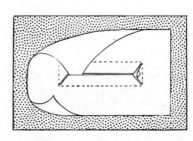

B38b

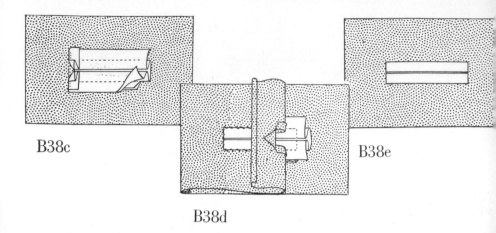

B38c

B38e

B38d

center joining; baste (B 38c). Stitch triangular pieces at ends to piping on inside. Sew fabric invisibly to stitching along buttonhole (B 38d). If facing is used, cut slit in facing through buttonhole; turn edges under and slip-stitch or hem down to buttonhole (B 38e).

Corded or Piped Buttonhole: Cut two corded or bias strips 1 inch longer than buttonhole. Stitch both strips to outside of garment, so that raw edges meet at center (B 39a). Do not stitch across ends. Slash between stitchings and clip diagonally to corners. Turn corded or piping strips through slash to inside (B 39b). Stitch only the triangular pieces at ends to piping. Overcast edge and finish same as for a bound buttonhole.

Loop Buttonholes: Loops may be made of bias tubing with or without cord, braid or thread. Cut loops correct size for continuous row of buttons or separately for each button; extend loops over edge and sew loops

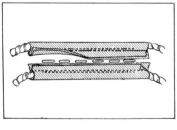

B39a

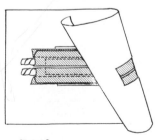

B39b

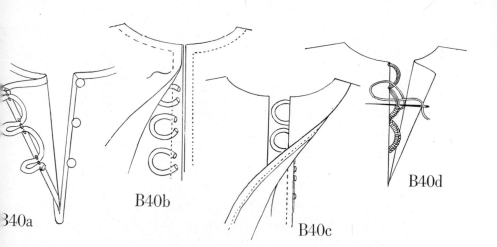

B40a

B40b

B40c

B40d

to wrong side (B 40a). If a facing is to be used, place loops on right side and with right sides of fabric together; then, stitch (B 40b). Turn facing under and hem (B 40c). For blanket-stitched loops, sew a number of strands of heavy twist as for a bar tack, drawing stitches over a pencil for the correct size of button. Cover foundation stitches very closely with blanket stitches or purled buttonhole stitch, forming a firm edge (B 40d).

Note: Always use a double thread for sewing on buttons, snap fasteners; and hooks and eyes.

Buttons: Conceal the knot under the button by first pushing the needle through from right side. If the button has holes, place a pin across top to keep threads loose; make enough stitches over pin to hold button firmly. (B 41a and b). In last stitch, pass needle through hole and between button and fabric; withdraw pin. Wind thread between button and fabric

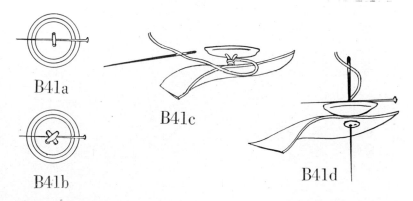

B41a

B41c

B41b

B41d

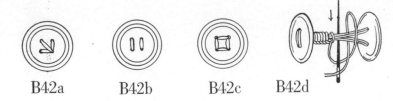

B42a   B42b   B42c   B42d

to form a neck or shank (B 41c); pass needle to wrong side and fasten thread with several buttonhole stitches or reenforce with a small button on wrong side (B 41d).

Link Buttons: Run thread several times through two buttons, leaving thread desired length for link. Work over thread with close blanket stitches as shown with needle inverted (B 42a, b, c and d).

Hooks and Eyes: Place hook so that end comes about ⅛ inch from edge, and eye so that it extends just over the edge. Sew both with an over and over stitch around the curved edges. Secure with several buttonhole stitches. Where the edges lap, the straight eye or blanket-stitched bar is set back from the edge, usually on the seam (B 43).

Snap Fasteners: Carefully mark position of socket on under lap and of the ball on the upper part so that the pressure will come from the ball part of fastener. Sew with over and over stitches like hooks and eyes. Secure with buttonhole stitches (B 44).

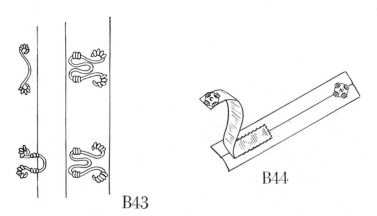

B43   B44

Pockets

Patch Pocket: This is the easiest type of pocket to make. It is advisable to stitch a piece of linen tape to the wrong side of the garment exactly on a line with the top of the pocket. The tape prevents the pocket from tearing the material of the garment. If pocket is plain, crease a tiny hem to wrong side, then fold hem or seam allowance to right side and stitch ends (B 45a). Trim, then turn hem to wrong side of pocket. Turn in raw edges on three sides and baste. Slash corners or curved edges; slip-stitch hem and press pocket (B 45b). Baste to garment, then top-stitch (B 45c). If made of heavy worsted, patch pockets are often lined. The lining is stitched to the pocket along sides and lower edge, placing right sides of material together. Trim, then turn pocket to right side. Fold hem over lining; slip-stitch hem; press and stitch pocket to position of garment. If pocket has a flap at top, stitch flap to right side of pocket, baste hem and stitch in place (B 45d).

Bound or Set-In Pockets: Mark position of pocket on garment. For a one-piece bound pocket, cut pocket at least 1 inch wider than slash line and at least twice as long as the pouch or depth. Mark piece so that upper half is one inch longer than lower half. With right sides together, place piece on garment, matching the markings. Baste; stitch ¼ inch each side of basting (B 46a) and across ends; slash between stitching and slash diagonally at corners. Pull pouch through slash to wrong side (B 46b). Allow material of pouch to form a narrow piping, or fold piece to meet in center of slash opening. Baste; stitch in position on outside (B 46c).

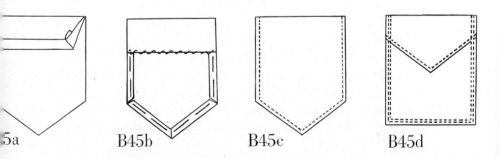

5a   B45b   B45c   B45d

B46c

B46d

B46a

B46b

Finally, stitch edges of pouch on inside, trim and overcast (B 46d). Finish ends of slit on outside with arrowhead tacks, if desired.

Slash Pocket in One Piece: Mark position of pocket on garment and cut piece in same manner as for Bound Pocket. Mark piece so that lower half is one inch longer than upper half. With right sides together, place piece on garment matching the markings. Baste, stitch and slash, then pull pocket to wrong side (B 47). Stitch, trim and overcast.

Welt or Stand Pocket: Mark position of pocket on garment. Cut piece for welt one inch longer than opening and twice as wide as desired welt (B 48a). Cut pocket in one piece. With right sides together, fold welt in half and stitch across ends. Trim, turn to right side and press. With folded edge of welt turned down, baste raw edges of welt to right side of garment along marking. With right sides together, stitch free edges of welt to lower edge of slash line and stitch one edge of pocket piece to upper edge or slash line (B 48b). Cut on slash line and slash at corners. Draw pocket through to wrong side. Turn welt up. Stitch at sides and lower edge close to seam (B 48c). With wrong side of garment facing,

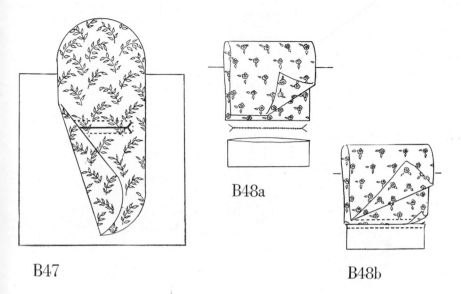

B47

B48a

B48b

turn pocket piece up and stitch free edge to raw edges of welt. Stitch, trim and overcast pocket (B 48d). For Pocket With a Diagonal Welt, cut welt with square or round corners, following grain of garment.

Welt Pocket with Flap: Mark position of pocket. Cut and finish the flap as in B 49a. Baste flap to right side of garment. Cut 2 pieces for pouch one inch wider than slash line. Stitch a piece of fabric at least 2 inches wide to each pouch piece. Baste pouch piece over flap. Stitch and finish in same manner as for a welt pocket. Press flap down (B 49b).

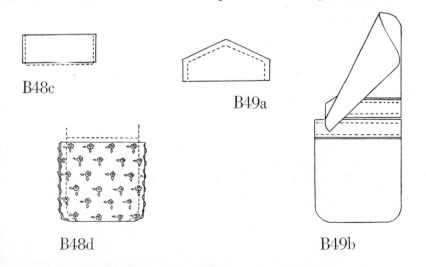

B48c

B49a

B48d

B49b

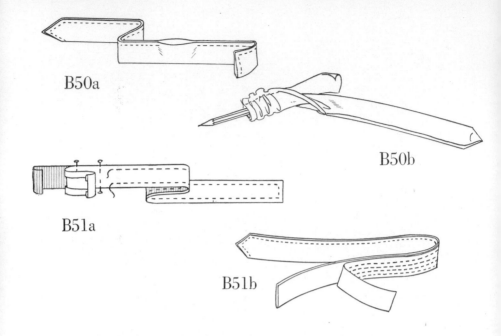

B50a

B50b

B51a

B51b

Belts and belt carriers

Belts: Cut on the lengthwise grain of the material. For an unlined belt, with right sides facing, stitch as shown leaving a 1 to 2 inch opening at center (B 50a). Pull inside out and slip-stitch along opening (B 50b). Interline belts of a lightweight fabric with preshrunk muslin or belting. With right sides together, stitch, leaving the straight end open (B 51a). Trim edges, turn inside out, press and slip-stitch opening together (B 51b).

Stiff Belts: Baste webbing or canvas to material; turn edges over, clipping along curves; pin and baste lining in place. Press and slip-stitch edges together (B 52).

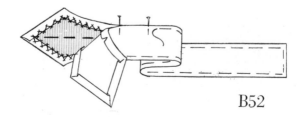

B52

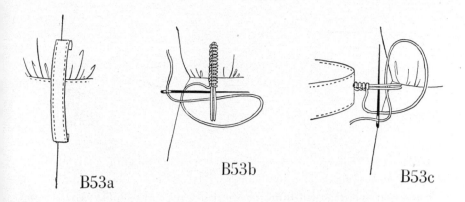

B53a

B53b

B53c

Fabric Belt Carrier: With right sides together, fold a narrow piece of fabric; stitch edges together. Turn, inside out, topstitch and press; then, stitch in place (B 53a).

Thread Belt Carrier: Allowing for width of belt, sew several loose strands of thread above and below belt line. Fasten securely. Using the eye-end of the needle to pass through loops, work blanket or buttonhole stitch over strands (B 53b). Or attached belt to garment as shown in B 53c.

Tacks

Bar Tack: Sew several strands of thread across ends of opening (B 54a). Cover these strands with overhand stitches, picking up a bit of the fabric at the same time (B 54b). Finish ends with small bar tacks (B 54c).

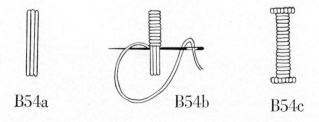

B54a

B54b

B54c

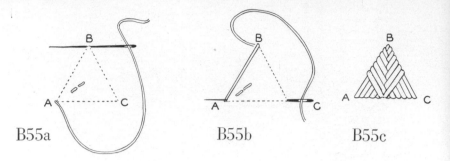

B55a   B55b   B55c

Arrowhead Tack: Mark outline of triangle. Beginning at left-hand corner A, bring needle to upper corner B (B 55a); take a small stitch from right to left, then bring needle to lower right-hand corner C and finally across underneath from C to A (B 55b). Continue placing stitches close until space is filled (B 55c).

Crow's Foot Tack: Mark outline of triangle. Beginning at left-hand corner A, pass needle to upper corner B (B 56a); take a small stitch from right to left; bring needle out at lower right-hand corner C, take a small stitch from left to right; pass needle down at A and take a small stitch from left to right (B 56b). Continue placing stitches close in this manner (B 56c) until the space is filled. The edges draw toward the center as the work progresses (B 56d).

Proper Pressing is important. Press as you sew is best rule to follow. Always test a sample piece of material to determine how much heat it will stand. Always press on wrong side of material. When it is necessary to press on right side, use a press cloth. The ironing board should be well and firmly padded. Do not have wrinkles in padding or cover as they will mark the finished work. When pressing rounded or curved parts, it is advisable to use a tailor's cushion.

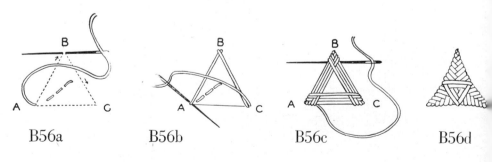

B56a   B56b   B56c   B56d

CHAPTER 3

SIMPLE EMBROIDERY

SIMPLE EMBROIDERY

➤➤➤ SIMPLE embroidery is the expression of self through the medium of a sewing needle and thread. It is a play of long and short, straight and curved lines in a manner that gives animation and color to a piece of plain fabric.

As a beginner, try one and all the basic stitches; practice those that come easily to you until you are a master of the stitches; then learn to group them to form a completed whole. Next, be fair and compare your work with that made by the professional as to stitch, symmetry of arrangement and the self-satisfaction it gives you. Then dare to be different—to use the sword, the stroke, the mock pekingese, the checkered chain or the couching stitch on fabrics, net, hand-knit pieces, etc., as it has never been used before. Dare to embroider a simple running stitch with yarn on metallic cloth for an evening wrap, or to embroider the triangular punch stitch with metallic thread on a machine or hand knit blouse.

It's fun and it's inspiring to create. A creative sense lies silent and still within each one of us. It awaits a call to action from self. A few earnest attempts can produce practical and artistic pieces of embroidery, similar, yet in direct contrast to our grandmothers—an expression of the vibrant, artistic understanding of our age.

Instructions for Embroidered Pictures (*Color Plate C, see pg 79*).

Ca

Cb

Cc

Design your own from color plate C

With a bit of ingenuity, you can design from embroidered pictures.

1. Enlarge design (Chapter 10, pg 339), omitting center motif; and use for needlepoint or hooked rug (Ca).
2. Use part of center motif for place mat and napkins (Cb).
3. Enlarge border designs for bedspread (Cc) in simple appliqué or trapunto quilting (Chapter 5).

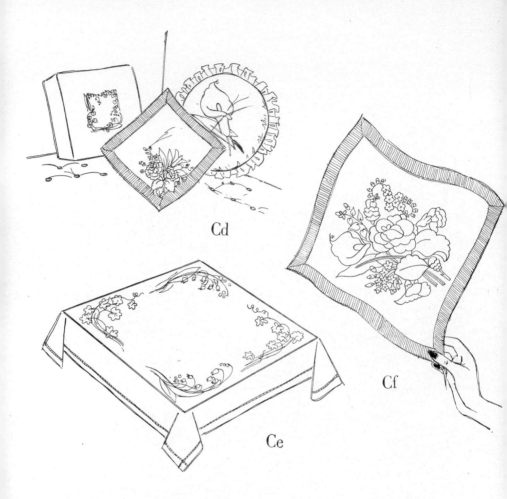

Cd

Cf

Ce

4. Use parts of design as is or enlarged for pillows (Cd and Chapter 13).
5. Use corner motifs for tea cloth (Ce), sampler, etc.
6. Use center motif for textile painted scarf (Cf and Chapter 14).

Ideas from the background of color plate C

For helpful hints, turn the pages.
1. Instructions for draperies, pillows, lamps (Chapter 13).
2. Use sofa design for tufting (Chapter 5).

Instructions for embroidered pictures
(color plate C)

Materials Required:

⅝ yard 36-inch white linen

6-strand embroidery cotton, 1 skein each of 4 shades of rose; 1 skein each
of 3 shades of blue; 2 skeins each of 2 shades of yellow green; 2 skeins
each of 3 shades of blue green; 1 skein each of 2 shades of lavender;
2 skeins of white; 1 skein each of beige, light yellow and black.

1 embroidery hoop

1. Scale to size design of picture (Cg), each square represents one inch.
To scale design to size: On plain white or tracing paper, measure off
14″ x 18″ oblong. Divide this oblong into 252 1-inch squares (the
same number shown in Cg) and copy, line for line, the part of the
design shown in each square.

2. Press linen, removing all creases.

3. With right side up place linen on smooth surface; lay carbon paper
face down on linen. Lay tracing paper face up on carbon paper,
centering design. With sharply pointed pencil trace design.

4. Split the six strand cotton and use two strands in the needle at one
time. Embroider solid sections of design in encroaching stitch (C 43);
stems in outline stitch (C 4); lilies-of-the-valley and clover leaves in
buttonhole stitch (C 49 and 50); and dots in satin stitch (C 39a to h).

5. Lay picture face down on a Turkish towel and press with a damp
cloth and moderate iron.

6. Cut a piece of cardboard the size you desire the finished picture.

7. Stretch embroidered piece over cardboard and hold in place by stitching back and forth from one side to the opposite side across back;
or glue edges down with gummed paper.

8. After stretching, place in frame, then cover back with second cardboard. Hold in place with small nails. Paste paper over back of frame.

9. Repeat for companion picture (Ch).

Cg

Ch

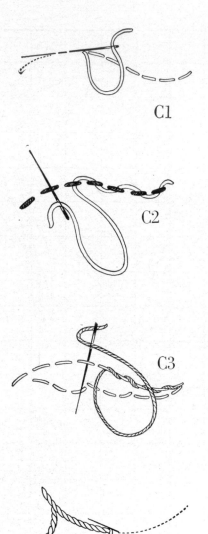

Running or Darning Stitch:
Pass the needle in and out of the material in a straight line. Always take several stitches on needle before drawing it through (C 1).

Threaded Running Stitch: Outline the design with the simple running stitch (C 1), then weave a thread in and out the running stitch. A contrasting thread can be used for weaving (C 2).

Whipped Running Stitch: Outline design with simple running stitch (C 1). Then, whip-stitch over running stitch (C 3).

Outline or Stem Stitch: Work from left to right and keep the thread below the needle. Bring needle up through fabric at lower end, take a short slanting stitch from right to left and bring needle out to left at the end of first stitch. Again pass needle forward at an angle taking another stitch to the right of first stitch and bring it out at end of last stitch (C 4).

Rambler Rose Stitch: The outline stitch begun as a single stitch for the center of the flower and continued around this center point (C 5). Always point the needle to the left and keep the thread below the needle.

C5

Whipped Stem Stitch: Outline design in stem stitch; then, whipstitch over stem stitch (C 6).

C6

Couching Stitch: Lay one or more strands of thread in position and take slanting stitches as shown (C 7a). Interesting effects are produced by working over the laid threads in blanket (C 7b), the open chain (C 7c) and the feather stitch (C 7d).

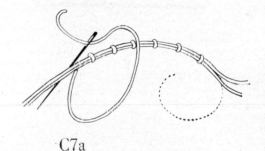

C7a

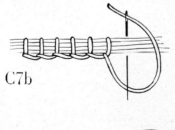

C7b

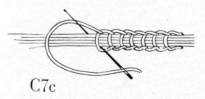

C7c

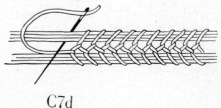

C7d

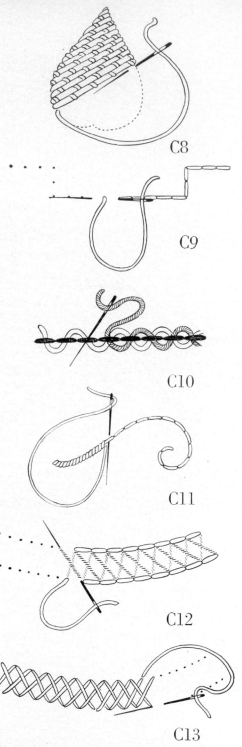

Bokhara Couching Stitch: The thread to be couched is laid across the space from left to right and this tied down on the return row by small slanting stitches at regular intervals (C 8).

Backstitch: Take a small running stitch, insert needle at end of running stitch, bring to wrong side and over twice as much space as original stitch on wrong side; bring needle to right side and repeat (C 9).

Threaded Backstitch: Outline design in simple backstitch (C 9). Weave in and out with one or two contrasting threads (C 10).

Whipped Backstitch: Outline design in simple backstitch, then whipstitch over backstitch (C 11).

Crossed Backstitch or Shadow Embroidery: On the right side this stitch resembles two rows of backstitch and on the wrong side the catch-stitch. Slanting the needle in same manner as for a catch-stitch (C 31), make a single backstitch (C 9) first on the lower side and then on the upper side (C 12).

Basket Stitch: The catch-stitch (C 31) so closely spaced as to make the stitches touch (C 13).

Chevron Stitch: Commenced in the same manner as the catch-stitch (C 31) and completed by taking a small stitch to the right of the first stitch and bringing the needle out at the same point as the down stroke of the first stitch (C 14a and b).

Chain Stitch: Bring needle up to right side; hold left thumb over loop of thread and insert needle near the place where it first came up. Do not pull thread tightly. Bring needle out a short distance forward and over the loop of thread (C 15).

Checkered or Double Chain Stitch: Use two threads of contrasting thread in one needle. Commence exactly as for ordinary chain stitch but when needle is ready to be pulled through over the two threads, slip the dark thread from underneath the needle point and permit it to lie over the needle. The needle is then pulled through over the light thread and forms an ordinary chain stitch. The second stitch is made in the same manner with the colors reversed, i.e. the light thread lies over the needle and the stitch is made with the dark thread. If, when making a light stitch, the dark thread shows, a slight pull will cause it to disappear (C 16).

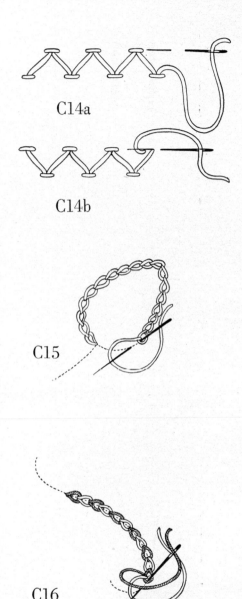

C14a

C14b

C15

C16

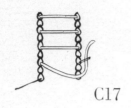

C17

Ladder or Step Stitch: Work two parallel rows of chain stitch; take a long single stitch through center of every second chain (C 17).

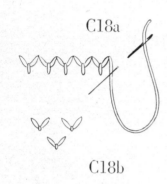

C18a

C18b

Y Stitch: Pass needle up through cloth, a little to the left of center, then place needle a little to the right of center and take a slant stitch bringing needle up through the center below the first stitch (C 18a). Take a straight stitch on the center line to complete Y and hold the horizontal stitch in position. The Y Stitch becomes a *Fly Stitch* when the stem of the Y Stitch is shorter than the horizontal stitch (C 18b).

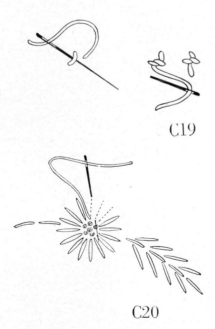

C19

Sword Stitch: Bring needle through cloth and insert a little to right and above center. Bring needle out a little to right and downward to center of first stitch. Pass needle over, then under strand of first stitch from left to right. Insert needle directly below at center of this stitch (C 19).

Stroke Stitch: Large single stitches used to form flowers, leaves or tiny squares (C 20).

C20

Fern Stitch: Work a long single stitch to right of center line; bring needle up at beginning of center line. Return to beginning of first stitch and up above and to left of center line. Insert at beginning of first stitch (C 21).

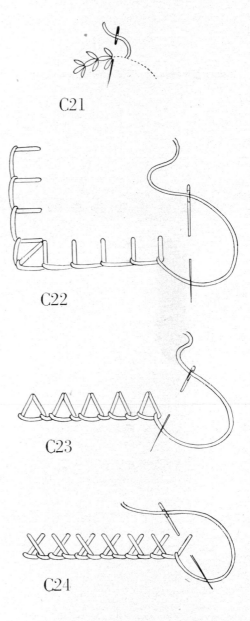

C21

Blanket Stitch: Pass needle up through cloth; holding thread under left thumb, form a loop and pass needle down through cloth again and up from under cloth and over thread (C 22).

C22

Closed Blanket Stitch: Pass needle through cloth in a slanting position and bring needle through the extreme edge of the work as shown. The second stitch is slanted in the opposite direction and meets the first stitch, thus forming pairs of stitches that are closed at top to form a pattern of points (C 23).

C23

Crossed Blanket Stitch: Work first stitch in same manner as for closed blanket stitch. The second stitch is slanted in the opposite direction and is crossed over the first stitch. As in the closed blanket stitch, the needle is brought through the edge of the work (C 24).

C24

87

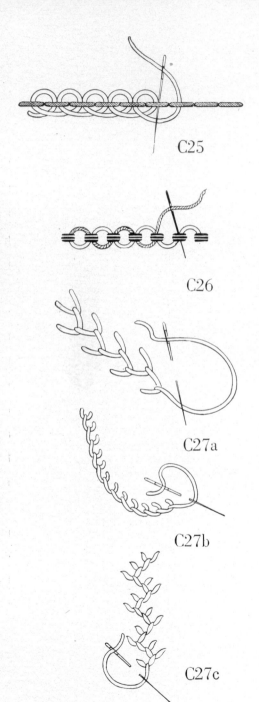

Pekingese or Chinese Stitch:
A combination of backstitch and an interlacing stitch as shown in C 25.

Mock Pekingese Stitch: Work closely three parallel rows of evenly spaced running stitches. Weave a contrasting thread in and out these groups of stitches. Repeat on opposite side with third color (C 26).

Feather Stitch: Work in same manner as blanket stitch. Take one short slanting stitch on the right side of line pointing needle to left, and the next stitch on the opposite side of line pointing needle to right with the thread to left (C 27a). This stitch can also be made in a variety of ways,—in C 27b, by keeping the stitches straight on one side of the center line,—in C 27c, by groupings of 2 and 3 stitches to right and to left of center line.

Closed Feather Stitch: Made in the same manner as the simple feather stitch only the stitches are made large and close together. Bring thread out at left, take a stitch to right and a little above starting point. With thread under needle, bring out needle directly below this stitch on right. Take stitch to left

C25

C26

C27a

C27b

C27c

and just below stitch above. With thread under needle, bring out needle directly below this stitch on left. Repeat (C 28).

Creton Stitch: A variation of the blanket (C 22) and feather stitches (C 27 and 28). With the thread always under the needle, the stitches are made at right angles to the work above and below a center line (C 29).

Fish-Bone Stitch: In forming this stitch the needle is slanted more than for the simple feather stitch and is brought out exactly on the center line (C 30).

Herringbone stitches

Catch Stitch: The first stitch of the herringbone group from which a number of stitches have been derived which are no more than the original catch stitch (C 31) combined with one or more stitches as shown.

Tacked Herringbone Stitch: Work a row of the catch stitch, then work a small single stitch over each point in either a horizontal or vertical position, where the stitches cross (C 32).

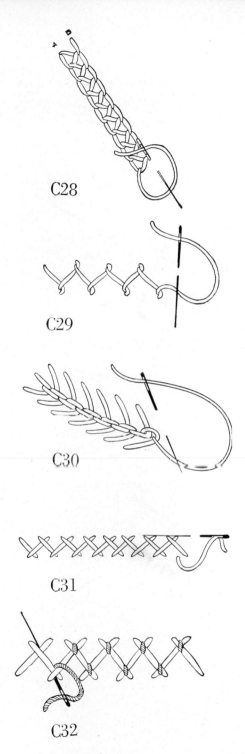

C28

C29

C30

C31

C32

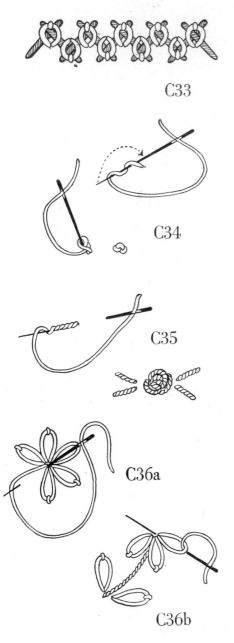

Ornate Herringbone Stitch: Work row of simple catch stitch, then work a large single chain stitch (C 15) over each point where the stitches cross (C 33).

French Knots: Bring needle to right side. Wrap thread around needle 2, 3 or 4 times, holding it near cloth. Insert needle in cloth near the point it came out. Draw thread close to form knot (C 34).

Bullion or Wheat Stitch: Bring needle to right side. Wrap thread around needle 4 or more times. Insert needle in fabric just far enough away to permit the stitches to lie flat (C 35). A raised rambler rose can be formed by working the bullion stitch in the same manner as the rambler rose stitch.

Lazy Daisy Stitch: Bring needle to right side at center of flower. Hold left thumb over a long loop of thread, the length of a petal, and insert needle as close as possible to place where thread came out. Take a long stitch the length of the petal on wrong side; bring needle to right side and keep loop under needle (C 36a). Fasten end of loop with a short stitch. Bring needle back to center for next petal (C 36b).

Cross Stitch: In the first row of single stitches, bring needle up at lower right hand corner; down at upper left-hand corner; repeat across row (C 37a). On return row, bring needle up at lower left-hand corner and down at upper right-hand corner. In working rows of cross stitches, work across the row from right to left forming the first slanting stitch, then work from left to right to complete the stitch (C 37b).

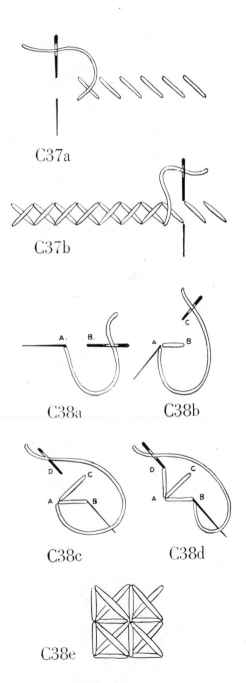

C37a

C37b

Two Sided Italian Cross Stitch: Really a cross stitch surrounded by a square. Each corner is emphasized by a small hole formed by drawing the thread tightly. It should be worked on coarse, loosely woven material, preferably linen. Two rows must be worked to complete the stitch. Make a horizontal stitch from left A to right B (C 38a). Beginning at A, make slant stitch to C directly above B (C 38b); again beginning at A, make a vertical stitch to D, directly in line with C (C 38c). Bring needle out at B, make a slant stitch to D (C 38d). Bring needle out at B and repeat across row. On second row be sure to keep crosses parallel to the first row (C 38e).

C38a

C38b

C38c

C38d

C38e

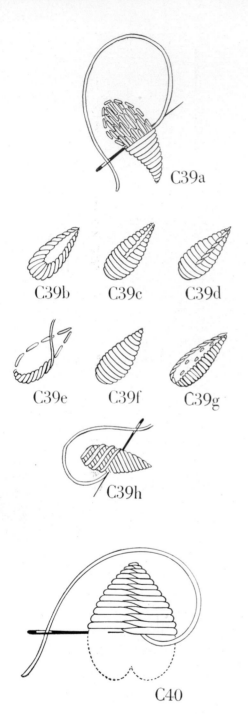

C39a

C39b   C39c   C39d

C39e   C39f   C39g

C39h

C40

Satin Stitch: Before working this stitch, the parts are padded with closely placed rows of running, back or outline stitches, to bring the design into relief. Always make the padding stitches in the opposite direction to the satin stitches. Working from left to right, make over and over stitches putting the needle in each time beside the preceding stitch (C 39a). Always keep the stitches close and perfectly even.

The satin stitch is used in many ways for flowers, leaves, border designs, etc. Variations of the satin stitch are used for leaves as shown in C 39b, c, d, e, f, g and h.

Horizontal Flat Stitch: Make a short horizontal stitch across the top of the leaf, then bring thread a little to the right of the center; place needle on left edge of leaf and bring it out a little to the left of center. Continue to alternate this horizontal stitch a little to the right and a little to the left of the center until leaf is completed (C 40).

Slanted Flat Stitch: Make a short vertical stitch at the top of the leaf, and bring thread out at the right. Now, alternate slant stitch, always placing the needle on the center line and bringing it out at the edge (C 41a and b).

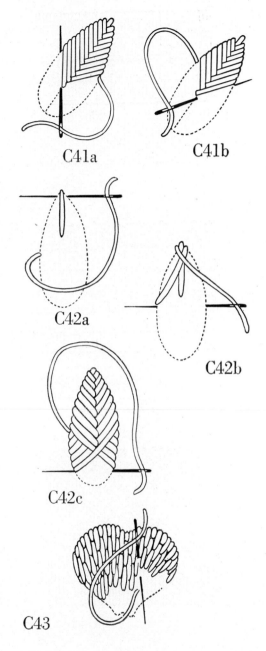

C41a

C41b

Dorondo Stitch or Self-Padded Leaf: Starting at the center top of the leaf, make a short vertical stitch at the top. Bring needle down ⅔ of leaf on the underside and come up at the left edge of the leaf. Again carry thread to top and bring down on the right side. Continue to alternate from left to right until the leaf is completed (C 42a, b and c).

C42a

C42b

C42c

Needle Painting, Kensington or Encroaching Stitch: Closely resembles the flat stitch but differs only from the latter in that the carrying out of the stitches varies in accordance with the shape and color of the design. It is a series of long and short stitches that fades into the material and completely covers the surface to be embroidered (C 43).

C43

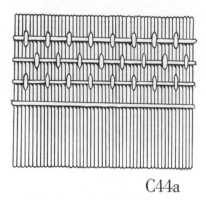

C44a

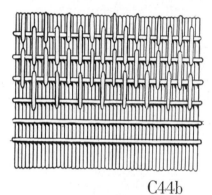

C44b

Oriental Stitches: Lay the vertical stitches first, keeping them close and perfectly even as in the satin stitch. Then, stretch threads horizontally across vertical stitches at even intervals. Fasten them with detached stitches about 5 or 6 vertical threads apart (C 44a). Or, work the fastening stitches over 2 horizontal threads (C 44b). The threads may also be stretched diagonally across the vertical threads and the fastening stitches made to correspond (C 44c).

Plaited Stitch: Lay the vertical threads, then beginning at the right, pass the needle over and under 3 or 4 of the foundation threads. To keep an even stitch, it is advisable to carry the thread underneath to the starting point at the right (C 45).

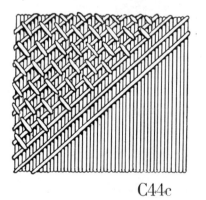

C44c

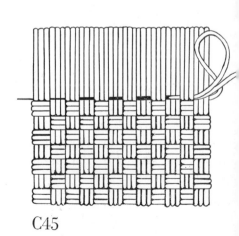

C45

Mosaic Stitch: This stitch is worked in the same manner as for the plaited stitch except that each stitch is made separately and must pass through the fabric itself so that the pattern stitches are raised (C 46).

Eyelet: Mark hole with padding stitches. Punch hole with stiletto. Work over edge with an overhand or blanket stitch. Eyelets may be of various sizes and graded widths (C 47a, b, and c). For eyelet leaves, slash material with scissors (C 47d).

Eyelet or Buttonhole Wheel: Bring needle through material on edge of circle and make two small back-stitches (C 9). Always draw stitches tightly to form holes. Bring needle back to starting point and make two small stitches into hole. Bring needle out on circle just far enough away from last stitch to make same sized back-stitch as preceding one. The circle can have as many stitches as desired. If made correctly, little holes appear around edges at each pair of stitches, and a large hole in the center (C 48).

Scallops: Pad scallop. Work over padding stitches in blanket stitch, placed close together in vertical lines. Work from left to right; make

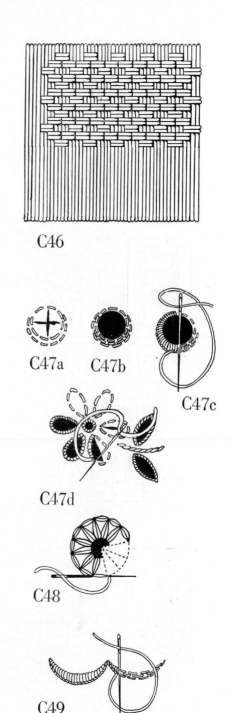

C46

C47a   C47b

C47c

C47d

C48

C49

95

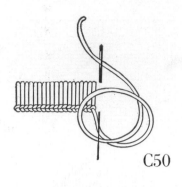

C50

no knots; conceal end of thread in padding stitches. Cut fabric away at edge (C 49). For firmer edge, use purled buttonhole stitch.

Purled Buttonhole Stitch: Bring needle to right side. Pass thread around point of needle from right to left. Draw needle through cloth and draw thread up close to form a purled edge (C 50).

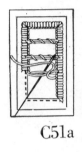

C51a   C51b

Buttonhole Bars: First work the simple buttonhole stitch along the entire line of one side, then work along the opposite line until you come to the placement of the bar. Carry thread across to finished row and bring needle up from below through one loop; bring needle through the last loop of the upper row and again carry thread across to lower row and through the next loop, thus laying three threads. Cover threads with overcast (C 51a) or buttonhole stitches (C 51b), being careful not to stitch through the fabric itself, which is cut away when the piece is completed.

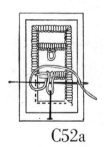

C52a

Buttonhole Bars with Picots: Work in same manner as above forming a simple picot in center of bar as shown in C 52a, an elongated picot as in C 52b and a buttonhole picot as in C 52c. For detailed explanation of picots see D 14 and 15.

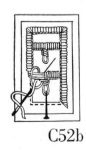

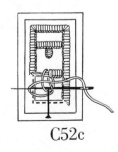

C52b   C52c

Punch Stitch: This stitch has the advantage of being able to be worked in any direction of the material. One should use a rather open mesh round weave linen and a very large round needle. Leave very little material between the spaces of the two parallel lines of the open work.

Simple Punch Stitch: Worked as indicated by the figures C 53a, b, c and d following the order of the letters.

Diagonal Punch Stitch: More frequently used. Beginning at the bottom on the right, make two stitches diagonally to the right, A to B (C 54a), then two stitches at the top to the left from C to B (C 54b); then two stitches from C to A (C 54c); then two stitches at bottom from D to A (C 54d and e).

Smocking: The most important step is the evenness of the gathering. Mark material on right side. Use a transfer or gauge dots by machine-stitching. For fine work, adjust machine for at least 8 stitches to 1 inch, and 6 stitches to 1 inch for heavy material. In using stitched lines, the presser foot gives the width and the size of the stitch, the length of your smocking stitch. When rows of stitching are com-

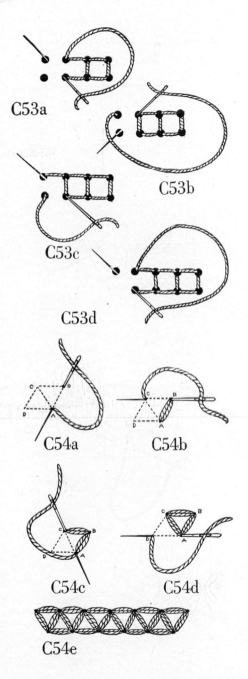

C53a

C53b

C53c

C53d

C54a   C54b

C54c   C54d

C54e

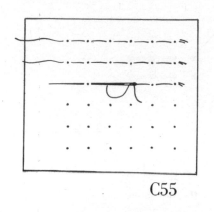

C55

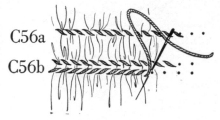

C56a
C56b

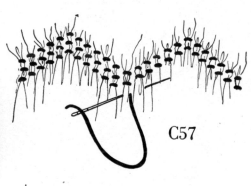

C57

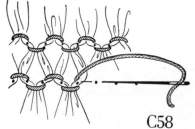

C58

pleted, clip threads about every 2 inches and remove a few at a time so as not to obliterate the marks made by machine needle. In hand-smocking, run uneven basting stitches across row with dots on top (C 55). Gather and fasten rows in pairs.

Outline Stitch: This is the simplest stitch used in smocking. Work from left to right. Bring needle to right side in the first dot and work across, always keeping thread below needle and taking a stitch over each dot. If the second row is to be worked in reverse direction, keep thread above needle, yet continue to work from left to right (C 56a and b).

Wave Stitch: Formed when the outline stitch is worked up and down in groups. Take a stitch over each dot. When working up, keep thread below needle and when working down, keep thread above needle (C 57); or reverse work.

Cable Smocking: Bring needle up through first dot. Take a stitch with first and second dots, keeping thread above needle, and draw dots together. Bring needle through third dot, keeping thread below needle and draw material to second dot. Continue across row reversing position of thread with each succeeding stitch (C 58).

Honeycomb Stitch or Seed Smocking: This stitch is formed by taking a stitch through two folds and drawing them together. Bring needle through first dot, take a stitch through second and first dots and draw them together (C 59a). Take another stitch through same dots and draw needle through to wrong side (C 59b). Work in pairs across row from left to right. Commence second row with second and third dots, thus forming the honeycomb pattern.

Diamond or Chevron Smocking: Work from left to right. Bring needle up in second row, taking up first and second dots and draw together. Keep thread on right side of material and work as for honeycomb stitch, taking one stitch through each pair of dots and on second row taking alternate pairs of dots to form diamond design (C 60).

Mock Smocking: Interesting smocking effects can be made by working embroidery stitches over machine gathers. For example, use the closed feather stitch as shown in C 61a, a fagoting stitch as in C 61b, and a back-stitch as in C 61c.

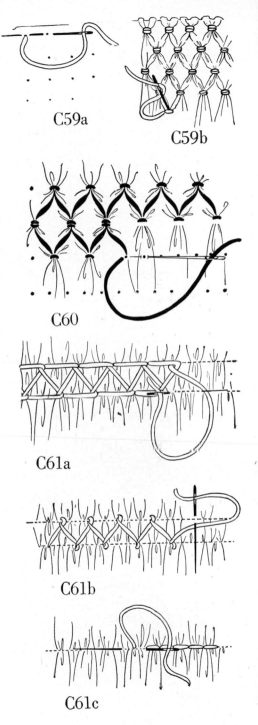

C59a

C59b

C60

C61a

C61b

C61c

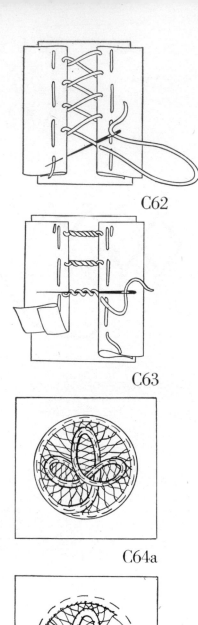

C62

C63

C64a

C64b

Fagoting Note: Always baste 2 edges of material to brown paper.

Criss Cross Fagoting: Baste folded, straight or bias strips of fabric to paper. Work from top to bottom. Bring needle up from under side of right-hand strip and slanting the needle downward, bring needle up from under side of left-hand strip. Pass the needle back of thread of preceding stitch and slanting needle downward, bring needle up from under side of right-hand strip. With needle under preceding stitch, repeat (C 62).

Ladder or Bar Fagoting: Bring needle out at left hand strip, pass it straight across to right hand strip. Twist the needle over and under this stitch and then draw needle through this twisted stitch and bring to under side of left-hand strip (C 63).

Fagoted Medallion: Baste bias binding or strips to heavy paper. Use criss cross fagoting in an irregular pattern to correspond to the design created in the binding (C 64a). Cut away paper and baste medallion to material. Cut material from under the medallion and whip raw edges to medallion (C 64b).

Hemstitching: First pull out the number of threads to make the open space. If there is to be a hem, baste hem to place (C 65a). With wrong side toward you and the open space over first finger of left hand, pass needle from right over to left, behind the desired number of threads (C 65b); draw thread close to edge; pass needle through fabric to complete stitch (C 65c).

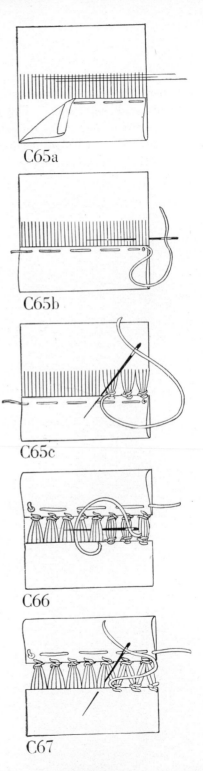

C65a

C65b

Double Hemstitching: Work same as for single hemstitching, then turn fabric around and work on opposite side. Pass needle back of same group of threads, thus forming straight bars of thread (C 66).

C65c

Diagonal Hemstitching: Work first row in same manner as for plain hemstitching. Second row: Turn and begin by taking second half of first group of threads, and first half of second group to form a cluster. Continue to pass needle back of half of each group of threads, thus making a zig-zag line of bars (C 67).

C66

C67

Hemstitching is a natural ending to this chapter on simple embroidery, as well as an appropriate beginning for the following chapter on advanced embroidery. Through hemstitching, the beginner is taught to arrange and group threads attractively. This principle is applied to the making of fringe, beaded festoons, netting, weaving, knitting, crocheting, and practically every phase of needlework.

CHAPTER 4
ADVANCED EMBROIDERY

ADVANCED EMBROIDERY

➤➤➤ EMBROIDERY and music need no interpreter. Embroidery is an international language for all lovers of beauty. From all corners of the world and from time immemorial come the stitches of this chapter; the expression of the skilled artist, an heritage that everyone admires and may make his own. Analysis of these advanced stitches in embroidery impresses us with the truth that beauty is basically simple. In this particular chapter the steps are repeated over and over again until their fineness and symmetry make one forget that the finished piece is a mere application of the satin, the buttonhole, the cross, the hemstitch or the darning stitches mentioned in the previous chapter—the a, b, c of the alphabet formed into words and colloquialisms that defy verbatim interpretation.

For instructions for Cutwork Tablecloth (Color Plate D, pg 107).

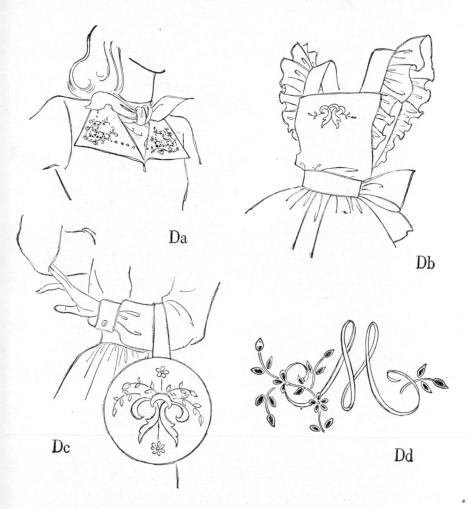

Da

Db

Dc

Dd

Design your own from color plate D

With a bit of ingenuity, you can design from a cutwork tablecloth.
1. Use Point Venise motifs (D 16d) for collar detail on dress (Da).
2. Use single motif (D 16c) in satin stitch on pinafore with eyelet spray (Db).
3. Enlarge (pg 339) single motif (D 16c) for crewel embroidered (pg 127) bag (Dc).
4. Use satin and eyelet motif to design monograms (Dd).

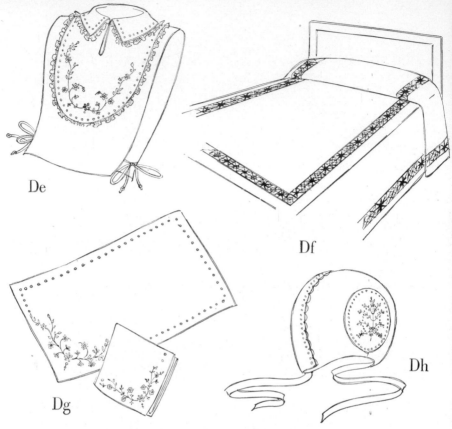

De

Df

Dg

Dh

5. Use simple satin stitch spray for dickey (De).
6. Make Point Venise motif with heavy cotton, for a bedspread (Df).
7. Use corner spray (Dj), as is, for place mats and napkins (Dg).
8. Use satin and eyelet stitch spray (D 16c) for baby bonnet (Dh).

Ideas from background of color plate D

For helpful hints, turn the pages.
1. Directions for making ruffles and flounces (Chapter 1).
2. Apply designs shown on wall paper for crewel embroidery (pg 127), net appliqué (Chapter 5), and textile painting (Chapter 14).
3. Apply floral arrangements or China dogs for embroidered pictures, needlepoint cushion, etc.

Instructions for Italian cutwork tablecloth (color plate D)

Materials Required:
2½ yards 72″ linen
1000 yards embroidery cotton in white

1. Scale and trace to size (Pg. 339) one quarter of the center design of cloth (Dj), each square represents 2 inches.
2. To form a second quarter of design, turn tracing made in Step 1 over, and trace face down on another sheet of tracing paper, overlapping center motif. Join these two pieces of tracing paper to form tracing for one half of the center design.
3. To form second half of design, turn tracing of first half made in Step 2 over, and trace face down on another sheet of tracing paper of the same size. Join these last two pieces of tracing paper to complete design for center of cloth.
4. Retrace entire design on a single sheet of tracing paper.
5. To make a transfer of this tracing, with a threadless machine stitch along all lines.
6. Lay perforated tracing paper on cloth, centering the design.
7. Rub stamping powder or ground cinnamon through holes. Or, using contrasting thread, form a running stitch (A 2) by weaving in and out the line made by the sewing machine needle.
8. Mark placement of cutwork corners (D 16d) and eyelet motifs (D 16c) on each side.
9. Embroider corners in cutwork stitches as explained from D 11a to D 16d, forming four, six or eight pointed motifs (Di) as desired.
10. Embroider center motif in satin (C 39) and eyelet stitches (D 16a) as shown in D 16c.
11. About 14 inches from center design, work one row of ornate hemstitching (D 3a). Corner detail is shown in D 7a.
12. Make a 2½ inch hem (pg 27) with single hemstitching (C 65a, b, c).
13. Press cloth, face down on a well padded board.

Di

Dj

Italian hemstitching

Italian Hemstitching: Draw out two parallel groups of thread; usually two threads are drawn out, four left in, two drawn out, but one must be guided in this regard by the quality of the material. In any case, the space between the drawn threads should be twice as wide as the open space left by the drawn threads. Work top edge in same manner as for plain hemstitching (C 65a, b), then collect into clusters the same vertical threads of the lower row. Pass the needle under the four threads of the lower row, then out in the upper row; pass needle under four threads at upper row and repeat (D 1a and b). Hemstitch the outer edge of the row. Threads for double Italian hemstitching should not be drawn all the way to the edge, as this will weaken the corner. They should be clipped a short distance from the edge at each side of the corner and tucked inside the hem. In many instances, the extreme outside edges are not hemstitched as shown in D 2. In this sketch the outer row is simple hemstitching, wrapping the long groups of threads at each side of the corner as they are reached. In the second row of stitches the left hand vertical stitch is omitted as the threads are already held by the finished row. The wide drawn space is taken care of as the inner row of hemstitching is done. The first stitch of the wide horizontal row is the simple Italian hemstitching; the second is the same as on the upper and lower rows, but instead of taking the second upright stitch over the four threads on the edge of the wide drawn space, take it over the center of the first group in this space, under the second, over the two groups again, then finally over the second group close to the outer edge. Now take the second stitch of the regular Italian hemstitching close against the edge. In D 3a, the clusters are merely knotted together. Fasten thread in the middle of the first cluster with chain stitch and draw together. Pass needle under next three clusters and repeat. For a wider area, apply this principle alternating from right side (D 3b) to left (D 3c). Repeat. It is important that the thread through center is not pulled tightly between the clusters.

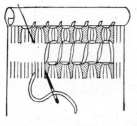

Dla

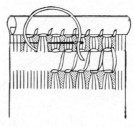

Dlb

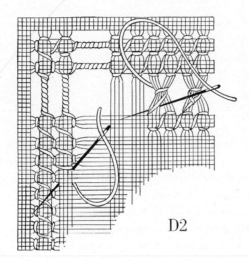

D2

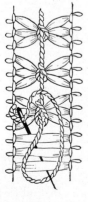

D3a

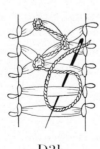

D3b

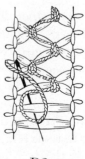

D3c

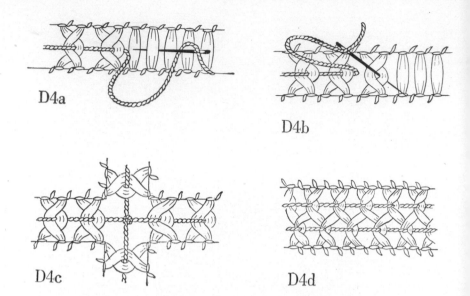

D4a

D4b

D4c

D4d

Simple Drawn Work Stitches: Draw threads and overcast or hem-stitch edges. Bring needle from right to left under the second cluster of threads (D 4a); turn needle before drawing through and pick up the second half of the first cluster of threads, which is then passed under and in front of the first cluster (D 4b). Be careful not to pull the working thread too tight. At a corner, twist the second thread at center to form a knot (D 4c). For a wider area, double twist as shown in D 4d.

Advanced Open Work Designs, Swedish or Needle Weaving: Draw out threads for desired width of border. Although not necessary, it is advisable to hemstitch the top and bottom edges where threads were drawn. As you hemstitch divide the threads into groups or sets, consisting of three or more threads. Begin weaving by running embroidery thread (no knot) into material a little above border. Bring needle out at first set and weave it over the first set and under second set as in darning (D 5a), until the set is completely encased with darning stitches. Be sure to pack threads closely. Push the darning stitches together as you work. This completes bar. Run thread down center of bar on wrong side and fasten off securely. Undo starting end of thread and finish off in the same way. All bars are made in this way and can be grouped to form many and varied patterns. In D 5b, following the above directions, weave over and under the first 2 sets until ½ of the border is covered. Then continuing across the upper space, weave over and under the second and third sets until the second half of the border is completed. Pass needle under stitches and repeat weaving over and under second set of first half. Continue in this manner until border is completed. In D 5c, an interesting border is achieved first by weaving over and under the two sets at the center, covering ½ of the border; second, by weaving over and under the two center bars of each set of four; and third by weaving over and under remaining single bar on each side. Repeat on opposite side.

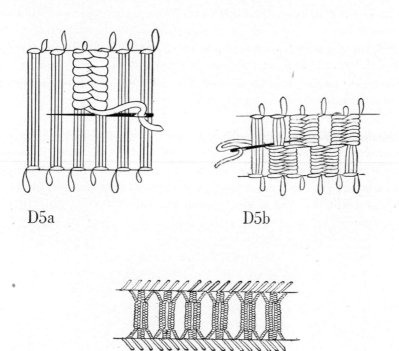

D5a

D5b

D5c

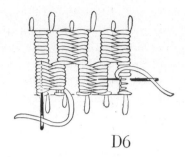

D6

Finishing: Overcast raw edges of material, then overhand with close stitches to give the appearance of a woven bar. Conceal ends of thread in woven bars (D 6).

Finishing Corners in Open Work: In a simple corner, cut and loosen threads on both sides. Conceal them in hem and fasten with a few stitches, overcast, hemstitch or buttonhole stitch (Chapter 2). The corners are finished as in Italian hemstitching or filled with attractive designs, combining the simple drawn-work stitches and a weaving stitch around the corner threads (D 7a and b).

Hardanger Embroidery: Must be worked on fabric in which the warp and woof threads are of the same thickness and equidistant from each other. Contrary to the openwork designs described above, in Hardanger embroidery the edges are embroidered before the threads are cut (D 8a). The two stitches used in this type of embroidery are the satin stitch for

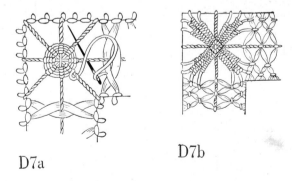

D7a

D7b

the solid parts and a weaving stitch for the drawn stitch. If the satin stitch is worked in parallel rows, the thread is brought up through the selected mesh and carried in a straight line over 4 warp threads (D 8b). If the satin stitch is worked on the diagonal, each stitch is lowered one mesh (D 8c). In many designs, the satin stitch is usually worked in groups, 5 stitches over 4 threads, though one can work as many stitches as desired, bearing in mind that there is always one more stitch than there are threads to be cut. In working a row of squares, when the first block is completed, the needle is brought up in the same line as the fifth stitch of the first block, but 4 meshes to the right. Draw thread through and again insert needle in the upper mesh of the last stitch. This forms the first stitch of the second block at right angles to the last group of stitches of the first block. Continue down this side, then carry thread under stitches on wrong side to the opposite side and commence third

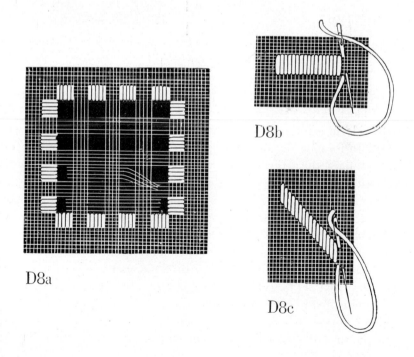

D8b

D8a

D8c

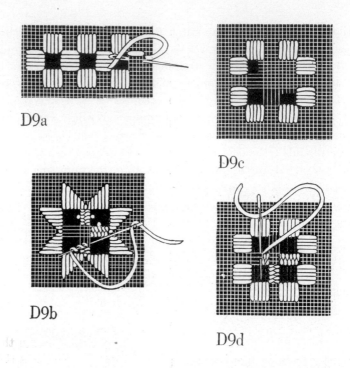

D9a

D9c

D9b

D9d

side of block in first stitch of fourth side of block above. Finally, form fourth side in same manner as first side at right angles to third side (D 9a). In forming diagonal blocks, this same principle is applied. For diagonal edges, the satin stitch is worked in graded lengths, applying the same principle (D 9b).

When all the embroidery has been completed, the work is removed from the frame and the threads cut. Care must be exercised in cutting the threads for the openwork design. Warp threads are always cut along the side of the block and never at their ends. Moreover, the threads cut inside a motif are removed first in one direction and then only in the opposite direction (D 9c). The web formed by the remaining threads is then ornamented by overcasting or darning stitches (D 9d). In the more elaborate pieces, the centers are ornamented in many ways as shown by the motif with twisted bars combined with the woven bars (D 9e);

the woven stitch combined with picots (D 9b); and the woven stitch combined with a loop stitch (D 9f and g).

Cutwork

Cutwork: As in Hardanger embroidery, the entire design is completed and then the material is cut away. The design is done in buttonhole stitch with all stitches the same width. When the buttonhole stitch is used, it is turned towards the side where the material is to be cut. When there are bars in the design as in *Richelieu embroidery*, it is preferable to outline

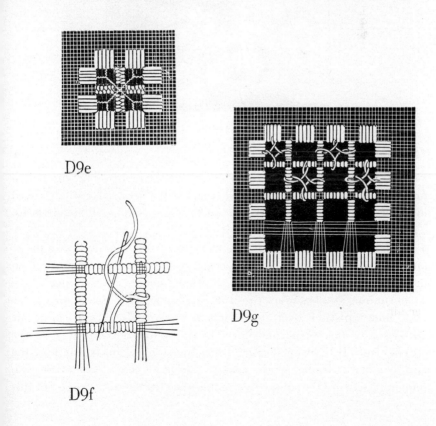

D9e

D9g

D9f

them, then work in buttonhole stitch (D 10). The bars forming the open-work are not taken into the material which is cut away from beneath them. When the *Richelieu embroidery* is elaborated with openwork it is called *Colbert embroidery*. When the design is heavily padded to give the appearance of *Venetian lace*, it is called *Venetian embroidery*.

Italian Cutwork: The name commonly given to a special type of embroidery in which the patterns are commonly marked on stiff paper or oil cloth, as a guide, and the stitches are woven on this skeleton foundation, However, some of the best examples of this work have come from Greece.

D10

France, Denmark (Hebedo Embroidery) and Mexico. The stitches in many ways are more detailed applications of the decorative stitches used in other types of drawn-work, flat embroidery and needle-made laces.

To Work a Simple Design: Sketch outline of design on brown paper and pin linen to paper. With fine stitches, baste in position about 1/8 of an inch from the outline of the sketch. Now commence embroidering. Make small running stitches from A to B, then from B carry thread diagonally to C and top-stitch over this diagonal back to B. Always form the stitches over the thread and never in the material (D 11a). Run the stitches from B to D, then carry it diagonally to A and D, catching the two diagonals together at the center. Complete the outline of the two remaining sides of the square by running the stitches to the center of this side, E. Now carry thread to the center of each side of the square F, G, H and back to E. Always pass the needle through the diagonal bars and catch it in the material on the running stitches (D 11b). Buttonhole over these strands, working picots (D 11c) in the center, if desired. Sometimes in solid *Gros Venise*, the couching stitch is used to fasten a foundation thread. There are two ways to make a point in this type of cutwork. For openwork effect, work in outline and satin stitch (D 11d); or in outline and buttonhole stitch as described above (D 11c). For a solid effect; baste linen to paper; using the couching stitch, outline the points (D 11e), then work in the *Point Venise* stitch over this structural frame of couching stitches.

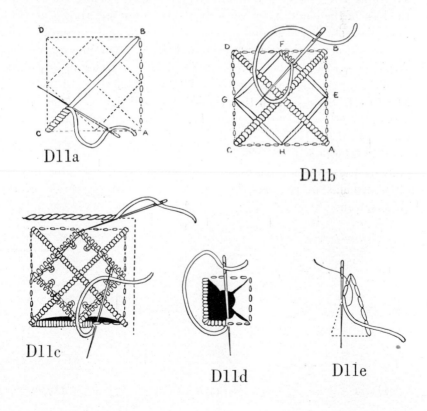

D11a

D11b

D11c

D11d

D11e

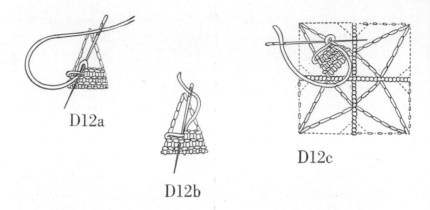

D12a

D12b

D12c

To Make the Point Venise Stitch: Work in couching stitch across
the base of the point. Then work over this foundation thread in a close
buttonhole stitch. On second row carry thread around the outline stitch
on the left, across the space and around the outline stitch on the right.
Work across in a close buttonhole stitch (D 12a), covering the foundation
or filling thread and going through each buttonhole stitch of the row below (D 12b). Always keep the stitches close and tight omitting the first
and last stitch of each row and work from right to left (D 12c). When
each point is finished, the thread is carried back to the base of the next
point by whipping down the side of the finished point. In forming ornate
points, parts of the point are made solid and parts worked in combination
of twisted and covered bars. This stitch can be used in a variety of ways
(D 13a, b and c).

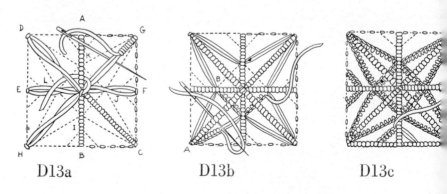

D13a

D13b

D13c

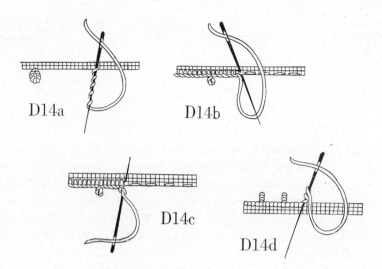

Picots: A very important and charming part of Italian cutwork. In making the single picot edge, do not wrap thread around needle, but turn needle around thread from 12 to 15 times. Draw thread through this spiral and insert the needle in the same place where it was drawn out. Carry the thread inside the hem for approximately ¾ of an inch and work next picots (D 14a).

Buttonhole Stitch and Picots: Make a running stitch the full length of hem and turn hem on this line. With edge of linen toward you, make several buttonhole stitches, then insert needle in last buttonhole stitch (D 14b)—not the material—pull it through to end of thread, then take another buttonhole stitch in the same thread. Now insert the needle *under* the last buttonhole stitch in the material and not over it (D 14c). The thread is now in the correct position to continue the buttonhole stitches across the desired space, usually five or six stitches. A simplified form of this edge can be worked by replacing the buttonhole stitch with the overcast stitch and the above single picot. This time the linen is held toward you and not the edge (D 14d).

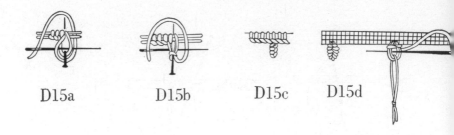

D15a   D15b   D15c   D15d

Enlarged Single Picot: Work in same manner as for single picot, holding the fold of the hem toward you. Sew into the hem, three loops over a pin or string which serves to keep them the size desired and to hold them down (D 15a). Keeping these loops close by this pin, weave over and under as in drawn work, from the hem to the top of this triple loop or work over triple strand in buttonhole stitch (D 15b). When picot is finished, slip needle through stitches on right side of loop back to hem (D 15c). If preferred, omit buttonhole stitches between picots. Carry needle between the fold of the hem to next picot. Draw holding pin or string out at the completion of each picot (D 15d).

Giant Picot or Point: Formed along the edge in the same manner as the Point Venise stitch, omitting the outline stitch. Merely work in buttonhole stitch over a foundation thread for the desired number of stitches and skip one stitch at the beginning of every row. A splendid example of cutwork is seen in these photographs, clearly expressing the beauty and depth of the padded satin stitch in the side-center motif (D 16a, b and c) and the symmetry of the picots, buttonhole and Point Venise stitches of the corner motif (D 16d).

D16a

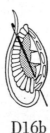

D16b

122

D16c

D16d

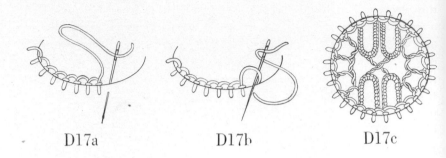

D17a   D17b   D17c

Hedebo Embroidery: The *Danish* form of cut and drawn work. In it,
one applies the stitches described in Italian cutwork and Hardanger embroidery, as well as the punch stitch (C 53 and 54). Delightful effects can
be obtained in Hedebo embroidery by working the openwork parts with
a strong, firmly twisted thread and the surface embroidery in a softer
but thicker, and lightly twisted linen thread.

To Work a Design: Mark outline of the motif on material, preferably
linen; work 2 rows of running stitches around the entire outline; following the grain of the material wherever possible, cut away the material
and outline edge in the Hedebo buttonhole stitch (D 17a and b). To
make the Hedebo buttonhole stitch, two separate movements are necessary. Holding the edge of the material away from you, insert the needle

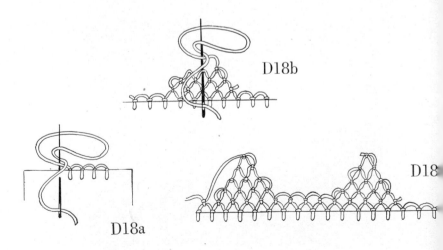

D18b

D18a   D18

downwards into the edge of the material (D 17a) and draw through until a small loop remains. Then slip needle through the loop and pull stitch and loop tightly with a slight jerk, thus leaving a small space between each stitch (D 17b). It is advisable to turn the material under with your needle as you form the stitch and take each stitch through the double thickness of the material. The second row in Hedebo embroidery is usually an application of this buttonhole stitch, simply worked more loosely. Skip one or two stitches of the row previous and omit the final jerk at end of each stitch. Complete row by whipping or overcasting looped edges. The surface embroidery consists chiefly in floral arrangements worked in satin stitch, while the edges are finished with the Hedebo buttonhole stitch arranged as loops, pyramids and rings (D 17c).

Armenian Needlepoint Lace: Another application of the buttonhole stitch. In this work, all loops and meshes are made with a knot stitch worked from right to left.

To Make the Knot Stitch: Hold the edge away from you and point the needle away from you. Fasten thread in material and insert needle in material. Place thread nearest the cloth over and in front of the needle; place the far end of the thread nearest the eye of the needle, under and over the needle; then pull needle through and tighten thread, bringing the knot close to the edge (D 18a). The next stitch is taken about ⅛ of an inch from previous knot. The succeeding rows of loops are made in the same manner, forming a knot in each loop (D 18b). When forming points, the edging may be made with or without cutting the thread (D 18c).

Gold Embroidery: This unquestionably holds the highest place in the various kinds of embroidery when we consider the effect produced. Now as in the 17th and 18th centuries, it is used primarily for the decoration of ecclesiastical vestments and ornaments, and is usually worked on heavy brocade, velvet, silk or leather. Gold embroidery requires a strong frame on which to mount the work, a spindle on which to wind the thread and a stiletto. First, fasten a strong piece of material to the frame as a

D19

lining, then stretching the material to be embroidered as taut as possible, sew material to lining. It is advisable to complete the outline or couching stitch and the flat stitches not requiring padding before commencing the more elaborate stitches.

Raised Gold Embroidery: The designs are padded in various ways; in the same manner as for the simple satin stitch; and by covering pieces of cardboard, blotting paper or leather, cut to the shape of the design. If couching is necessary, it is done with a matching silk thread.

Flat Gold Embroidery: A thick or a double strand of gold cord is laid on the foundation and commonly fastened with gold thread to make the stitches invisible. The design must be worked without any break as the passing of the thick cord will deface the fabric and spoil the appearance of the work. To eliminate as much strain as possible, push a blunt-end needle through the material at the beginning of the motif and draw end of cord or double strand through to wrong side for ½ inch.

The gold cord is then couched down with silk thread in two distinct movements, up to the right of the thread and down on the left. When the needle enters the material, be certain to insert it well under the threads of the previous row to prevent the cord from moving. Before beginning to work on an elaborate piece of gold embroidery, it is necessary to study carefully the design itself, determining beforehand the proper direction of your stitch. A change in the slant of your stitch not only gives diversity to your design but gives the life and character that has placed this embroidery in such an enviable position (D 19).

Crewel or Jacobean Embroidery: A combination of many embroidery stitches usually worked in wool (D 20). It, however, can be carried out in silk and cotton. Chain, encroaching, satin, chevron, brick, herringbone, blanket, feather stitches all play a part in crewel embroidery. The designs are usually free and graceful, worked on a heavy fabric for bedspreads, draperies, wall hangings and furniture covers.

D20

127

Assisi embroidery

Assisi Embroidery: A variation of the cross stitch (Page 91). In this work, the stitch is the same but the principle of design is reversed—the background is embroidered and the design itself left plain or merely outlined for emphasis (D 21). For a more detailed explanation of the application and designing of charts see pgs 454 to 458.

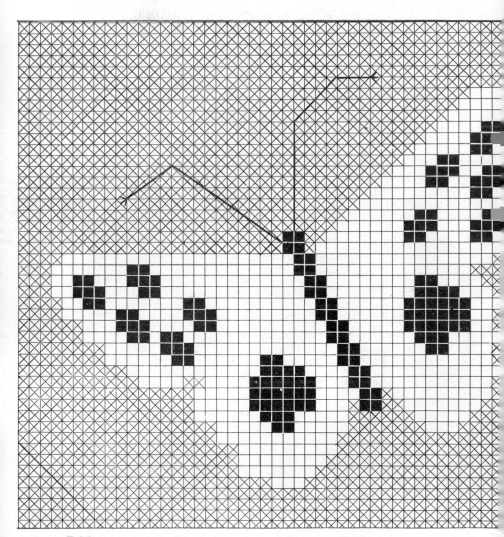

D21

CHAPTER 5

APPLIQUÉ, QUILTING, PATCHWORK AND TUFTING

APPLIQUÉ, QUILTING, PATCHWORK AND TUFTING

➤➤➤ "AUNT DINAH's quilting party" may make us feel that the patch-work quilt is an American creation, but, both patchwork and quilting take us to ancient Egypt. In the International Encyclopedia we read of a garment called "gambeson"—"a medieval armor, a protection for the body, composed of layers of cloth, tow or similar material, quilted on a lining of canvas or leather; worn by the infantry as their only defense and by knights under mail shirts. It is the most ancient of all armor used by the ancient Egyptians." And so our gay and colorful quilts of today are an outgrowth of need.

As in all works of art, there is no end to what can be created from the application, of not only the primer steps but of kindergarten methods, as the folding of paper into quarters and cutting away part of the folded edges to form an appliqué design, or a motif for shadow quilting, or a geometric scroll for trapunto quilting. To the genius, and we all are potential masters of what we desire to know, real satisfaction lies, not in copying what has been planned by another, but in what is designed by the trial and error system.

Instructions for Quilted Bedspread (Color Plate E, see pg 134)

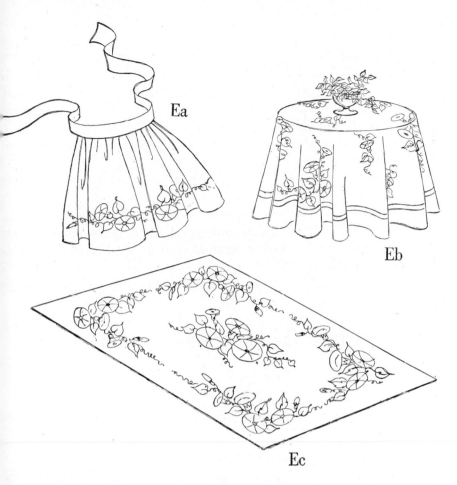

Ea

Eb

Ec

Design your own from color plate E

With a bit of ingenuity, you can design from a quilted bedspread.

. Scale (pg 339), trace and cut stencil of design, entire or in part, and paint on material (Textile Painting, Chapter 14) for apron (Ea). For accent, use embroidery stitches (Chapter 3).

. Scale, trace and use design, entire or in part, in simple appliqué (pg 139), outline stitch (C 4), crewel embroidery (Chapter 4), machine-embroidery (Chapter 14), etc. for tablecloth (Eb).

. Scale (pg 339) and trace design (Ek and l) of sham or spread as is, for a hooked or needlepoint rug. For a large rug, duplicate design at opposite end (Ec).

4. Scale, trace and cut stencil of design, entire or in part and paint on material (Textile Painting, Chapter 14) for spread, place mat (Ed), dresses, bags, etc. For accent, use embroidery stitches (Chapter 3), beads and sequins, (Chapter 14).
5. Scale, trace, and reverse (pg 340) corner design of spread for housecoat (Ee).
6. Scale, trace, and reverse corner design of spread for dressing table skirt (Ef).
7. Allowing space between corner-designs, use for double spread (Eg).
8. Scale, trace and use design entire or in part in simple appliqué, outline stitch (C 4), machine-embroidery (Chapter 14), etc. for sheets and pillow cases (Eh).
9. Scale, trace and use design for valances (Ei), headboard of bed (Ej), slip covers, etc.

Ideas from the background of color plate E

For helpful hints, turn the pages.
1. For lampshades and curtains, see Chapter 13.
2. For detail explanation of tucks, see Chapter 1.

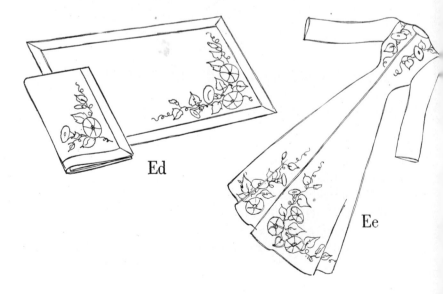

Ed

Ee

Ef

Eg

Eh

Ei

Ej

Instructions for quilted bedspread and sham (color plate E)

Materials Required:

10½ yards blue chintz 36″ wide (8 yards for ruffles, 2½ yards for flowers, cording and border)

2¾ yards white chintz

¾ yard dark green chintz for leaves and vines

⅓ yard chartreuse chintz for leaves and vines

⅓ yard shrimp chintz for flowers

2¾ yards white cotton lining 40″ wide

3 yards heavy comforter padding or 10 sheets 40″ x 40″ of cotton wadding (use double).

1 roll cotton batting for trapunto quilting

10 yards cable cord

3 spools white sewing cotton, 2 blue, 1 each of dark green, chartreuse, shrimp

1 skein each embroidery cotton—blue, dark green, shrimp

Directions for Bedspread

1. Cut white chintz 78½″ x 36″; 2 pieces of blue chintz for side flounce 152″ x 24½″; 1 piece of blue chintz for end flounce 76″ x 24½″; 2 pieces blue chintz for side border 80″ x 2¼″; 2 pieces of blue chintz for end border 40½″ x 2¼″; 2 pieces of blue chintz in bias strips 1¼″ wide for cording; padding same size as white chintz; and cotton lining 80″ x 40½″.

2. Baste padding to white chintz. Quilt 5″ squares on direct bias across entire quilt.

3. Allow ½″ for seams, join and mitre side borders to end border.

4. Make cording (pgs 25 and 26) to fit around outer edge of blue border, allowing for ease at corners.

5. Stitch 1″ hem along bottom and end of each side flounce piece.

6. One-half-inch from top edge, gather each side flounce to 78″.

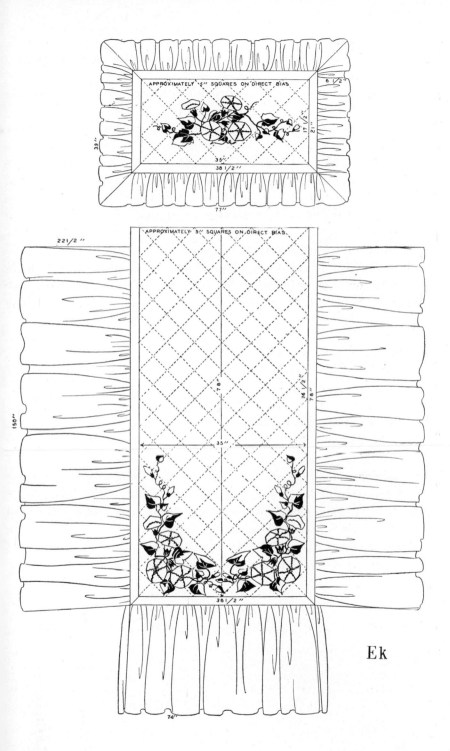

APPROXIMATELY 9" SQUARES ON DIRECT BIAS

6 1/2"

17 1/2"

21"

39"

35"

38 1/2"

77"

APPROXIMATELY 9" SQUARES ON DIRECT BIAS

22 1/2"

78"

76 1/2"

78"

150"

35"

38 1/2"

74"

Ek

135

7. Allowing 1″ hem, stitch to cording and border on each side, beginning 4″ from each top end (Ek).
8. Stitch; gather to 38½″; and join end flounce to border in similar manner (Ek).
9. Scale and cut appliqué flowers and sections of leaves (Em), allowing ½″ on all sides (¼″ for seams and ¼″ to allow for trapunto quilting). Make each flower and leaf 6 times the size in sketch.
10. Scale and trace design (El) in proper position on quilted piece Ek.
11. Cut bias strip (A 67) ¾″ wide for vines in dark green chintz. Form double bias and stitch. Following traced design, slip stitch to quilted piece.
12. Match and join sections to complete leaves. (El).
13. Following tracing lines, appliqué (E la to d) pieces to spread—leave a ½″ opening for insertion of cotton batting (E 8c).
14. Use outline stitch (C 4) for veins of leaves and flowers in matching embroidery cotton. (El)

Directions for Sham
1. Cut white chintz 19½″ x 36″.
   2 pieces blue chintz for side flounces 41″ x 7½″
   2 pieces blue chintz for bottom and top flounces 79″ x 7½″
   2 pieces blue chintz for bottom and top borders 40½″ x 2¼″
   2 pieces blue chintz for side borders 23″ x 2¼″
   blue chintz in bias strip 1¼″ wide for cording
   padding same size as white chintz and cotton lining 40¼″ x 23″
2. Follow steps 2, 3 and 4 of bedspread directions.
3. Make ⅛″ hems along bottom edge of flounce pieces, join (Ek).
4. One-half-inch from top edge, gather side flounce pieces to 21″; bottom and top flounce pieces to 38½″. Stitch to cording and border.
5. Follow steps 9 to 14 of bedspread and charts Ek and m.

136

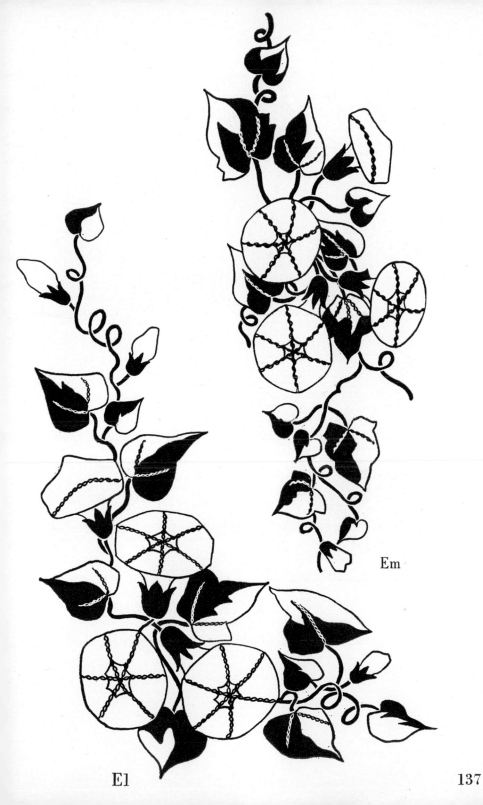

Em

El   137

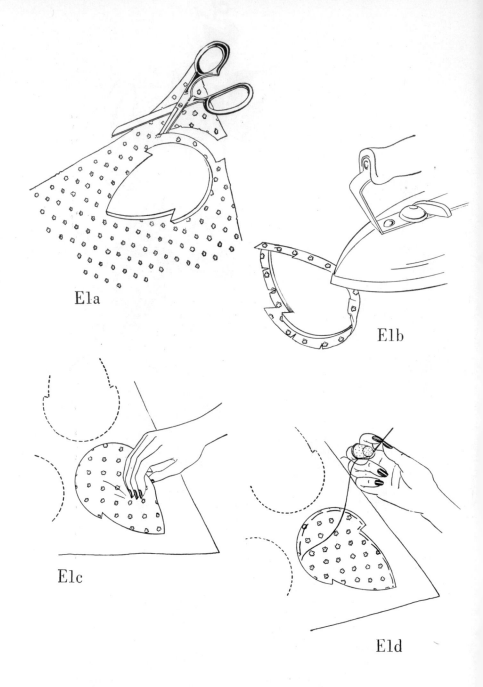

Ela

Elb

Elc

Eld

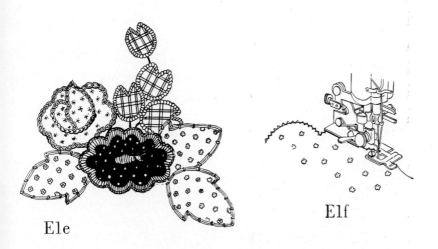

Ele

Elf

Appliqué, quilting, patchwork and tufting

Appliqué: The cutting out of pieces of material so as to form a design and laying them on the surface of another. The applied material should be in direct contrast in texture or color to the foundation material to make it stand out in bold relief from the background. It is advisable in this type of work, to make a pattern of the design in cardboard; then cut design in material (E 1a). Felt and leather require no seam allowance, however. Turn seam allowance over cardboard design and press (E 1b). Slash edges, wherever necessary, to make them lie flat. Remove the cardboard (E 1c). Lay the "appliqué" with edges turned under on foundation cloth being careful that the grain of the "appliqué" corresponds with the straight of the background material. Baste into place (E 1d). The pieces may be applied to the foundation cloth in many ways . . . by invisible hemming, buttonhole, chain and fine herringbone stitches; by couching stitches over a cord or heavy thread; in fact, by almost every kind of hand (Chapter 3) and machine stitch (E 1e). In machine-sewing, the zigzagger attachment that swings from side to side is very effective for appliquéing (E 1f).

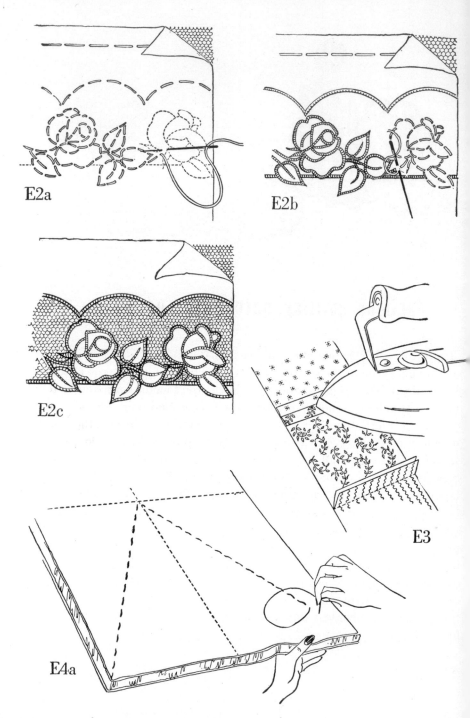

E2a

E2b

E2c

E3

E4a

140

Net Appliqué: Contrary to the ordinary appliqué, in net appliqué the design is *not* cut out first. Apply the net to the back of the foundation material (E 2a). Baste firmly, then, going through both layers of material, outline the design in a running stitch. Work over this line in a buttonhole, couching, slanting satin or straight and very close raised stem stitch (E 2b). Now, add any surface embroidery to the appliqué pieces, as desired. When the embroidery is finished, pull out basting thread and carefully cut away the material around the design. The net appears, forming an insertion on which the embroidery design stands out in relief (E 2c). Many times, touches of embroidery are added to the net to complete the design.

Patchwork: The art of piecing together fabrics of various types and colors to form a design. Prepare patches or units in same manner as for appliqué. Press back seam allowance of each unit, thus making a guide line for sewing. As in quilting, commence the joining of the units from the center out. Join units together with a running stitch or by machine on wrong side. Press the seams frequently to make a perfect quilt. In simple block design, the block units are joined in strips and then the strips are joined together (E 3). The border is always sewed on last. Embroidery stitches are often used to enhance the design as in appliqué.

Quilting: Merely a group of close running stitches arranged to form an effective design and commonly worked through two layers of material and a soft interlining. Many patchwork quilts are quilted only along the seams and this can be done holding the quilt on the lap or supporting it on the table. However, a frame is necessary for hand-quilting a large piece. The purpose of the frame is to hold the work smooth and taut. Cut the backing and the top the same size unless you wish to bring the edges of the backing over the top for a binding. Lay the lining flat, smoothing it out. Place cotton batting on top of lining, again smoothing it out to eliminate wrinkles. Place top over these two layers and baste together very carefully. Always start basting at center and always baste through three layers. Baste out to side; then diagonally to each corner (E 4a). Finally, baste all outer edges together.

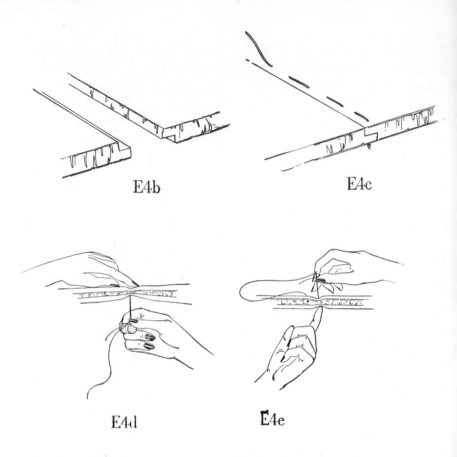

E4b

E4c

E4d

E4e

To Mark the Top for Quilting: For straight line quilting, mark with a ruler and a soft pencil or with a chalked cord held taut and quickly snapped, leaving a straight mark to follow in quilting. If a stiff cardboard or a stencil pattern is used, follow the design lightly with a soft pencil. Pencil marks left on the top of the quilt can usually be removed with an "art gum" eraser. Another method of marking, one that keeps the top clean, is to mark around the cardboard or stencil pattern with a large needle. This type of marking is done after the quilt is on the frame and only a small space is marked at a time. If the design is sketched on tracing paper, a perforated pattern can be made by perforating the design from the right side with a large needle or with an unthreaded sewing machine set to a medium stitch. Transfer this design to the quilt top with stamping powder or ground cinnamon. Place pattern in position and dust

142

over the perforations with a pad dipped in the powder. Remove the pattern and trace lightly over the marking with a soft pencil, if necessary.

To Join Two Pieces of Batting: Split the thickness about one inch from the edges of both pieces to be joined. Then, cut away the upper half from one edge and the lower half from the other edge, about ¾ of an inch back (E 4b). Lap the two half thicknesses over one another and baste together with long stitches (E 4c). This even seam will add nothing to the thickness and will not interfere with the quilting.

To Quilt: Thread a sharp needle with a thread that will not fray and make a knot at one end. Wax thread for better results. Place the forefinger of left hand over the place where the needle should come through. With right hand, force needle from underneath up through the three layers of material until the needle touches the tip of forefinger of the left hand, thus indicating that it is coming through at the correct spot (E 4d). With right hand, draw the needle and thread through until the knot is concealed in the interlining. Place forefinger of left hand under the spot where the needle should come through. With right hand, force needle down through the three layers (E 4e). With right hand, draw the needle and thread through. To protect your fingers, wear the tips of old kid gloves thin enough not to interfere with the sense of touch. Work in close running stitch in this manner, taking care to fasten securely the end of each thread. When the quilting is completed, bind the edges. Bias binding is necessary for scalloped edges. The machine-quilter with an attached guide is effective and helpful for large pieces of work as well as a time-saver (E 5).

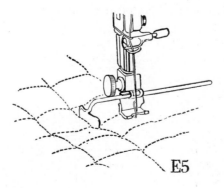

E5

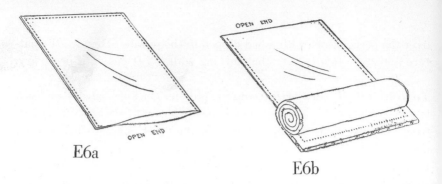

E6a

E6b

Tufted or Quilted Comforter: Sometimes where more warmth is required in a quilt, the interlining is made of wool, feathers, two layers of batting or similar material. In a comforter, sew pieces together to form a tube or bag which is opened at one end (E 6a). With wrong side out, spread cover out on a flat surface, unroll the double batting or interlining and place smoothly and evenly on top of the cover, allowing the interlining to extend beyond the edges of the cover about one inch on all sides (E 6b). This gives the edges of your comforter when completed, a nice rounded finish. Baste interlining to all four sides of the top cover and turn right side out as you would a pillow slip, reaching inside for the two far corners and drawing them back through the open end. Sew up the end and complete your comforter by tacking or quilting. To quilt a comforter, use the same principles explained above but use a very simple design.

To Tuft: Use heavy wool or soft rug cotton and a thick needle to make a big enough hole for the yarn to go through. Cut a long strand of yarn and thread the needle with it, pulling the ends even. Force the needle down through the various layers of material and pull it through to the

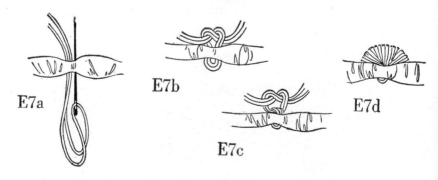

E7a

E7b

E7c

E7d

144

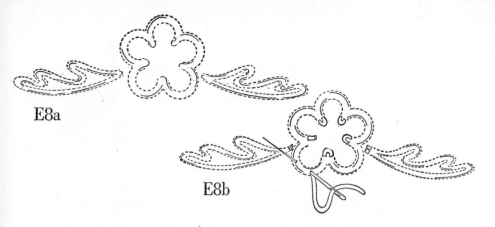

E8a

E8b

wrong side; then force it up to the right side again, about a quarter of an inch away from the spot where it went in (E 7a). Pull yarn through and tie in a firm double knot (E 7b and c). Cut off, leaving half an inch at the ends to make the little tufts. Trim neatly with scissors (E 7d). If woolen yarn is used, the tufts may be steamed, which will cause them to fluff and appear much larger.

Trapunto, Italian or Stuffed Quilting: Using double lines, trace a design, preferably onto cheesecloth or any thin, loosely woven material. With wrong sides facing, baste design to the top piece of material, usually taffeta or satin, and follow the lines of your design with a fine running stitch (E 8a). Using a blunt-end needle and heavy rug yarn, jiffy wool or cord, insert the yarn from the back between the rows of stitches to emphasize the design as shown (E 8a). At any definite curve, bring needle out and insert again through the same hole, then continue threading (E 8b). At a sharp angle, bring needle out at corner, leave the yarn or cord loose forming a loop; then, insert needle again just beyond the hole and continue threading (E 8b). Use as many strands as is necessary to fill the space between the double rows of stitches. If animals or flowers are used, the entire motif can be raised by forcing batting or absorbent cotton through the cheesecloth with a large-headed needle or crochet hook (E 8c). If cotton batting is unavailable, with four strands of wool in needle, draw wool across the length of the motif and cut, leaving an end of ½ inch at each end. Continue in this manner until the entire design is padded; then, cut off ends of wool close to cheesecloth (E 8d). Another method is to baste pieces of cheesecloth under the portions to be

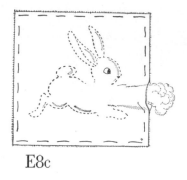

E8c

E8d

padded before the top is quilted. Sew these pieces with tiny running stitches following the design, leaving a small opening at one corner and stuff the extra cotton in and complete quilting (E 8c). The parts that have been padded will show on the quilt back as unquilted spaces. If appliqué pieces are to be padded, do not quite complete whipping the appliqué; leave an opening and push the cotton through with a crochet hook; then finish whipping.

Shadow Quilting: An outgrowth of simple quilting that lends itself only to thin materials. The material, of necessity, must be transparent as China silk, voile, marquisette or any thin rayon material. Any color can be used but since the outer layer of the material dulls the tone of the background or second layer, it is essential to bear this in mind when choosing the colors for the design. The thin outside layer is usually white, cream or ivory. Baste cotton batting to under sides of background (E 9a). If a patchwork effect is desired, cut out the motifs of your design in the desired colors, press back seam allowance and pin in place on the right side of the background (E 9b). Turn the background to wrong side and pin the pieces through again from this side (E 9c). Remove pins from upper side, then lay the transparent top over it (E 9d). Baste the design in place catching the three layers of material. Make the bastings close enough to keep the pieces from slipping or wrinkling. Remove all pins. Now outline the design with small running stitches in silk or fine cotton, then add a few inside touches to each motif as veins for leaves or di-

agonals in a geometric design. This may be all the quilting desired. However, in a large piece, it is advisable to cover the entire background with
an all-over quilting design (E 9e). A very attractive type of shadow quilting is obtained when the design is applied directly to the material with
textile paints (Chapter 14, Page 451), the highlights accented with
simple embroidery stitches (Chapter 3) and the background quilted.

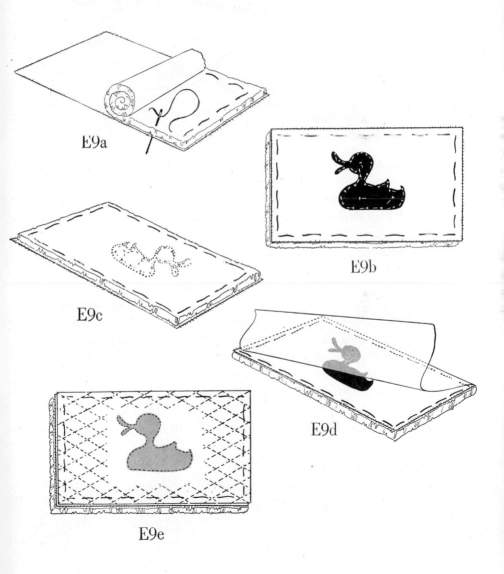

E9a

E9b

E9c

E9d

E9e

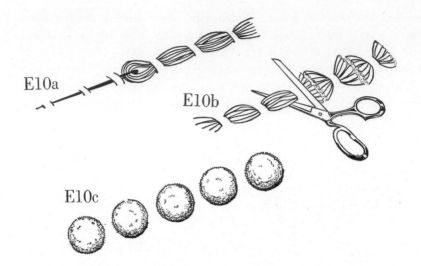

E10a

E10b

E10c

Candlewicking or Tufting: Merely long running stitches worked with a large needle and with several strands of cotton yarn. Outline the design with dots or lines on any coarse cotton or linen material. Cut several long strands of cotton yarn, preferably four strands; thread a candlewick needle or any thick needle with a large eye and pull the ends even. Following the dots or lines, work in running stitch, forming stitches at least ¾ of an inch in length (E 10a). In olden days, the stitches were raised on the surface by passing the loop over a small twig. Clip the stitches (E 10b); dip piece in water and stretch out to dry without ironing (E 10c). In candlewicking, many times, tassels or the ancient *Maltese stitch* is used. In this stitch, each tassel is made separately. Begin the stitch from the right side of the material in the center of the dot or horizontal line. Leaving an end which is a cluster of strands about one inch in length, bring the needle in again a few strands to the right of the center (E 11a). Again bring the needle out at the center and cut the strands to the length of the first cluster (E 11b).

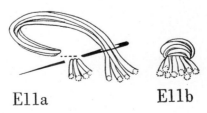

E11a

E11b

CHAPTER 6

KNITTING

KNITTING

>>> KNITTING, too, is an ancient art. It is an interlacing of lines, more specifically an interlacing of loops formed by the combined motion of two long, pointed needles. Not until one has tried does one realize what can be created with such an insignificant medium. From the interlocking of loops, fabrics unlimited in pattern and design can be created; and from these swatches of texture the individual as well as the designer can give personality to a simple sweater, dress or bedspread.

It is fun to play with knits and purls, yarn-overs and knit-2 together, even to drop a stitch and forget to pick it up, if it adds interest to the pattern—to give birth as it were, to your very own brain child.

Instructions for Ski Sweater (Color Plate F, see pg 154).

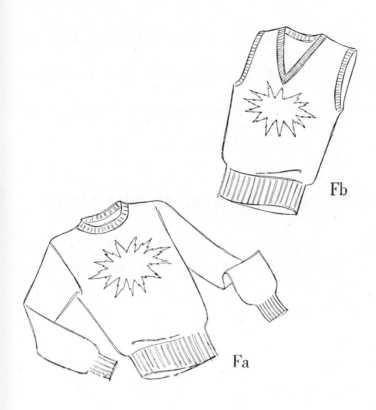

Fb

Fa

Design your own from color plate F

With a bit of ingenuity, you can design from a ski sweater.
1. For round neck sweater, rib only for one inch around neck (Fa).
2. Omit sleeves and make length to armhole one inch shorter, and length of armhole one inch longer for sleeveless sweater. Rib around armholes (Fb).
3. Use design for shopping bag (Fc).
4. Use chart for cross-stitch design (Fd) for crocheted afghan (Chapter 7) or crocheted rug (Chapter 11).
5. Trace and enlarge (pg 339) design for hooked rug (Fe and Chapter 11).
6. Scale design to size (pg 339) for potholders (Ff).
7. Use design for appliqué (Chapter 5) pillow (Fg and Chapter 13).

8. Trace and enlarge design for needlepoint (Fh), or pompon rug (Chapter 11).
9. Scale design to size (pg 339) for needlepoint footstool (Fi and Chapter 10).
10. Work sunburst design on plain handmade or machine-made sweater in duplicate stitch (F 1a to d).
11. Make simple sweater omitting design.

Ideas from the background of color plate F

For helpful hints, turn the pages.
Use design on chair for textile painting (Chapter 14), simple embroidery (Chapter 3), or crewel embroidery (Chapter 4).

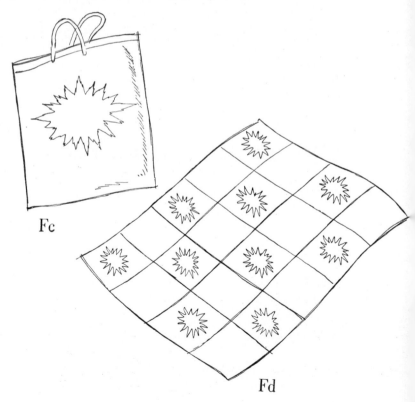

Fc

Fd

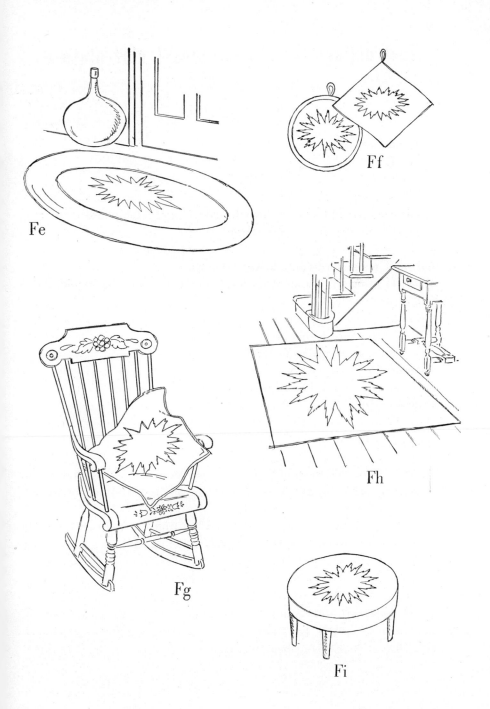

Fe

Ff

Fh

Fg

Fi

Instructions for ski sweater (color plate F)

Sizes 34, 36 and 38

Materials Required:
Knitting Worsted:
For sizes 34 and 36; 16 oz. red; For size 38: 18 oz. red.
For all sizes: 2 oz. white.
1 pair each straight knitting needles Nos. 3 and 6 (standard).
1 set D.P. needles No. 2 (standard).

Gauge: 6 sts = 1 inch; 8 rows = 1 inch.
When knitting the sunburst design, work with two balls of red and 1 ball of white (F 37).

Note 1: Be sure to check and watch your stitch gauge (pg 162). A change in yarn or needles will change your stitch gauge and consequently the size of the sweater. (See chart for possible stitch gauge with different yarns and needles and for all sizes from 6 to 44—see page 157).

Note 2: In following the chart Fj each square represents a stitch and each row a round or row. (Abbreviations—pg 160).

Note 3: Underline the numbers for the size desired. The first number in each group is for size 34, the second for size 36; and the third for size 38.

Back: On No. 3 needles and with red knitting worsted cast on (F 4a to F 5c) 104 (110–116) sts. Rib (pg. 168) in K 1 and P 1 for 3 ins. Change to No. 6 needles and work throughout in stockinette st (K 1 row and P 1 row, F 11). Work even for 14 (15–16) inches.

To Shape Armhole: Still keeping the continuity of the pattern stitch, bind off 6 (7–7) sts (F 16a and b) at the beg of the next 2 rows (once each side). Dec 1 st (F 15) at beg and end of every other row 6 (7–7) times.

Work even on 80 (82–88) sts until armhole measures approximately 7 (7½–8) ins.

To Shape Shoulders: Bind off 9 sts at beg of next 6 (4–2) rows; then bind off 0 (10–10) sts at beg of next 0 (2–4) rows—27 (28–29) sts for each shoulder. Leave remaining 26 (26–30) sts in center on holder for neck.

Note: If preferred, work Front in red in stockinette stitch, and embroider sunburst design in duplicate stitch (F 1a to d) when finished.

Front: Work in same manner as for Back until piece measures 9½ (10–11) ins. Now follow chart Fj to form sunburst design and to shape armholes. When neck is reached, work both sides at same time. Still following chart, dec 1 st at neck edges every other row or as indicated on chart until 27 (28–29) sts remain for each shoulder. Work even until same length as back.

To Shape Shoulders: At armsides, bind off 9 sts 3 (2–1) times; then bind off 0 (10–10) sts at beg of next 0 (1–2) rows. Fasten off.

Sleeves: On No. 3 needles and with red yarn cast on 52 (56–60) sts. Rib (pg. 168) in K 1 and P 1 for 3 ins. Change to No. 6 needles and work throughout in stockinette st. Work even for 4 rows, then inc 1 st at beg and end of every 4th row 8 times then every 6th row until there are 76 (80–84) sts on needle. Work even until desired length to armhole—approximately 17 (18–19) ins.
To Shape Cap: Bind off 5 sts at beg of next 2 rows (once each side). Dec 1 st at beg of next 20 rows (10 times each side). Bind off 2 sts at beg of next 8 rows (4 times each side). Bind off 4 sts at beg of next 4 rows (twice each side). Bind off remaining sts.

Finishing: Join side, shoulder and sleeve seams. Set in sleeves (pg 208).

Turtle-Neck Band: With No. 2 d.p. needles, pick up 104 (108–112) sts (F 18) and rib in K 1 and P 1 for 5 ins. Bind off loosely in ribbing.

155

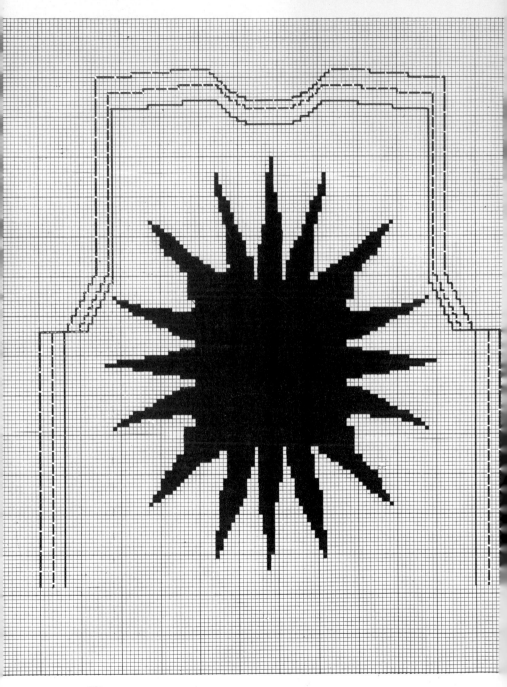

Fj

Special Note: Stitch gauge chart (Fk) and the size-chart (Fl) are for knitters who wish to apply the principles for planning a garment explained on pages 184 to 209. Be sure to check your stitch gauge (F 3a) with chart (Fk) and reread above mentioned pages before writing your own instructions. Please note that size-chart (Fk) covers all possible stitch gauges and chart Fl is a draft in inches of sizes—6–10–14 for standard measurements given below:

Stitch gauge chart (Fk)

If Your Stitch Gauge Measures:	Cast On Stitches For Size:										
	6	8	10	12	14	34	36	38	40	42	44
5 sts = 1 in.	62	68	72	78	82	88	92	98	102	108	112
5½ sts = 1 in.	68	74	80	84	90	96	102	106	112	118	124
6 sts = 1 in.	74	80	86	92	98	104	110	116	122	128	134
6½ sts = 1 in.	80	86	94	100	108	114	120	126	132	140	146
7 sts = 1 in.	86	94	100	108	114	122	128	136	142	150	156
7½ sts = 1 in.	92	100	108	116	122	130	138	146	152	160	168
8 sts = 1 in.	98	106	114	122	130	138	144	152	160	168	176
8½ sts = 1 in.	104	114	122	130	138	148	156	164	172	182	190
9 sts = 1 in.	110	120	128	138	146	156	164	174	182	192	200

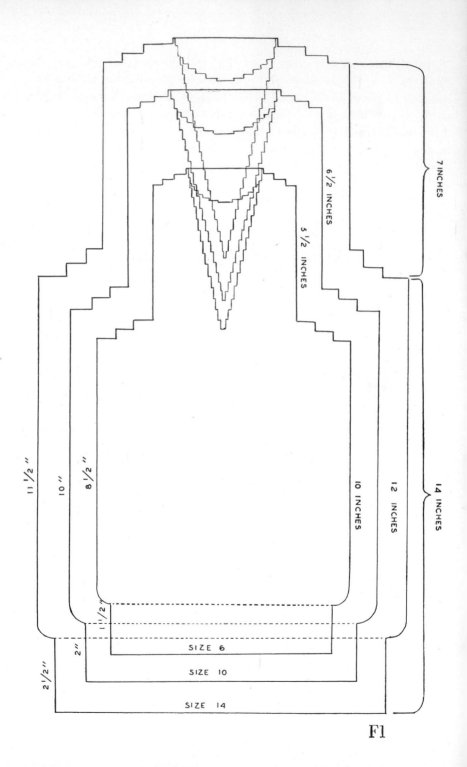

7 INCHES

6 1/2 INCHES

5 1/2 INCHES

11 1/2 "

10 "

8 1/2 "

10 INCHES

12 INCHES

14 INCHES

1 1/2 "

2 "

2 1/2 "

SIZE 6

SIZE 10

SIZE 14

F1

158

Standard body measurements

FOR INFANTS AND CHILDREN

		Chest	Waist	Hips
Size	6 Months	19		
	1	20		
	2	21		
	3	22	20½	23
	4	23	21	24
	5	23½	21½	25
	6	24	22	26
	8	26	23	28
	10	28	24	30

FOR MISSES AND WOMEN

	Bust	Waist	Hips
Size 12	30	25 −26	33
14	32	26½−27	35
16	34	28 −29	37
18	36	30 −31	39
20	38–40	32 −33	41

FOR MEN

	Chest	Waist
Size 36	36	32
38	38	34
40	40	36
42	42	38
44	44	40

Every specialty has its own lexicon and knitting is no exception to this rule. There are certain terms we must learn and certain symbols we must recognize. Without a knowledge of these abbreviations, a knitting direction sheet will seem like so much Greek or hieroglyphics. However, if we learn the simple abbreviations shown below, we will have a clear and adequate key to the mysteries of a direction chart.

Abbreviations and glossary

K....knit (F 4a to F 8)

P....purl (F 10a and b)

st(s)....stitch(es)

y.o.....yarn over. In pattern stitches, wrap your yarn as if to purl, if it precedes a knit stitch (F 17a). If, however, it precedes a purl stitch, wrap yarn completely around needle, being sure to make a new stitch (F 17b).

sl....slip. This means the transference of a stitch from the left-hand needle to the right-hand without knitting it (F 13). Unless otherwise instructed, always slip a stitch purlwise.

p.s.s.o.....pass slipped stitch over knit stitch (F 16a and b).

dec....decrease (F 15)

inc.....increase (F 14)

in(s)....inches

rd(s)....round(s)

d.p.....double pointed

*....an asterisk. This indicates that the instructions following are to be repeated across row or for the number of stitches or times specified.

A row is once across the needle.

A ridge is 2 rows, back and forth (F 9).

Work even, means to continue in pattern stitch always keeping the continuity of the original design.

In all instructions, always measure straight up and down unless otherwise stated.

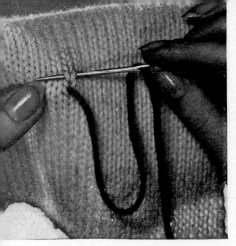

Fla   Flb

Duplicate Stitch: Thread blunt-end needle with contrasting yarn and
* from purl or wrong side, bring needle to knit or right side through the
center of the stitch. Following the outline of the knit stitch above (F 1a),
draw the yarn across the back of the 2 strands of this stitch, then return
needle to the center of the same stitch (F 1b) and draw yarn through.*
When forming the next stitch above, bring the needle through the
center of the stitch just completed (F 1c). Repeat between *'s for each
stitch to be covered in this manner, or for each stitch marked with an X
on the chart (F 1d). This stitch can only be embroidered on a stockinette
background. For example, the sunburst design, (Chart Fj), the butterflies (Charts Gn and Go); the prancing ducks (Charts K 18b) and the
needlepoint designs (Charts Jj to Jn) can be used very effectively for
the duplicate stitch on a machine or hand knit sweater.

161

lc   Fld

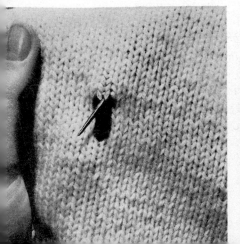

F2

F3a

Pattern Stitch: Always make a swatch of your pattern stitch before commencing garment and as you knit your swatch study the trend of the stitch. This knowledge is necessary in the shaping of your garment.

A marker is used whenever it is necessary that increases and decreases be made to form a continuous line, as in the forming of the seams of a raglan sweater. Make the marker of contrasting wool or thread; place it on right-hand needle and continue to slip the knot from left to right-hand needle in successive rows as directed (F 2).

Stitch Gauge: A true understanding of stitch gauge, which appears at the beginning of all instructions for knitting and crocheting, is most important to size and fit. Gauge is the number of stitches per inch *you* knit with a certain size needle and a specific yarn. To measure your stitch gauge, cast on 20 to 30 stitches, or the necessary multiple of stitches required for at least one repeat of the pattern stitch and knit in the desired pattern stitch for at least 3 inches or the completion of 3 pattern motifs. If possible, block piece with a damp cloth and moderate iron, then calculate the number of stitches to one inch and number of rows to one inch that *you* knit with the needle and the yarn to be used in the knitting of a specific article. The gauge can be measured with a ruler or with a guide cut in cardboard. The photograph indicates that the gauge in this swatch is 5½ stitches = 1 inch (F 3a). To impress you with the importance of the gauge, two knit sweaters are shown (F 3b). The same instructions were used for both sweaters. Merely a change of yarns and needles produced the difference. So, always overemphasize gauge. If you are in

To Cast On: *Method 1*—Make a slip knot, leaving a long end (allow 1 inch for each st) and slip needle into the loop (F 4a). * With the loose end make a loop over left thumb and with the strand attached to the ball, make a loop over the left forefinger; insert needle into this loop and draw through yarn attached to ball (F 4b). Drop yarn from thumb and tighten slightly the stitch on needle (F 4c). Repeat from * for desired number of stitches. Experienced knitters never release the strand from the ball on the forefinger, they tighten the stitch as they return the loose end to the left thumb (F 4d). It is advisable to cast on over 2 needles with this method, to insure a loose edge with sufficient stretch.

F5a

Method 2—Make a slip knot on left-hand needle (F 4a). * Insert right-hand needle into this loop from below (F 5a); pass yarn around point of right-hand needle and draw yarn through, slip this loop from right-hand needle onto left-hand needle (F 5b), then insert right-hand needle from left to right (F 5c). Repeat from * for desired number of stitches.

F5b

165

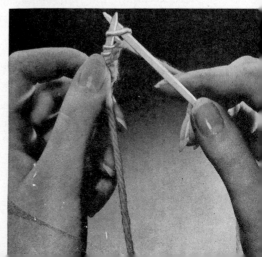

F5c

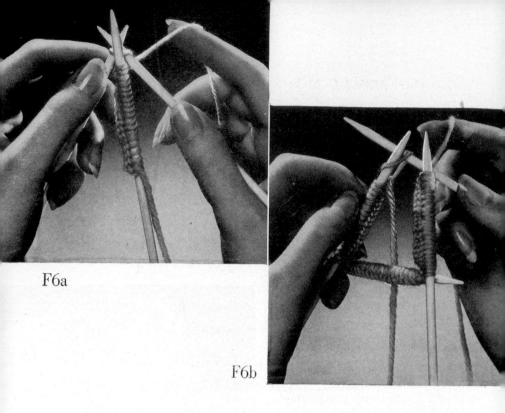

F6a

F6b

To Cast on Three Needles: When the desired number of stitches have been cast on first needle (F 5c), make an extra stitch and leave it on the right-hand needle. Change this needle to the left hand and continue to cast on in usual manner (F 6a). Repeat for third needle. Lay all three needles on a flat surface if possible, making sure that the cast-on edge does not twist. The point of the triangle, formed by the 3 needles, should be toward the knitter. Pick up the first needle in the left hand and the free needle in the right hand. Knitting is begun by inserting the 4th needle into the 1st stitch on the left-hand needle (F 6b).

To Cast on and Knit on a Circular Needle: Cast on the desired number of stitches. Lay the needle on a flat surface if possible, the same as for three needles, making sure that the cast on edge does not twist. Insert point of needle in right hand into first stitch on left-hand side, and begin to knit (F 7). In working on a circular needle the stitches always go in same direction. To form the stockinette stitch, knit continually.

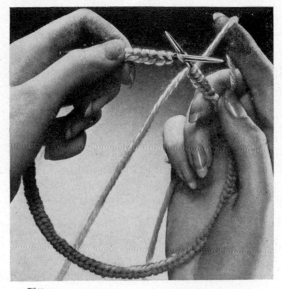

F7

To Knit: Hold needle with cast-on stitches in left hand between thumb and index finger. Place yarn in back of work. Insert the right-hand needle through the first stitch on the left-hand needle, taking it from front and below. Pass yarn around the point of the right-hand needle with a circular movement, going first behind and then in front and draw yarn through, thus forming a stitch on right-hand needle (F 8). Slip the stitch off the left-hand needle and pull the new stitch tight enough to be easy to knit in the next row. Knitting plain in this manner for a number of rows is known as the garter stitch (F 9).

167

F8

F9

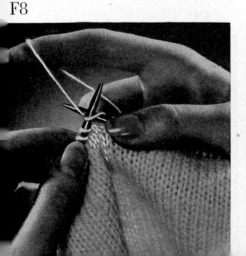

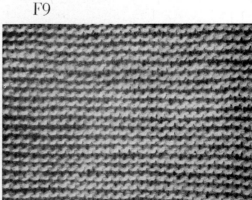

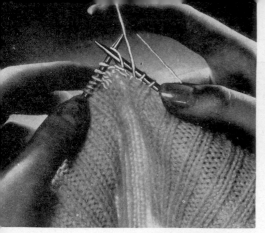
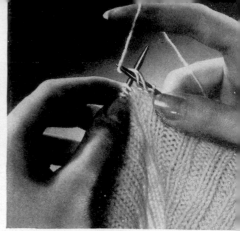

F10a   F10b

To Purl: The needles are held in the same way as for plain knitting but the wool is held in front of the work. Insert the point of the right-hand needle through the front of the first stitch on the left-hand needle from right to left (F 10a). Pass yarn around back of right-hand needle, taking the wool over and below the needle (F 10b). Draw this loop through the stitch. Slip the stitch off the left-hand needle and keep yarn to the front of the work. Pull the stitch to required tension. The purl stitch is never used alone. It is always combined with other stitches.

Stockinette Stitch: Knit across and purl back. Repeat these 2 rows (F 11).

Ribbing: This consists of alternate panels of knit and purl stitches. The most popular form of ribbing is knit 2 and purl 2. To try this ribbing stitch, cast on a number of stitches divisible by 4. * K 2 sts,
168

F11   F12

bring yarn forward and P 2 sts, repeat from * across row and end P 2. Repeat this row. Note that in ribbing, when the smooth side of stitch is toward you, the stitch is to be knitted; and when the rough side of stitch is toward you, the stitch is to be purled. In some pieces of work it is advisable for the purpose of symmetry to cast on a multiple of 4 stitches plus 2 extra; in that case, the row will begin and end with K 2 and the following row with P 2 (F 12).

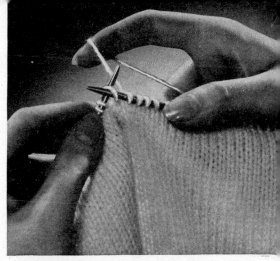

F13

To Slip a Stitch: With the yarn in back, insert right-hand needle into stitch from the front, as if to purl and take it from left-hand needle to right-hand needle, without knitting or purling (F 13).

To Increase: Knit twice in the same stitch. Knit the stich as a plain stitch and before taking it off the needle, knit again into back of same stitch (F 14). Also, to increase one purl stitch, purl twice in same stitch. Purl into front and then into back.

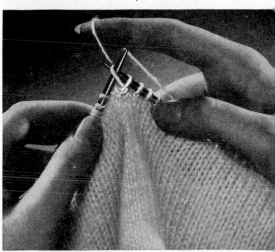

F14

To Decrease: The most common manner consists merely of knitting two stitches together (F 15). In the second method, commonly used

169

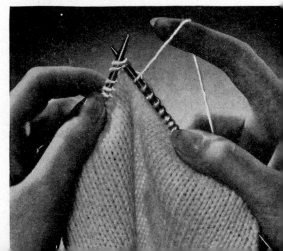

F15

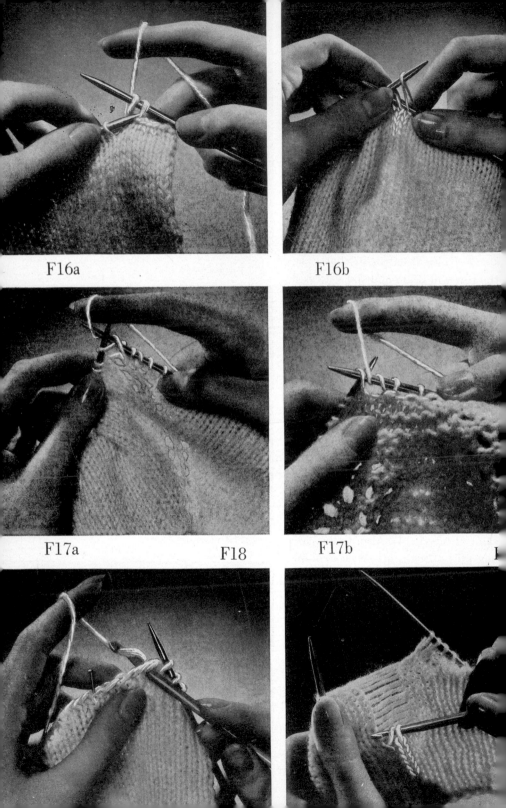

F16a

F16b

F17a

F18

F17b

in the heel of a sock, slip 1 stitch, knit 1 stitch, then pass the slipped stitch over the knit stitch on right-hand needle as in binding off. (F 16a and b).

To Bind Off: Knit 2 stitches (F 16a). * Pass the first stitch on the right-hand needle over the second stitch (F 16b), leaving one stitch on right-hand needle. Knit another stitch, again having two stitches on right-hand needle. Repeat from * until desired number of stitches is bound off.

To Yarn Over: Before a *knit* stitch, bring yarn in front of right-hand needle (F 17a) and knit the next stitch. Thus a loop is formed on the right-hand needle and an extra stitch added. Before a *purl* stitch, wrap yarn completely around right-hand needle and purl the next stitch in the usual way (F 17b). Thus a loop is formed on the right-hand needle and an extra stitch is added.

To Pick Up Stitches: Around neck and armholes hold work with right side toward you and work from right to left. * Insert crochet hook into first row or stitch and draw yarn through, thus forming stitch (F 18). Place stitch on knitting needle. Repeat from * until the desired number of stitches have been picked up within a specific area. In picking up a specified number of stitches, for example, around an armhole; it is advisable to divide the space into 4 equal parts (use pins or contrasting yarn) and be certain to pick up ¼ the desired number of stitches in each allotted segment to insure a smooth finished surface. To prevent holes in picking up, go through 2 strands of the stitch or row.

Dropped Stitches: In stockinette or rib stitch, always pick up with the K stitch toward you. Using a crochet hook, * insert hook in loop of dropped stitch, draw yarn of row above through loop (F 19), thus forming a new loop. Repeat from * until you reach the row being worked and slip loop on needle. Be careful not to twist stitches. If a dropped stitch is found in a completed piece, pick up in same manner as described above until closed space is reached. Draw loop through stitch of row above and fasten on wrong side.

To Weave Stockinette: Thread a tapestry needle and bring pieces to be joined close together. Fasten the thread to right-hand edge of upper piece. Insert needle from right side in the first stitch on lower edge and bring up through the next stitch on lower edge from wrong side (F 20a). Draw up yarn. Insert needle from right side in first stitch on upper edge * and bring up through next stitch on upper edge from wrong side (F 20b). Draw up yarn. Insert needle from right side in same stitch as before (last one threaded) on lower edge and bring up through next stitch on lower edge from wrong side (F 20a). Draw up yarn. Insert needle from right side with same stitch as before (last one threaded) on upper edge (F 20b). Repeat from * until all are joined.

To Graft Toe or Kitchener Stitch: Holding the needles side by side, with the right sides out, * insert the worsted needle in the first stitch on the front needle, as though you were going to knit it. Let the stitch slip onto the worsted needle, and insert the needle in the second stitch on the front needle as though to purl (F 21a). Pull the yarn through both these stitches (one off and one on the knitting needle). Drawing the yarn up close but not tight, insert the worsted needle in the first stitch on the back needle, as though you were going to purl. Let the stitch slip off the knitting needle onto the worsted needle. Insert the worsted needle in the second stitch on the back needle, as though you were going to knit (F 21b). Pull the yarn through the 2 stitches (one off and one on the knitting needle). Repeat from * until all stitches are used. There are al-

172

F20a   F20b

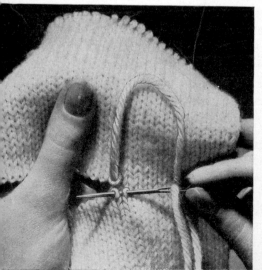

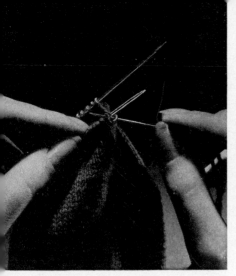
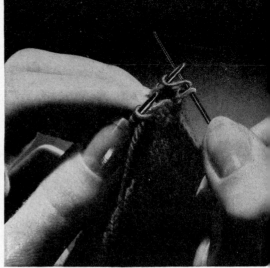

F21a   F21b

ways 2 operations on each needle with the loss of 1 stitch each time on
each needle.

Pattern Stitches: After one has attained some measure of skill and
ease in knitting, different effects that will lend distinction to the finished
piece are sought. The following stitches serve to satisfy the desire for in-
dividuality.

Moss, Seed or Rice Stitch: Cast on an uneven number of stitches.
Row 1: * Knit 1 st, and P 1 st, repeat from * across row and end K 1.
Repeat this row. In moss stitch, always be certain to K above the P sts
and P above the K sts on the following row (F 22).

F22

Simple Rib Stitch: Multiple of 7 sts plus 2 extra sts. Row 1: * P 2, K 5, repeat from * across row and end P 2. Row 2: * K 2, P 5, repeat from * across row and end K 2. Repeat these 2 rows for pattern stitch (F 23).

Oblique Rib Stitch: Cast on a number of stitches divisible by 7 and 2 extra stitches, commonly referred to as a multiple of 7 sts plus 2. Row 1: * P 2, K 5, repeat from * across row and end P 2. Row 2: * K 3, P 4, repeat from * across row and end K 2. Row 3: * P 2, K 3, P 1, K 1, repeat from * across row and end P 2. Row 4: * K 2, P 2, K 1, P 2, repeat from * across row and end K 2. Row 5: * P 2, K 1, P 1, K 3, repeat from * across row and end P 2. Row 6: K 2, * P 4, K 3, repeat from * across row and end K 3. Repeat these 6 rows for pattern stitch (F 24). These 2 examples will show you how to create new pattern sts.

Smocked Rib Stitch: Make a swatch in a simple rib pattern of K 5, P 1. The P 5–K 1 side is the right side of the garment. Gather the knit-ribs with tacking stitches as in ordinary smocking. For example: Thread blunt-end needle with contrasting yarn. ** Working from left to right, bring needle from wrong side to right side to the left of the first knit stitch; * insert needle from right to left under the second knit stitch and at same time from right to left under first knit stitch (F 25a). Draw yarn tightly through both stitches, thus forming a gather. Repeat from *, then bring needle to wrong side at the right of the second knit stitch **. Repeat between ** for each group of two knit stitches across the same

174

F23

F24

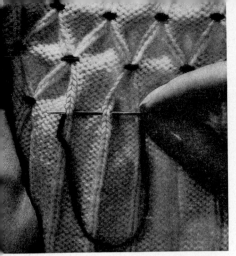

F25a   F25b

row. Skip 8 rows. Omit the first knit stitch and gather together the second and third knit stitches. Repeat the double tacking stitch for each
pair of two knit stitches across row, thus alternating the gathers of the
previous tacking row. Skip 8 rows. Repeat these 18 rows for pattern
stitch (F 25b, wrong side). This smocking stitch can be embroidered on
any type of rib pattern and the number of skipped rows varied to suit
the yarn and the whim of the designer.

Block Stitch: Cast on a number of stitches divisible by 10, commonly
referred to as a multiple of 10 stitches. Row 1: * K 5, P 5, repeat from *
across row and end P 5. Repeat Row 1 for 6 rows. Row 7: * P 5, K 5, repeat from * across row and end K 5. Repeat Row 7 for 6 rows. Repeat
these 12 rows for pattern stitch (F 26).

F26

F27

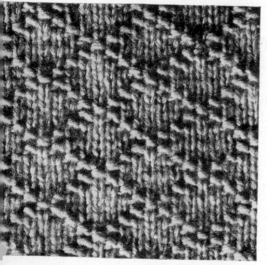

F28

Diagonal Rib Stitch: Cast on a multiple of 8 stitches. Row 1: * K 4, P 4, repeat from * across row and end P 4. Row 2: P 1, * K 4, P 4, repeat from * across row and end P 3. Row 3: K 2, * P 4, K 4, repeat from * across row and end K 2. Row 4: P 3, * K 4, P 4, repeat from * across row and end P 1. Row 5: * P 4, K 4, repeat from * across row and end K 4. Row 6: K 1, * P 4, K 4, repeat from * across row and end K 3. Row 7: P 2, * K 4, P 4, repeat from * across row and end P 2. Row 8: K 3, * P 4, K 4, repeat from * across row and end K 1. Repeat these 8 rows for pattern stitch. Note: In forming a diagonal rib st, any number of K and P sts can be used and the bias-effect attained by merely moving the K and P st one st to right on one side and one st to left on reverse side (F 27).

Diamond Stitch: Multiple of 8 sts plus 1 extra. Row 1: K 4, * P 1, K 7, repeat from * across row and end P 1, K 4. Row 2: P 3, * K 1, P 1, K 1, P 5, repeat from * across row and end P 3. Row 3: K 2, * P 1, K 3, repeat from * across row and end K 2. Row 4: * P 1, K 1, P 5, K 1, repeat from * across row and end P 1. Row 5: * P 1, K 7, repeat from * across row and end P 1. Row 6: Same as Row 4. Row 7: Same as Row 3.

176

F29

Row 8: Same as Row 2. Repeat these 8 rows for pattern stitch (F 28).

Woven Stitch: Cast on a multiple of 4 stitches plus 2 extra. Row 1 (right side): * K 2, yarn forward (in front of needle) slip 2 sts, yarn back. Repeat from * across row and end K 2. Row 2: P 1, * yarn back (when sts are slipped on wrong side, the yarn must always be on knit side), slip 2 sts, yarn forward, P 2. Repeat from * across row and end P 3. Row 3: * Yarn forward, slip 2 sts, yarn back, K 2. Repeat from * across row and end, yarn forward, slip 2 sts. Row 4: P 3, * yarn back, slip 2 sts, yarn forward, P 2. Repeat from * across row and end P 1. Repeat these 4 rows twice (12 rows in all), then shift pattern to produce slant effect in opposite direction. Change to contrasting color. Row 1: * With yarn forward, slip 2 sts, yarn back, K 2. Repeat from * across row and end with slip 2 sts. Row 2: P 1, * yarn back, slip 2 sts, yarn forward, P 2. Repeat from * across row and end P 3. Row 3: K 2, * yarn forward, slip 2 sts, yarn back, K 2. Repeat from * across row and end K 2. Row 4: P 3, * yarn back slip 2 sts, yarn forward P 2. Repeat from * across row and end P 1. Repeat these last 4 rows twice (12 rows in all). Repeat these 24 rows for pattern stitch (F 29).

Mock Cable: Cast on a multiple of 6 sts, plus 3 extra. Row 1: * P 3 and K 3. Repeat from * across row and end P 3. Row 2: * K 3 and P 3. Repeat from * across row and end K 3. Row 3: * P 3, K into third st on needle and leave on needle (F 30a), K into first st on needle then K into second st on needle, drop 3 sts off left-hand needle. Repeat from * across row and end P 3. Row 4: Same as Row 2. Repeat these 4 rows for pattern stitch (F 30b).

177

F30a

F30b

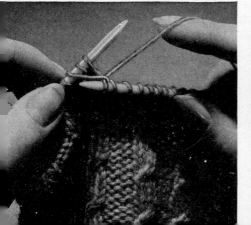

F31a

Simple Cable: Multiple of 14 sts. Rows 1, 3, 5, 7 and 9: K 2, * P 10, K 4, repeat from * across row and end K 2. Rows 2, 4, 6 and 8: P 2, * K 10, P 4, repeat from * across row and end P 2. Row 10: P 2, * slip next 5 sts onto d.p. needle and drop to back of work, K next 5 sts (F 31a), then K 5 sts from d.p. needle, P 4, repeat from * across row and end P 2. Repeat these 10 rows for pattern st (F 31b).

Plaited Cable: Multiple of 14 sts plus 1. Rows 1 and 3: * P 1, K 2, P 9, K 2, repeat from * across row and end K 2, P 1. Row 2: * K 1, P 2, K 9, P 2, repeat from * across row and end P 2, K 1. Row 4: * K 1, P 2, slip next 3 sts onto d.p. needle and drop to front of work, K next 3 sts, then K 3 sts from d.p. needle, K 3, P 2, repeat from * across row and end K 3, P 2, K 1. Rows 5 and 7: Same as Row 1. Row 6: Same as Row 2. Row 8: * K 1, P 2, K 3, slip next 3 sts onto d.p. needle and drop to back of work, K next 3 sts, then K 3 sts from d.p. needle, P 2, repeat from * across row and end P 2, K 1. Repeat these 8 rows for pattern st (F 32).

Lattice Cable: Multiple of 4 sts plus 2 extra. Rows 1, 3, 5 and 7: * K 2, P 2, repeat from * across row and end K 2. Rows 2, 4 and 6: * P 2, K 2, repeat from * across row and end P 2. Row 8: * P 2, slip next 4 sts onto d.p. needle and drop to back of work, K 2 from left-hand needle, slip 2 P sts from d.p. needle to left-hand needle and P these 2 sts, K 2 from d.p. needle, repeat from * across row and end P 2. Rows 9, 11, 13 and 15: Same as Row 1. Rows 10, 12 and 14: Same as Row 2. Row 16: P 2, K 2, * P 2, slip 4 sts onto d.p. needle and drop to front of work, K 2 from left-hand needle, slip 2 P sts from d.p. needle to left-hand needle and P these 2 sts, K 2 from d.p. needle, repeat from * across row and end P 2. Repeat these 16 rows for pattern st (F 33).

1b

32

3

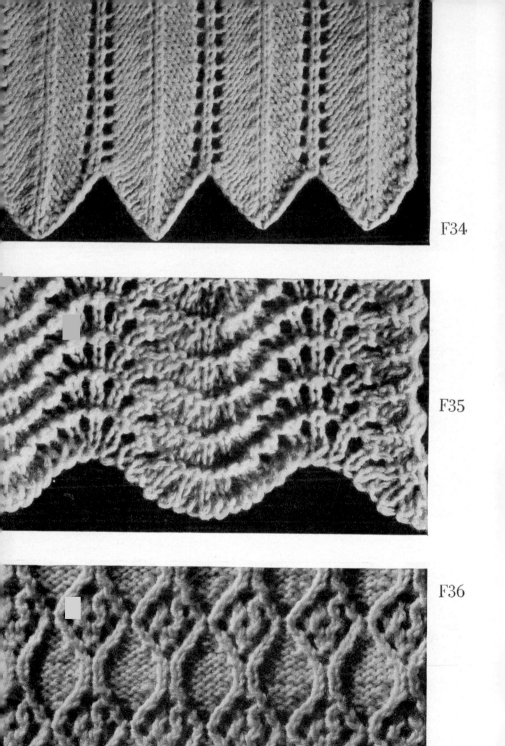

F34

F35

F36

Lace Stitch Forming Pointed Border: Cast on multiple of 13 sts, plus 1 extra. Row 1: P. Row 2: * K 1, y.o., K 4, K 2 tog twice, K 4, y.o. Repeat from * across row, end K 1. Repeat 2 rows for pattern st (F 34).

Lace Stitch Forming Scalloped Border: Multiple of 18 sts. Row 1: Knit. Row 2: Purl. Row 3: K 2 tog 3 times, * (y.o. and K 1 for 6 times), K 2 tog 6 times, repeat from * across row and end K 2 tog 3 times. Row 4: Knit. Repeat these 4 rows for pattern stitch (F 35).

Medallion Lace Stitch: Multiple of 8 sts plus 2 extra. Row 1: K 1, P 3, * K 2, P 6, repeat from * across row and end K 2, P 3, K 1. Row 2: K 4, P 2, * K 6, P 2, repeat from * across row and end K 4. Row 3: Same as Row 1. Row 4: Same as Row 2. Row 5: K 1, P 2, * K 2 tog, y.o., slip 1, K 1, p.s.s.o., P 4, repeat from * across row and end K 2 tog, y.o., slip 1, K 1, p.s.s.o., P 3. Row 6: K 3, * P 1, K into back of next st, then K into the front of the same st, P 1, K 4, repeat from * across row and end K 3. Row 7: K 1, P 1, * K 2 tog, y.o., K 2, y.o., slip 1, K 1, p.s.s.o., P 2, repeat from * across row and end P 2. Row 8: K 2, * P 6, K 2, repeat from * across row and end K 2. Row 9: K 1, * K 2 tog, y.o., K 2 tog, y.o., slip 1, K 1, p.s.s.o., y.o., slip 1, K 1, p.s.s.o., repeat from * across row and end K 1. Row 10: K 1, P 3, * K into the front and back of the next st, P 6, repeat from * to last 5 sts, then K into the front and back of the next st, P 4. Row 11: K 1, * y.o., slip 1, K 1, p.s.s.o., y.o., slip 1, K 1, p.s.s.o., K 2 tog, y.o., K 2 tog, repeat from * and end y.o., K 1. Row 12: K 1, K into back of next st * P 6, K into the front and back of the next st, repeat from * and end K into back of next st, K 1. Row 13: K 1, P 1, * y.o., slip 1, K 2 tog, p.s.s.o., y.o., K 3 tog, wrap yarn around needle (be sure to make a stitch), P 2, repeat from * across row and end wrap yarn around needle, P 2. Row 14: K 2, * K into back of next st, P 1, K into the front and back of the next st, P 1, K into back of next st, K 2, repeat from * across row and end K 2. Row 15: K 1, P 2, * y.o., slip 1, K 1, p.s.s.o., K 2 tog, wrap yarn around needle, P 4, repeat from * across row and end P 2, K 1. Row 16: K 3, * K into back of next st, P 2, K into back of next st, K 4, repeat from * and end K 3. Repeat the last 14 rows (Rows 3 to 16 inclusive) for pattern st (F 36).

F37

Changing Color in Knitting: When working with 2 or more colors for wide spaces, always be certain to twist the colors to prevent holes. Bring second color over first color as shown in F 37.

Fair Isle Knitting: The name given to designs knit in several colors. There are 2 methods of carrying the yarn across the wrong side of the work. Method 1: When only 2 colors are being used and the spaces between are not more than 4 stitches wide; the yarn not in use is stranded across back (F 38a), never taut, but rather at same tension as knitting (F 38b). Working in stockinette st (F 11) follow chart (F 38c) for design. Method 2: When the distance between colors is more than 4 stitches wide, the colors should be woven in while knitting (F 39a). It is advisable to work with both hands and to hold 1 thread in the left hand for knitting and 1 thread in the right hand for carrying (F 39b). The latter thread should be held taut at all times so that it does not change the gauge of your stitches. Knit 1 stitch in the usual manner but before catching thread to knit, be sure needle is over the yarn you are carrying. In this manner you are weaving the color not being knit, into every other stitch. In Fair Isle knitting, it is fun to work designs from cross stitch patterns as well as to plan one's own designs on graph paper, using symbols similar to those illustrated (F 38c and F 39d) to designate the different colors.

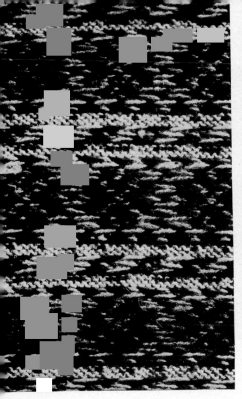 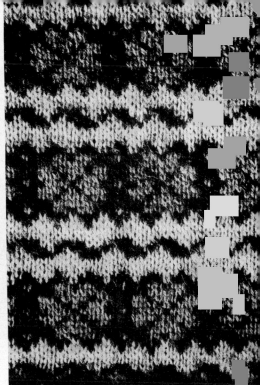

F38a

F38b

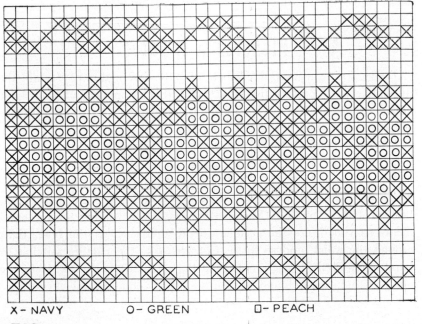

X - NAVY   O - GREEN   □ - PEACH

F38c

183

F39b

Fair Isle knitting should be done in bright colors, using contrasts. The background may be subdued but the pattern should contrast sharply. Adaptations of this type of knitting are used to decorate sport sweaters and mittens.

Planning a sweater

Today, knit garments are most carefully designed. They retain the durability and comfort that first made them popular but they have added an elegance of style. They proudly take their place with the smartest creations.

As a consequence, when we attempt a knit garment, we are confronted with a need for careful planning and for a knowledge of the basic principles of dressmaking. Only in this way can we achieve the success for which the yarn is pleading. The method of gauging stitch or tension has been explained (pg 162). So we will suggest your taking the measurements as you desire the garment to fit—loose across the bust, tight around the waist, and so forth. Consider too, the pattern stitch (the number required for each motif and the extra stitches), the stretching quality of a lace stitch and the tautness of woven and cable effects.

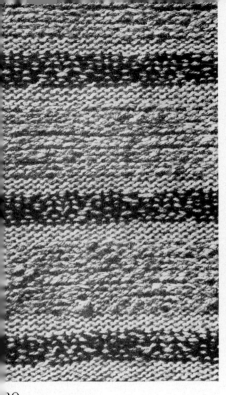

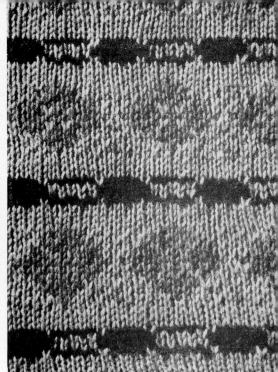

39a   F39c

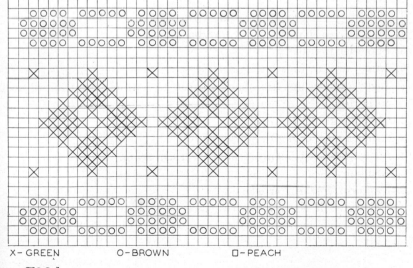

X - GREEN   O - BROWN   □ - PEACH

F39d

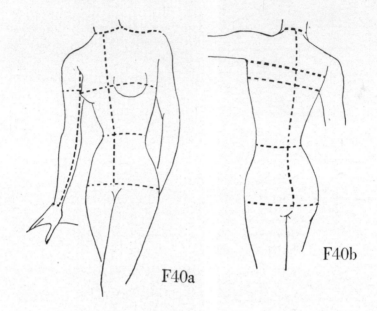

F40a

F40b

The following measurements are essential (F 40a and b):

1. Chest or bust (across front from seam to seam; across back).
2. Waist.
3. Measurement around bottom of sweater.
4. Shoulder to shoulder, front and back.
5. Shoulder to waist.
6. Under arm to waist.
7. Length of sweater from back of neck to bottom, also front of neck to bottom.
8. Shoulder to neck.
9. Around neck or depth of V-neck.
10. Sleeve length: Underarm seam, overarm seam.
11. Armhole.
12. Top arm, forearm, wrist.

At all times it is advisable to chart each piece singly and to check constantly, your inch measurement as well as your stitch gauge, while you knit.

For a simple sweater in which no apparent shaping is desired, knit a swatch in the desired pattern stitch on needles and with yarn to be used for body of sweater. In a man's sweater, merely divide the chest measurement in half; multiply the number of inches by the number of stitches for an inch and cast on that sum for back or front of sweater. It is always advisable to knit ribbing on a needle 2 sizes smaller to insure elasticity around the bottom. In a woman's sweater, take special measurements for front and for back. For example, for a 36 inch bust, the front measurement is usually 20 inches and the back, 16 inches. *For example:* Chest *36* (18); Stitch gauge: 6 sts to 1 inch. 18 x 6 = 108 sts to be cast on. In all calculations we will assume the pattern stitch is the stockinette stitch (F 11).

In a shaped sweater, when no ribbing is desired, you must take the measurement around the bottom of the sweater, around the waist, and around the bust. Calculate the number of stitches at each of these points

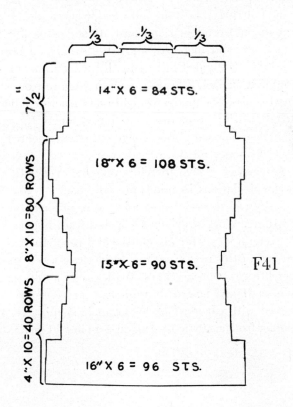

and bear in mind the number of rows and inches between the first measurement and the next.

For example (F 41):

Stitch gauge—6 sts to 1 inch; 10 rows to 1 inch

Bust (back)—18 ins.

Waist (half)—15 ins.

Bottom of sweater (half)—16 ins.

Bust 18 ins × 6 = 108 sts

Waist 15 ins × 6 = 90 sts

Bottom 16 ins × 6 = 96 sts

Length from bottom to waist—4 ins.

Length from waist to armhole—8 ins.

Gauge: 4 ins × 10 = 40 rows

   8 ins × 10 = 80 rows

Length from shoulder to bottom—19½ ins

Length from armpit to shoulder—7½ ins

Difference in sts between bottom and waist, 6 sts; 6 ÷ 2 = 3 decreases.

Difference in sts between waist and bust, 18 sts; 18 ÷ 2 = 9 increases.

As the decreases and increases are made evenly on both sides, the number of stitches is divided in half to find the number of decreases or increases required on each side. In calculating the row on which the decrease or increase is to be made, disregard any fractional part and work the extra length at the completion of each part, or for the exact number of inches before commencing work for next measurement. For example 40 rows ÷ 3 decreases = 13⅓, therefore, decrease every 13th row. 80 rows ÷ 9 increases = 8⅔, therefore increase every 8th row.

With these calculations in mind, plot the back of your sweater accordingly. Cast on 96 sts and decrease 1 st at beginning and end of every 13th row, 3 times. Work even until 4 inches from bottom (waist line). Then work even on 90 sts for an additional 8 rows. Increase 1 st at beginning and end of this row. Continue to increase 1 st at beginning and end of every 8th row 8 more times. Work even on 108 sts until 12 ins from bottom or desired length to armhole.

Now proceed with calculations for armhole shaping (F 41). For example: Shoulder from armhole to armhole—14 ins; 14 ins. × 6 (gauge) =

4 sts. Difference in sts required for bust and for shoulder—24, or 12 decreases. Therefore, 12 sts to be taken off for each armhole. For armpit, always allow about 1 in. Therefore, bind off 6 sts at each end or once on each side, and continue to decrease 1 st at the beginning and end of every other row 6 times.

Work even on 84 sts until you have the desired length from armpit to shoulder, or the difference between the length from shoulder to bottom and the length from bottom to armpits, allowing ½ inch for shaping shoulder (7½ ins).

In a simple sweater, the stitches required for shoulder from armhole to armhole are divided by 3, leaving ⅓ number of stitches for each shoulder and ⅓ for the back of the neck (F 42). The stitches for each shoulder are again divided by 3 and the stitches bound off in thirds for a slightly shaped shoulder. For example: 84 sts divided by 3 = 28 sts for each shoulder and neck. 28 sts (shoulder) divided by 3 = 9 sts and 1 extra. Therefore, to shape the shoulders and neck for the back of the sweater, work until the armholes measure the desired length to shoulder (7½ ins); then bind off 9 sts at beginning of next 4 rows or twice at each end; bind off 10 sts at beginning of next 2 rows or once at each end (28 sts bound off for each shoulder). Finally, bind off remaining 28 sts for neck (F 42).

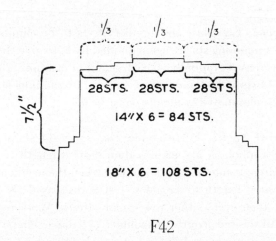

F42

For Square Neck: Applying the same principle described in the last paragraph at desired depth from the completion of the shoulder, for example, knit across 28 sts for shoulder and leave on holder, bind off center 28 sts for neck and knit across remaining 28 sts for second shoulder. Work on 28 shoulder sts, until you have attained desired depth for the armhole (7½ ins) then shape shoulder same as back shoulder, i.e., at armside only, bind off 9 sts at beginning of next 2 rows and finally bind off remaining 10 sts. Work other shoulder in same manner (F 43).

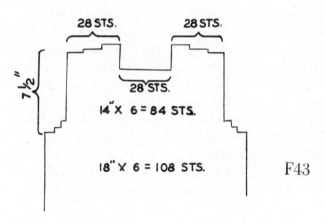

28 STS.   28 STS.

28 STS.

14" X 6 = 84 STS.

7½"

18" X 6 = 108 STS.   F43

For Round Neck: Calculate the number of sts to be eliminated and divide by 2. The remaining sts are again divided by 2, to give the number of sts that are decreased gradually on each side. For example: 28 neck sts divided by 2 = 14 sts to be bound off in center. 14 remaining sts divided by 2 = 7 sts to be eliminated gradually on each side.

A Simple Round Neck: For example, the center 14 sts are usually bound off when armhole is 2½ ins less than desired length to shoulder (5 ins). For children, commence neck shaping when the armhole is 1 to 2 ins less than desired length to shoulder. 1 st is decreased (K 2 tog) at neck edge only, then every other row 6 more times. Work even on 28 shoulder sts until desired length to shoulder (7½ ins). Shape shoulder the same as for a square neck described above (F 44).

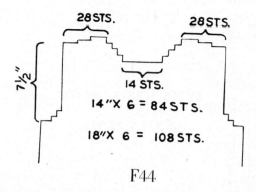

28 STS.   28 STS.

7½"

14 STS.

14" X 6 = 84 STS.

18" X 6 = 108 STS.

F44

For High Round Neck: Commence shaping 1 inch from shoulder (6 ins), bind off more than half the sts (18 sts) in center and bind off 2 sts at neck edge only until the proper number of shoulder sts remain (28 sts). Shape shoulder same as usual.

For V-Neck: This neckline requires a little more calculating than the other types. The shaping is usually commenced about 1″ above armpit. Leave ½ of sts (42 sts) on holder and work on remaining 42 sts. Calculate number of rows to be knit from point of V to shoulder; divide this number by number of decreases for each side of V to determine on what row decreases at neck edge are to be made. *For example:* 28 sts for neck divided by 2 = 14 decreases for each side of neckline. 60 rows from point of V to shoulder divided by 14 = 36/7 rows, i.e. dec 1 st at neck edge every 3rd row 14 times. Therefore, work on 42 sts and dec 1 st at inside edge for neck every 3rd row until 28 sts remain for shoulder. Work on 28 sts until desired length to shoulder. Shape shoulder same as described for square neck (pg 190). Work other side in same manner (F 45).

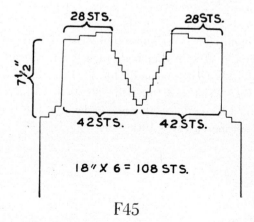

28 STS.   28 STS.

7½"

42 STS.   42 STS.

18" X 6 = 108 STS.

F45

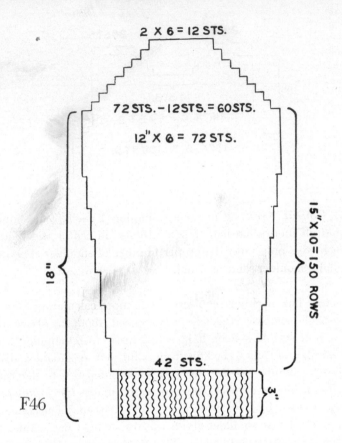

Sleeves: The seams of the sleeve are increased in the same manner as the body of the sweater from waist to armhole. Use this as a guide:

Length of underarm seam—18 ins.

Length of overarm seams—23 ins.

Top of arm—12 ins (72 sts if your st gauge is 6 sts = 1 inch)

Wrist 6 ins × 6 sts (gauge) = 36 sts.

As width of hand is larger than actual wrist measurement, add 1″ or 6 sts for necessary stretch. As for body of sweater, rib cuff sts on a small needle for greater elasticity—usually for 3″. Proceed as follows:

Difference between wrist and top arm—30 sts or 15 increases.

15 ins (18 minus 3 for cuff) × 10 rows (gauge) = 150 rows.

150 divided by 15 increases = 10th row.

Therefore, after ribbing cuff on small needles for 3″ (42 sts), change to large needles and inc 1 st at beg and end of every 10th row. Work on 72 sts until 18″ from beg, or desired length to armhole (F 46). Shaping of the cap of sleeve is important. Consider length of cap and type of cap to be made. •

Simple Cap: Allow 2 ins to be bound off for completion of cap. Then proceed as follows: bind off at each end same number of sts bound off for armpits of back and shape gradually as for seam. For example: 72 sts — 12 (6 sts each side) = 60 sts remaining; 2 ins (for very top of sleeve) × 6 (gauge 6 sts = 1 inch) = 12 sts bound off at completion of sleeve. 60 remaining sts — 12 sts = 48 sts to be eliminated from armpit to completion. 48 sts divided by 2 = 24 decreases each side of cap. 5 ins (length of cap) × 10 rows (gauge 10 rows = 1 inch) = 50 rows.

Therefore, to shape cap bind off 6 sts beg of next 2 rows or once at each side and continue to dec 1 st at beg and end of every 2nd row (50 rows ÷ 24 decreases = 2) until 12 sts remain. Bind off these 12 sts. With this as a foundation, almost any type of sleeve may be designed (F 46).

For a Short Puff Sleeve: Calculate increases from bottom of sleeve to armpit in same manner as for long sleeve. Rib on small needles for 1 inch, or as desired. For cap: Bind off 6 sts at each side, same as described for long sleeve. Then dec 1 st at beg and end of every second row for 6 times or for one inch on each side. Work on remaining sts (48 sts) for desired length of cap (5 ins), decrease gradually for final shaping. Bind off 2 sts at the beg of every row until 12 sts remain. Bind off (F 47).

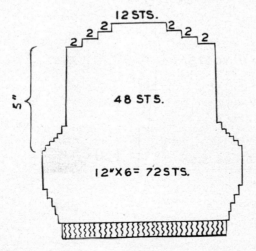

F47

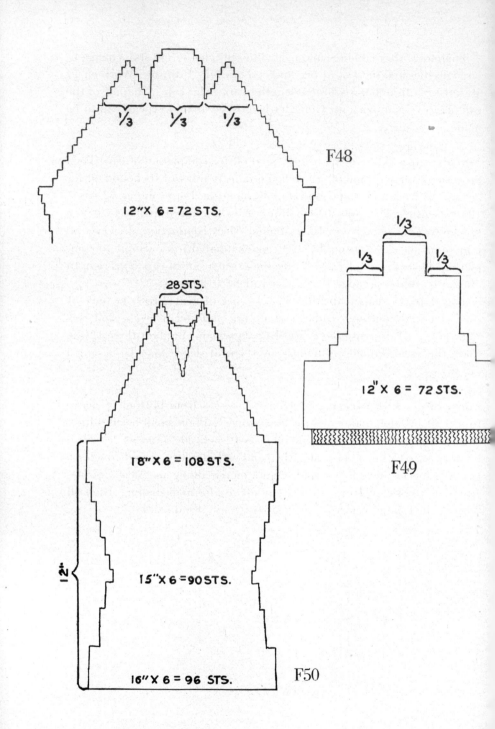

1/3 1/3 1/3

F48

12"X 6 = 72 STS.

28 STS.

1/3 1/3 1/3

12" X 6 = 72 STS.

F49

18" X 6 = 108 STS.

12"

15" X 6 = 90 STS.

16" X 6 = 96 STS.

F50

The Darted Cap: If darts are to be sewed in, shape as for puff sleeve and mark off 4 darts about ½ inch apart on each side of center. However, if darts (usually 2) are to be knit in, shape sleeve cap in usual manner and when it is 2 inches shorter than desired length (3 ins), divide sts in thirds: continue to shape outside edges of cap as originally planned and at the same time at inside edge of first and last thirds, decrease 1 st at beginning of every row until all sts are eliminated. Knit even on the center third for 1 inch, then decrease 1 st at each end of every other row until half the number of sts remain. Bind off (F 48).

For a Square Cap: Work in same manner as puff sleeve until cap is 1½ inches shorter than desired length for cap (3½ ins). Divide sts in thirds. Bind off first and last thirds, work even on center third for 1½ ins. Bind off (F 49). Sew bound-off thirds on each side to sides of center piece. The shape of this sleeve is improved by the use of shoulder pads.

Raglan Sweater with Set-In Sleeve: The body shaping is the same as for an ordinary sweater. The difference lies only in the shaping of the armholes. To shape the armholes for back, deduct the number of neck sts from the total number of sts, then calculate the decreases as for normal sleeve cap.

For example; For body of sweater
108 sts minus 28 neck sts = 80 sts.
80 sts minus 12 (6 sts for each armpit) = 68 sts.
68 sts divided by 2 = 34 decreases.
7 ins × 10 (gauge 10 rows = 1 inch) = 70 rows.
70 rows divided by 34 decreases = 2 ($\frac{1}{17}$) rows, i.e. decrease 1 st at each
   end of every second row.

Therefore, to shape armholes, bind off 6 sts at beginning of next 2 rows (once each side) and decrease 1 st at beginning and end of every second row, until 28 sts remain for neck (F 50). For the front of sweater, decrease for armpits and armholes in same manner and at the same time calculate neck-shaping in the same manner as described for a simple sweater with set-in sleeves (F 50).

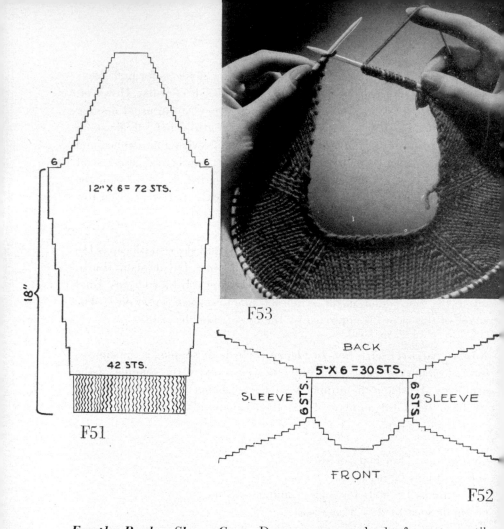

12″ X 6 = 72 STS.

18″

42 STS.

6   6

F51

F53

BACK

5″ X 6 = 30 STS.

SLEEVE   6 STS.   6 STS.   SLEEVE

FRONT

F52

For the Raglan Sleeve Cap: Decrease same as back of sweater until length of sleeve cap is same as length of armholes, then bind off remaining sts. For example; 72 sts for top arm minus 12 sts for armpit = 60 sts or 30 decreases. Length of cap = $7\frac{1}{2}''$—same as armhole of sweater. $7\frac{1}{2}'' \times 10$ (gauge 10 rows = 1 inch) = 75 rows. 75 divided by 30 = $2\frac{1}{2}$ rows, i.e., dec 1 st each side of every second row until cap is same length as armhole of sweater. Therefore, dec 1 st at beg and end of every second row until sleeve cap is same length as armhole of sweater. If sts are being eliminated too quickly, when cap is $\frac{1}{2}$ its desired length, dec 1 st every third row until desired length. Bind off remaining sts (F 51).

Knit-In Raglan Sweater: This style of sweater is the reverse of the set-in raglan. Calculate the width at the back of the neck, allow 1 inch for each sleeve, 8 sts for raglan increasing, plus 4 seam sts, and 1 st for each side of front. For example: Neck 5 ins × 6 (gauge 6 sts = 1 inch) = 30 sts; 6 sts for each sleeve. 30 for neck plus 12 sts for sleeves, plus 8 sts for increasing, plus 4 sts for seams, plus 2 sts for fronts = 56 sts.

Therefore, to commence sweater on circular needle, cast on 56 sts. Work back and forth, increasing on each side of 4 seam sts and at beginning and end of every alternate row until neck is completed. Then join and work round and round (F 52).

For example: Row 1: K 1 (front), inc in next st, K 1 (seam), inc in next st, K 6 (sleeve), inc in next st, K 1 (seam), inc in next st, K 30 (neck), inc in next st, K 1 (seam), inc in next st, K 6 (sleeve), inc in next st, K 1 (seam), inc in next st, K 1 (front). Row 2: P back.

Mark 4 seam sts with a marker (F 2) and increase before and after each of these 4 seam sts *every knit row. At same time shape neck.* For a Round Neck, increase one st at beginning and end of every second knit row 7 times or as desired. Then cast on number of sts required for completion of neck (F 53). The number of sts for front must equal or excel number of sts in back section. Therefore, if there are 58 sts in back section and 20 sts in each front section, cast on 18 sts. Join and work round and round in plain knitting. At same time continue to inc before and after each of 4 seam sts every other round until raglan (measure the line formed by seam st) is required length and there is the required number of sts for front and back. Work on 1 sleeve only and leave remaining sts on string or the sts for each section on a stitch holder to be worked later.

To sleeve sts, add ½ inch (3 sts) each side for armpits and work downwards, decreasing in same manner as set-in sleeve was increased (F 51). Work second sleeve in same manner. To body sts, add ½ inch (3 sts) on each side of front and back for armpits, join and work downward on total number of sts of back and front until desired length. Rib at waistline as desired. Bind off.

If a shaped sweater is desired, select 2 sts at each armpit for seamline for body, and dec 1 st on each side of these 2 sts of each seamline in same manner as seams of body of simple sweater was increased (F 50).

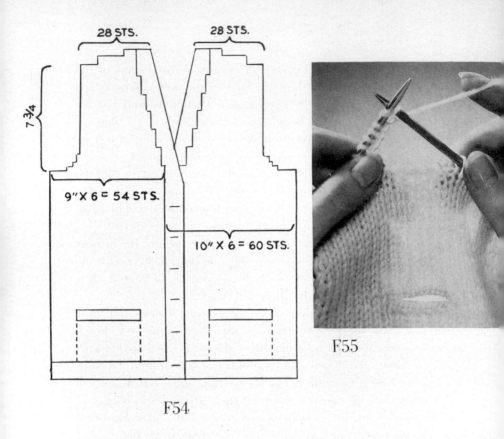

28 STS.   **28 STS.**

7 ¾

9" X 6 = 54 STS.

10" X 6 = 60 STS.

F54

F55

For V-Neck, reverse shaping, increasing as you decreased for sweater with set-in sleeves (F 50). Join when the total number of front sts equals the number of sts in the back section, then continue in same manner as described above. For an open-raglan substitute a "yarn over" for each "increase stitch."

Cardigans: Calculations for a cardigan are the same as for a slip-on, with this exception: all measurements for front, excluding the shoulder are divided in half, and 1 inch added to each side for lap (F 54). *For example:* Chest 18 ins divided by 2 = 9 ins plus 1 inch for lap = 10 ins; 10 ins × 6 (gauge 6 sts = 1 inch) = 60 sts to be cast on for each front. Now follow calculations as explained for slipon remembering the additional inch for lap. If bands are to be put on later, divide measurements of bottom, waist and chest in half—54 sts instead of 60 sts.

Horizontal Buttonholes: In planning a cardigan or neck opening with buttonholes, it is advisable to knit the opposite or button side first. Then plan the placement of the buttonholes. For example, knit as far as the first buttonhole. Consider how wide to make the hole—usually 3 or 4 stitches. * Knit 2 or 3 sts for edge. Bind off 3 or 4 sts for buttonhole and knit across remainder of row. On return row, turn right or knit side toward you and cast on 3 or 4 sts above those bound off to complete buttonhole (F 55). Turn wrong side toward you. Purl to end of row. * Now continue to knit front as planned until the placement for the next buttonhole is reached. Repeat between *'s to form buttonhole.

Vertical Buttonhole: Formation of this buttonhole is more complicated. The first step is to knit garment to the base of the buttonholes. With right side of work facing, knit along row as far as the base of first buttonhole. Turn work and knit back and forth in stockinette st (F 11) on these stitches for depth of hole. Break off wool. Slip these sts onto holder or leave on needle. Now join wool at first st at base of first buttonhole. Knit across desired number of sts for space between buttonholes. Knit back and forth on these sts until this section is as deep as the first. Break off wool and slip these sts onto holder or leave on needle. Repeat last process (F 56) as many times as required. Do not break wool at end of last section. Slip all sts onto one needle, so arranging sts that knitting will begin on a wrong or purl side. Knit or purl that row, thus joining all separate sections. Continue knitting as usual for remainder of garment. If a knit band is desired, divide sts of band in half at buttonhole placement. Knit 2 separate pieces for desired depth and join. Repeat for formation of each buttonhole.

F56   199

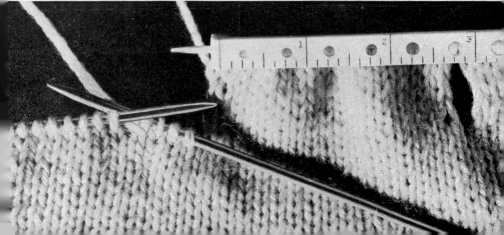

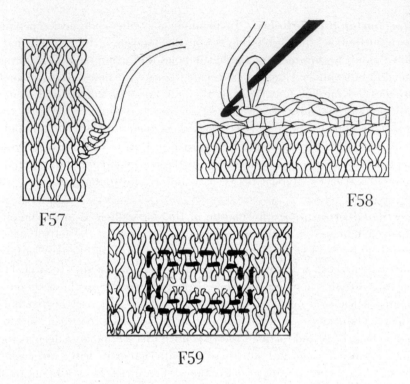

F57

F58

F59

Loop-Buttonholes: Mark space on edge of opening for placement of buttonhole and attach 2 strands of yarn along this space, allowing for the thickness of the specific button. Buttonhole stitch over this double strand with 1 or 2 strands of yarn as desired (F 57).

Crocheted Buttonholes: This type of buttonhole is usually part of the single crochet (G 3a and b) edge of small openings. Mark placement of buttonholes on edge of opening; work in sc to base of buttonhole, chain stitch (G 2) for number of sts required for the button, skip this space on edge and work in sc to placement of next buttonhole (F 58). If a wide crocheted band is desired, as for a cardigan; work 2 or 3 rows of sc, form buttonholes as explained above, on next row. On the following row, work as many sc sts in buttonhole-space as you skipped on the previous row. Work at least 1 or 2 more rows in sc to complete band.

Cutting Buttonholes: Mark placement of buttonhole; stitch twice around marker, preferably by machine; cut along marker between double row of stitching (F 59); buttonhole stitch around hole (B 36 and C 50).

Small Opening: When planning an opening for a sweater blouse, first calculate size of band, usually 8 sts. If it is a center opening, divide sts on needle in half. Slip 4 sts from underlap side to upper or buttonhole side. Slip remaining sts of underlap side onto holder. Work on sts of overlap side, forming buttonholes as described for cardigan. To complete underlap side pick up sts from holder. At center or buttonhole edge, cast on 8 sts for underlap. There are now as many sts on needle as on buttonhole side just completed. Knit underlap to correspond to buttonhole side (F 60). If opening is off-center, place marker at opening, slip 4 sts of underlap to overlap side and proceed as explained above.

Patch Pocket: Simplest kind of pocket to make. It is a piece knit separately in any shape, square or fancy and sewed on garment as desired. For sample pocket (F 61): Cast on 22 sts. Row 1: * K 2, P 2, repeat from * across row. Repeat Row 1 for 26 rows. Divide sts in half. Slip last 11 sts onto stitch-holder and work on first 11 sts. Still keeping continuity of pattern st, at inside edge decrease 1 st every row until all sts have been eliminated. Fasten off. Slip last 11 sts from stitch-holder onto needle and join yarn at center. Still keeping continuity of pattern stitch, decrease 1 st at inside edge every row until all sts are eliminated. Fasten off. Work 1 row of sc over top or shaped edge to conceal irregularity of the decreased edge (F 61).

201

F60   F61

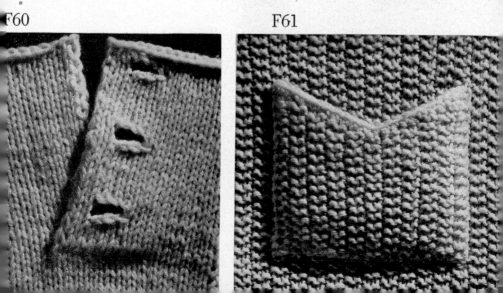

F62

F63

Set-In Pocket: (Pattern st used in this sample (F 62) is: Row 1: Knit across. Row 2: * Knit 1, P 1, repeat from * across row. Use garter st for border.) Knit the body of sweater to proper placement of pocket. Bind off number of sts desired for width of pocket. Knit to end of row. Drop this piece temporarily. On separate needles, cast on same number of sts as bound off for width of pocket and knit for desired depth of pocket. Be sure to end piece on same row as sts of body of sweater were bound off. Drop this piece of work. Pick up body of sweater. Knit across row as far as space made by sts bound off; pick up needle with small pocket piece, slip these sts onto left-hand needle and knit across these sts, thereby replacing the sts bound off. Knit to end of row. Continue knitting as usual. When garment is completed, sew pocket lining to body of garment on wrong side (F 62).

Revers: Calculate additional width desired for each rever. Then increase evenly on 1 side, either on outside edge or just inside desired width of revers. For example: Additional width of revers—2 ins × 6 sts (gauge 6 sts = 1 in) = 12 sts to be added to each front or side of sweater. Depth of revers—6 ins × 10 rows (gauge 10 rows = 1 in) = 60 rows. 60 rows divided by 12 st = 5 rows, i.e., increase 1 st every 5th row or every row as shown in F 63. Therefore, to form revers, increase 1 st every 5th row 12 times, then bind off all sts of revers, i.e., 12 increased sts and all sts not required for shoulder shaping. For example: If there are 52 sts on needle and shoulder shaping requires 30 sts, bind off 22 sts for revers, i.e., 12 increased sts plus 10 extra sts.

For a simple narrow rever: Merely work straight to shoulder. Shape shoulder and bind off remaining sts for revers (F 64).

Simple Round Collar: Made by calculating the number of sts required for entire neckline, then work for desired depth. Bind off loosely. Sew firmer edge to neckline of garment (F 65).

Pointed Collar: Cast on number of sts required for neckline and increase 1 st at beginning and end of every other (alternate) row until desired depth is attained. Sew cast-on edge to neckline of garment (F 66).

203

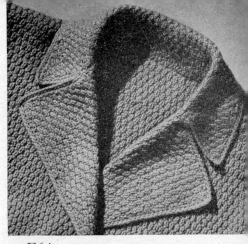

F64

F65

F66

Skirts: Strangely enough, the knitting of a skirt on a circular needle is the simplest form of knitting. In planning a shaped skirt, 5 measurements are essential—the waist, the length from hip to waist, the hip, the width at bottom of skirt and the overall length of skirt.

Straight Skirt: The width at the bottom is usually 10 ins wider than the hip measurement. To simplify the calculations, cast on a number of sts divisible by 10 and plan all decreases for 10 sts in 1 round (F 67). For example: Waist 30 ins; 30 × 6 (gauge 6 sts = 1 in) = 180 sts. Hip; 40 ins; 40 × 6 (gauge) = 240 sts. Length from hip to waist 6 ins; 6 × 10 (gauge 10 rows = 1 in) = 60 rows. Length of skirt 30 ins, 30 × 10 (gauge) = 300 rows. Width at bottom 50 ins; 50 × 6 (gauge) = 300 sts. 300 sts for bottom minus 240 sts for hip = 60 sts to be eliminated in 24 ins (30 ins length of skirt minus 6 ins distance from hip to waist) or 240 rows. 60 sts to be eliminated divided by 10 decreases in round = 6 decreasing rounds. 240 rows divided by 6 decreasing rounds = 40th round, i.e., decrease 10 sts every 40th round. Therefore, to shape the skirt from the bottom to the hip, at even intervals decrease 10 sts every 40th round or every 4 ins for 6 times (F 67). For example: Cast on 300 sts on circular needle. Join, being careful not to twist sts. Knit even for 39 rounds. On 40th round decrease 10 sts in round as follows: * K 28, K 2 tog. Repeat from * for 1 round (10 times). Knit even on 290 sts for 39 rounds. On the second decreasing or 80th round, decrease as follows: * K 27, K 2 tog. Repeat from * for 1 round—280 sts on needle. The decreases from the hip to waist are calculated in the same manner. For example: 240 sts minus 180 sts for waist = 60 sts to be eliminated in 6 ins or 60 rows (gauge 10 rows = 1 in). 60 sts divided by 10 rows = 6 decreasing rounds. 60 divided by 6 decreasing rounds = 10th round, i.e., decrease 10 sts every 10th round. Therefore, from hip to waist decrease 10 sts in every 10th round for 6 times. Knit even on 180 sts until skirt is desired length. Bind off.

In planning a skirt, allow for stretch in length. Allow about 1 inch or more if the fulness of the skirt and the elasticity of the yarn demand it. Dirndl skirts and rayon yarns usually have more "stretch" than straight skirts and virgin yarn.

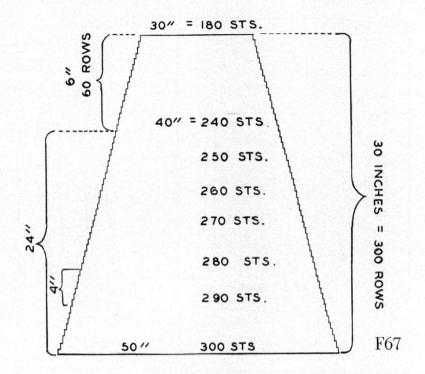

F67

Circular or Flared Skirt: Planned in a similar manner with added fulness from bottom to hip, usually bottom width is 15 ins wider than hip measurement, sometimes even wider. The decreases are planned to occur 6 or 8 times in a round with decreases at bottom of skirt farther apart (more rounds between decreases) than they are as the skirt reaches toward the hip measurement. For example: Instead of decreasing every 40th round evenly as described for a straight skirt; knit even for 10 ins, then decrease every 40th round twice, every 30th round 3 times and so on. This type of decreasing produces a graceful flare.

The same effect may be secured, when knitting a pattern stitch by changing size of needle about 3 times as you knit without decreasing. For example for a child's skirt: K with a #6 needle for 6″ (or to hip). Change to #4 needle. Knit for 2″. Change to #2 needle and knit for 1″. This example shows the importance of stitch gauge (pg 162).

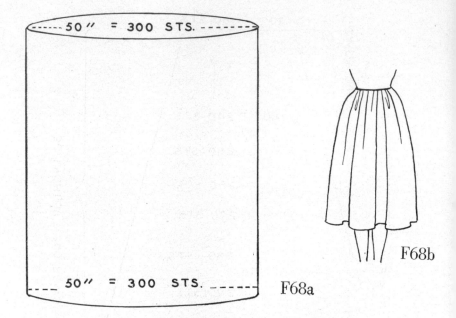

F68a 50″ = 300 STS. 50″ = 300 STS.

F68b

Dirndl skirt: Cast on number of sts desired, usually 1½ to twice the width of hip measurement. Knit even for desired length, allowing for "stretch." Bind off (F 68a and b). Make casing as shown in F 70 or knit a 2-inch band desired waist measurement. Run basting through top of skirt, shirr to desired size of waist and attach to waistband (B 29).

Pleated Skirts: Achieved mainly by a ribbed stitch. For example, cast on 300 sts and work in a pattern st of K 15, P 15, forming 10 K and 10 P gores. The decreases usually are made alternately in the K and P gores, applying the principle explained for a circular skirt.

Godets: Planned in a manner similar to a raglan with the decreases made within the allotted section and not at beginning and end of the row (F 69). For example: Width of godet 10 ins; 10×6 (gauge 6 sts = 1 inch) = 60 sts. Depth 8 ins; 8×10 (gauge 10 rows = 1 inch) = 80 rows or rounds. 60 sts divided by 2 decreases in a row = $2\frac{2}{3}$ rows, i.e., decrease 1 st on each side of the godet section every 2nd or 3rd round or row. Therefore, to shape godet, knit 3 rounds or rows. First decrease K as far as the 60 sts of the godet, then K 2 tog, K 56, K 2 tog, K to end of round. Knit 3 rounds. Second decrease—K to within 58 sts of the godet, then K 2 tog, K 54, K 2 tog, K to end of round. From now on decrease 1 st at beginning and end of the godet sts every second round until all sts of the godet section (original 60 sts) are eliminated (F 69).

Panel Skirts: Can be knit in separate panels, 2, 4 or 6 panels, as desired. In these skirts, the calculations are the same as for a godet, with the proper allowance made for the top width of panel. In a panelled or gored skirt it is advisable to use a skirt pattern, omitting the hem allowances. The pieces are then sewed together and the finishing is similar to a fabric skirt with a waistband and a zipper opening (B 29), or with beading as in skirt knit on a circular needle (F70).

Beading or Casing for Top of Skirt: With right sides facing, work several rounds of sc (G 3a and b) around top of skirt, usually one to two inches in width. With wrong side facing, work 1 sc in first st on first round and * ch 5 (G 2), skip 5 sts on last round and work 1 sc in the

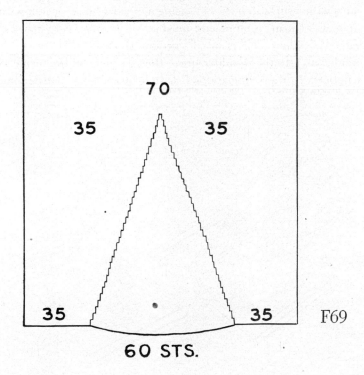

F69

60 STS.

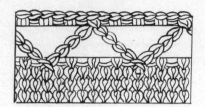

F70

sixth st. Ch 5, skip 5 sts on first round and work 1 sc in sixth st. Repeat from * for entire round (F 70). End with a slip st (G 11) in first sc. If the total number of sts at the top of the skirt is not a multiple of 6, then skip only 4 sts at regular intervals to produce an "even beading."

Blocking Hand-Knits: Blocking is the little miracle that transforms a homely mass of sts into the professional garment we all desire. Your yarn may be the finest, you may knit or crochet with great skill, but your garment will lack distinction and perfect fit if it is not blocked properly. There are two methods that may be used. In the first, join the seams with a slip stitch (G 11), using a crochet hook, or join with a back-stitch (C 9), using a blunt-end needle. Always take care in setting in the sleeves; overlook the pointed corners of the cap, to give a smooth, rounded arch to the shoulder line—these corners on the inside never will be noticed. Now provide yourself with heaps of tissue paper, some ½ inch

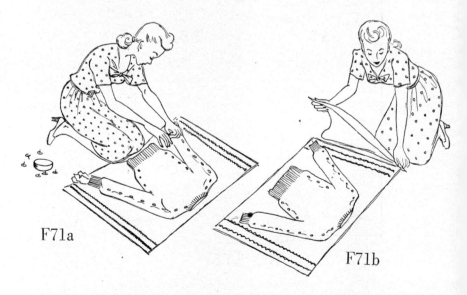

F71a

F71b

rust-proof thumbtacks, and a flat surface on which to work. (Protect surface against moisture). Immerse in cold water enough Turkish towels to cover both sides of the garment. Wring dry, and lay ½ of them on the table or floor space. Lay the garment on the moist towels. Crush the tissue paper into long strips and place inside the edges of the sleeves, along the shoulder seams and down the side seams. Naturally, you should be sure the tacks are rustproof. If not, watch them closely. Press in thumbtacks an inch apart at the shoulder seams, just inside the exaggerated ridge made by the crushed tissue paper. Then stretching the armhole to the proper size and bearing in mind the size of the bust or chest, press in tacks one inch apart, again inside the ridge of the side seams. Keep the bust measurement for at least 4 inches below the armpit. Now start graduating to the waist measurement. Always keep the ribbing as small as possible, to retain its natural elasticity (F 71a). For sleeves and skirt, follow the same principle. Finally cover the garment with moist towels and let it dry thoroughly before removing towels (F 71b); then steam seams lightly. The purpose of the crushed tissue paper is to prevent that ugly "pressed-in-seam" look. The weight of the moist Turkish towels acts as a natural presser and does not affect the elasticity of the yarn.

In the second method, with the strictly dressmaker finish, each piece is blocked separately. Cut heavy paper to the exact sizes you desire the knit or crocheted pieces to measure, allowing for small seams. It is advisable, especially when combining a fabric and a knit or crocheted piece, to use a regular dress pattern, cutting exact duplicates of the tissue-paper sections in heavy paper for knit or crocheted parts. Baste knit or crocheted parts to paper pieces. Place a damp pressing cloth over pieces and steam, but do not press. Never allow the weight of the iron to rest on the garment. Let the pieces dry thoroughly before removing them from the heavy paper. Remove basting threads and join seams, handling knit or crocheted pieces as you would any piece of fabric. Set in sleeves, easing fulness of cap around top of armhole and being careful not to bind the armhole with tight stitches. Make darts, tucks, shirrings, etc., as in tailoring (Chapter 2), to obtain that custom-made appearance. It is advantageous and essential to perfect fit to baste all pieces together. Try on, and make necessary adjustments for your figure, before actually sewing the garment. After sewing, slightly steam all seams.

Classic sweaters

Instructions For

Pullovers: Round Neck, Turtle Neck, V Neck—Long and Short
Sleeves

Sleeveless Pullovers: Round Neck and V Neck

Cardigans: Round Neck and V Neck

Sizes: 6–10 children, 12–20 women, 36–42 men

Materials Required For Pullover (F 72a and c):
(Light Weight)

Sizes:	6	8	10	12	14	16	18	20	36	38	40	42
3 ply fingering yarn............Oz.	5	6	6	7	8	9	10	11	11	12	13	14

Short Sleeve Pullover (F 72b) requires 1 ounce less than quoted for pullover.
Long Sleeved Cardigan (F 72d and e) requires 2 ounces more than
quoted for pullover.
Short Sleeved Cardigan requires 1 ounce more than quoted for pullover.
Sleeveless Pullover (F 72f and g) requires 2 ounces less than quoted for
pullover.

Knitting Needles: 1 pair each of No. 1 and No. 3 (standard); 1 set
d.p. No. 1 (standard)

Gauge: 7 sts = 1 inch, 10 rows = 1 inch (see stitch gauge, pg 162).

Pattern Stitch: Stockinette Stitch (F 11—pg 168).

Note: A rib of K 2 and P 2 can be used instead of a rib of K 1 and P 1,
if preferred (pg 168).
Chart Fl indicates in inches the changes for sizes 6, 10 and 14.

Pullovers

Sizes: 6 8 10 12 14 16 18 20 36 38 40 42

Pullover (F 72a and b): *Back:*

	6	8	10	12	14	16	18	20	36	38	40	42
On small needles cast on.(F 4)...sts	92	96	100	104	108	116	124	132	128	136	140	144
Work in rib (pg 168) of K 1 and P 1 for...ins	1½	1½	2	2	2½	2½	3	3	3	3	3	3
Change to large needles and work in pattern st throughout. Work even until back measures...ins	10	11	12	13	14	14	15	15	16	16	16	16
Shape armholes as follows: Bind off (pg 171)...sts	5	5	5	6	6	6	7	7	6	6	7	7
at the beg of the next 2 rows (once each side). Dec (F 15) 1 st at beg and end of every other row...times	5	5	5	5	6	7	7	7	6	7	7	7
Work even on...sts	72	76	80	82	84	90	96	104	104	110	112	116
until armhole measures...ins	5½	6	6½	7	7	7½	7¾	8	8	8¼	8½	9
Shape shoulders as follows: Bind off...sts	8	8	8	9	9	10	10	11	11	12	12	12
at the beg of the next 6 rows (3 times each side). Bind off remaining sts for back of neck...sts	24	28	32	28	30	30	36	38	38	38	40	44

Front:

	6	8	10	12	14	16	18	20	36	38	40	42
On small needles cast on...sts	92	96	100	112	120	124	132	144	128	136	140	144

Work in same manner as for back to armholes

For Round Neck Pullover (F 72a):
Shape armholes in same manner as for back.

	6	8	10	12	14	16	18	20	36	38	40	42
When armhole measures...ins	3½	4	4½	5	5	5½	5½	6	6	6	6	6½
Work across...sts	28	29	29	32	34	35	36	40	40	40	40	40
Leave center...sts	16	18	22	26	28	28	32	36	24	30	32	36
on holder. Tie in a second ball of yarn and work both sides at the same time. Work across remaining...sts	28	29	29	32	34	35	36	40	40	40	40	40
Dec 1 st at center edges every other row until...sts	24	24	24	27	27	30	30	33	33	36	36	36
remain. Shape shoulder as follows: At armside bind off...sts	8	8	8	9	9	10	10	11	11	12	12	12

at the beg of 3 rows. Fasten off.

For V-Neck Pullover (F 72b):
Divide work in half. Tie in a second ball of yarn and work both sides at same time. Shape armholes in same manner as for back and at same

time shape for V-neck as follows:

	6	8	10	12	14	16	18	20	36	38	40	42
Dec 1 st every other row . . . . . times	4	4	5	5	5	5	6	6	5	5	5	5

Dec 1 st every 3rd row until there

	6	8	10	12	14	16	18	20	36	38	40	42
are . . . . sts	24	24	24	27	27	30	30	33	33	36	36	36

Work even until armhole is same length as for back.
Shape shoulders to correspond to back shoulders.

Long Sleeves for Pullover (F 72a):

	6	8	10	12	14	16	18	20	36	38	40	42
On small needles cast on . . . . sts	48	48	48	52	56	60	60	64	64	72	72	72

and work in rib of K 1 and P 1

	6	8	10	12	14	16	18	20	36	38	40	42
for . . . . ins	2	2	2½	2½	3	3	3	3	3	3	3	3

Change to large needles and work throughout in pattern st. Inc. 1 st at the beg and end of the row every

	6	8	10	12	14	16	18	20	36	38	40	42
½ inch . . . . times	4	4	4	5	5	6	6	7	7	8	8	8

then every ¾ of an inch until there

	6	8	10	12	14	16	18	20	36	38	40	42
are . . . . sts	68	72	78	84	90	96	100	106	106	110	112	114

on the needle. Work even until

	6	8	10	12	14	16	18	20	36	38	40	42
sleeve measures . . . . ins	12	14	15	16	17	18	18	19	20	20	21	21

Shape sleeve cap as follows: Bind

	6	8	10	12	14	16	18	20	36	38	40	42
off . . . . sts	4	4	5	5	5	6	6	7	7	7	7	7

at the beg of the next 2 rows (once each side). Dec 1 st at the beg and end of every other row until . . . . . sts

	6	8	10	12	14	16	18	20	36	38	40	42
remain.	28	28	28	30	30	32	32	36	36	36	40	40

Bind off 2 sts at the beg of 4 rows (twice each side). Bind off the remaining sts.

Short Sleeves for Pullover (F 72b):

	6	8	10	12	14	16	18	20	36	38	40	42
On small needles cast on . . . . sts	64	68	72	76	80	84	88	92	92	96	96	96

and work in rib of K 1 and P 1 for 1 inch. Change to large needles and work throughout in pattern st. Inc 1 st at beg and end of every 4th row until there are . . . . sts

	6	8	10	12	14	16	18	20	36	38	40	42
	68	72	78	84	90	96	100	106	106	110	112	114

on needle. Work even until sleeve

	6	8	10	12	14	16	18	20	36	38	40	42
measures . . . . ins	3	3	4	4	4½	4½	5	5½	5½	6	6	6

Shape sleeve cap in same manner as for long sleeve

Round Neck Band for Pullover:
On small d.p. needles and with right side of work facing you, pick

	6	8	10	12	14	16	18	20	36	38	40	42
up (F 18) . . . . sts	104	108	112	112	120	120	124	128	132	132	132	132

and work in rib of K 1 and P 1 for 1 inch. Bind off loosely in ribbing.

212

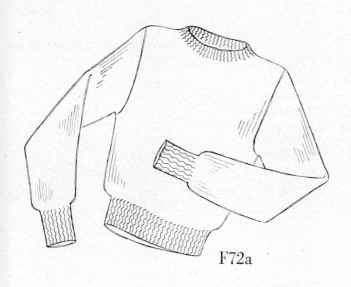

F72a

F72b

V-Neck Band for Pullover:
On small D.P. needles and with right side of work facing you, pick up..........................sts
Rib of K 1 and P 1 throughout. Place marker at center front of V-neck and dec 1 st on each side of marker every other round until 1 inch in depth. Bind off in ribbing.

For Turtle Neck Pullover (F 72c): Pick up same as Round Neck Band (pg. 212) Rib for 5 ins. Bind off in ribbing.

Sizes:	6	8	10	12	14	16	18	20	36	38	40	42
pick up ...sts	128	132	136	140	144	148	152	152	156	156	160	160

Cardigans

Sizes:	6	8	10	12	14	16	18	20	36	38	40	42

Cardigan (F 72d and e): *Back:*
Work in same manner as for pullover back, with these changes: Make back 1 inch longer to armhole and make armhole ¼ inch longer. For Boys and Men, form buttonholes on left front. For Girls and Women, form buttonholes on right front. To form buttonholes, work as follows: At center front edge work 2 sts, bind off..................sts
Work to end of row. On return row cast on......................sts
above those bound off. Form buttonholes......................ins apart (F 55).

Sizes:	6	8	10	12	14	16	18	20	36	38	40	42
2 sts, bind off ...sts	3	3	3	3	4	4	4	4	4	4	4	4
cast on ...sts	3	3	3	3	4	4	4	4	4	4	4	4
buttonholes ...ins apart	1½	1½	2	2	2½	2½	2¾	2¾	3	3	3	3

Note: It is advisable to work front without buttonholes first, then work first buttonhole 6 rows from the beg of front. Mark on plain front, just completed, the placement of each buttonhole for opposite front, being careful that last buttonhole is formed on row before neck is commenced.

214

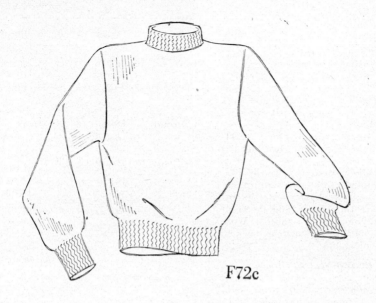

F72c

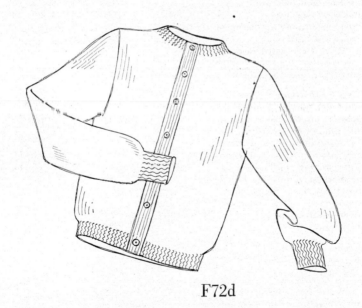

F72d

	Sizes:	6	8	10	12	14	16	18	20	36	38	40	42

Left Front of Cardigan:

On small needles cast on.......sts

58	62	66	70	72	76	80	84	84	88	92	96

and work in rib of K 1 and P 1 for.........................ins

1½	1½	2	2	2½	2½	3	3	3	3	3	3

Change to large needles and work as follows: Work in pattern st to within the last................sts

6	6	6	6	8	8	8	8	8	8	8	8

then rib in P 1 and K 1 for......sts

6	6	6	6	8	8	8	8	8	8	8	8

On return row, rib in K 1 and P 1 for.........................sts

6	6	6	6	8	8	8	8	8	8	8	8

Work in pattern st to end of row. Continue in this manner, thus keeping the body of the sweater in pattern st throughout, and the front band in a rib of K 1 and P 1. Work even until same length as back to armholes.

For Round Neck Cardigan (F 72d):
At seam edge shape armhole in same manner as for back. Work even until armhole measures....ins

3½	4	4½	5	5	5½	5½	6	6	6	6	6½

At center front edge leave.....•.sts

18	18	20	20	22	22	24	24	28	28	30	30

on holder. Continue to dec 1 st every other row until..........sts remain. Work even until armhole measures same as for back. Shape shoulder to correspond to back.

24	24	24	27	27	30	30	33	33	36	36	36

For V-Neck Cardigan (F 72e):
At seam edge shape armhole in same manner as for back and, at the same time at center front edge, dec 1 st inside of band of K 1 and P 1 every other row.........times

6	7	8	9	10	10	11	11	11	11	12	12

then every 3rd row until.....sts remain. Work even until armhole is same length as back. Shape shoulder to correspond to back shoulder.

30	30	30	33	35	38	38	41	41	44	44	44

Work even on rib sts for........ins Bind off.

1½	1½	1½	2	2	2	2½	2½	2½	3	3	3

Right Front:
Work to correspond to left front.

Sleeves for Cardigan:
Work same as for pullover sleeve, with this change: cast on 4 sts additional and keep these 4 additional sts throughout shaping.

216

F72e

Sizes:	6	8	10	12	14	16	18	20	36	38	40	42
Round Neck Band for Cardigan: On small needles and with right side of work facing you, pick up.....sts Work in rib of K 1 and P 1 for 1 inch. Bind off in ribbing.	91	95	99	103	107	111	113	115	117	119	121	123

Sleeveless Pullovers

Sizes:	6	8	10	12	14	16	18	20	36	38	40	42
Sleeveless Pullover (F 72f and g): **Back:** Work same as for pullover until back measures..............ins	9	9	10	10	11	11	12	12	13	13	13	13
Shape armhole as follows. Bind off.........................sts	5	5	5	6	6	7	7	7	6	6	7	7
at the beg of the next 2 rows (once each side). Dec 1 st at beg and end of every other row..........times	9	9	9	10	10	11	11	12	11	11	11	11
Work even on................sts	64	68	72	72	76	80	88	94	94	102	104	108
until armhole measures........ins	6½	7	7½	8	8	8½	8½	9½	9½	10	10	10
Shape shoulders as follows: Bind off.........................sts	6	7	7	7	8	8	8	9	9	10	10	10
at the beg of 6 rows (3 times each side). Leave remaining sts on holder for back of neck or bind off.												

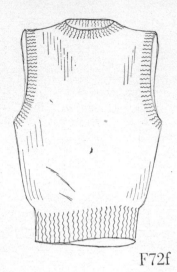

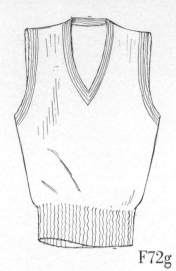

F72f   F72g

	Sizes:	6	8	10	12	14	16	18	20	36	38	40	42

Front:
Work same as for pullover front to armhole.

For Round Neck Sleeveless Pullover (F 72f):
Shape armholes same as for back. Work even until armhole measures....................ins $4\frac{1}{2}$, 5, $5\frac{1}{2}$, 6, 6, $6\frac{1}{2}$, $6\frac{1}{2}$, 7, 7, 7, 7, 7

Work across................sts 24, 26, 27, 29, 31, 31, 32, 36, 32, 34, 35, 36

Leave center................sts 16, 16, 18, 22, 26, 26, 32, 34, 30, 34, 34, 36
on holder. Tie in second ball of yarn and work both sides at same time.

Work across remaining.......sts 24, 26, 27, 29, 31, 31, 32, 36, 32, 34, 35, 36
Dec 1 st at center edges every other

row until...................sts 18, 21, 21, 21, 24, 24, 24, 27, 27, 30, 30, 30
remain. Work even until same length as back.

Shape shoulder to correspond to back shoulder.

For V-Neck Sleeveless Pullover (F 72g):
Shape armhole same as for back and, at the same time, when armhole measures...............ins $\frac{1}{2}$, $\frac{1}{2}$, 1, 1, 1, 1, $1\frac{1}{2}$, $1\frac{1}{2}$, $1\frac{1}{2}$, $1\frac{1}{2}$, $1\frac{1}{2}$, $1\frac{1}{2}$

divide work in half. Tie in second ball of yarn and work both sides at the same time. At center edges dec 1

Sizes:	6	8	10	12	14	16	18	20	36	38	40	42
st every other row.........times	5	5	6	6	6	7	7	7	7	8	8	8
then every 3rd row until.......sts	18	21	21	21	24	24	24	27	27	30	30	30

remain. Work even until armhole is same length as back. Shape shoulder to correspond to back shoulder.

Neck Bands for Sleeveless Pullover:
Work in same manner as for pullover.

Armbands for Sleeveless Pullover:
On small d.p. needles and with right side facing you, pick up....sts

128	132	136	140	144	148	152	152	160	160	160	160

and work in rib of K 1 and P 1 for 1 inch. Bind off in ribbing.

Finishing:
Join seams. Set in sleeves. Block to size (pg 208). If desired, sew ribbon on each front band of cardigan. Make buttonholes (F 59), using buttonhole-stitch (B 36 and C 50) in matching color. Press lightly.

Socks

As in all knitting, the essential factors in planning the anklet, regulation (F 73a) sock and knee-length sock are the measurements and stitch gauge. The measurements required are the width or circumference of the calf, the width of the ankle and the length of the foot. As the purpose of the ribbing at the top of a sock is primarily for its elasticity, it is often knit on smaller needles than the remainder of the sock, though it is not necessary to proper fit. Again it may be suggested that a beginner, and one who is uncertain of her stitch gauge, use a rib stitch throughout the leg of the sock and across the instep to insure a closer as well as a more adjustable fit. In planning the anklet and regulation sock, one rarely decreases in the leg section, yet a precaution to be taken is to be certain that the stitches are cast on loosely; casting on, preferably, over a larger needle or over 2 needles of the same size as those to be used for knitting

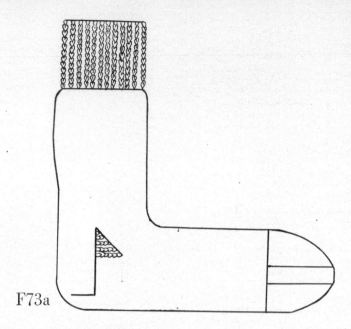

F73a

the sock itself. In the knee-length sock consideration must be given to the difference in the size of the calf and of the ankle. A seamline of one or two sts is selected as a guide; and a stitch decreased on each side of this seamline at even intervals until the number of the sts required for the ankle is reached.

For example, in planning a knee-length sock this is the method used:

Gauge: 6 sts = 1 inch, 10 rows = 1 inch.

Width of calf = 14 inches (14 × 6 (gauge 6 sts = 1 inch) = 84 sts).

Width of ankle = 10 inches (10 × 6 (gauge 6 sts = 1 inch) = 60 sts).

Length of sock to top of heel = 12 inches.

Calculations for shaping: 8 inches more to top of heel × 10 rows per inch = 80 rows; 84 sts for calf and 60 sts for ankle = 84 − 60 = 24 sts less at ankle; 24 divided by 2 = 12 decreases; 80 rows divided by 12 decreases = $6\frac{2}{3}$.

For example: On No. 2 needles cast on 84 sts (28 on each of 3 needles). Join (F 6b) being careful not to twist sts, and rib in K 2 and P 2 for 1 inch. Change to No. 3 needles and knit even for 3 inches. Mark 2 sts as seamline at center back of sock and dec 1 sts on each side of this seamline every 6th round 12 times.

Work even on 60 sts until sock measures 12 inches. Now divide sts in half, keeping half the sts on one needle for the instep (30 sts), and work back and forth on the remaining half (30 sts) for the heel. For added reenforcement at heel and toe work with a strand of yarn and a strand of ordinary sewing thread.

There are three types of heel—French (F 73b), most common, Dutch or square (F 73c), and Auto heel (F 73d). These three types of heel can be used interchangeably, and the formation of each of these is as follows:

To Shape the French Heel (F 73b):
** *Row 1:* Slip (F 13) 1 st, P back.
Row 2: * Slip 1, K 1, repeat from * across row and end K 1.

Repeat these 2 rows for 2 ins. or desired length to form a square ending with a P row. ** Turn heel as follows: K across half the number of sts on the needle plus 2 extra sts—K 17 (15 + 2) sts. K 2 tog., K 1, turn. Row 1: Slip 1, P 5, P 2 tog., P 1, turn. Row 2: Slip 1, K 6, K 2 tog., K 1, turn. Row 3: Slip 1, P 7, P 2 tog, P 1, turn. Continue in this manner always having 1 more st before dec, thus always knitting or purling the 2 sts tog on each side of the hole, until 16 sts remain on needle. K 8 sts and leave on needle.

Needle No. 1: K 8 sts (remaining half of heel sts) and with same needle pick up (F 18) 15 sts or required number of sts along side of heel piece. Needle No. 2: Work in pattern st across 30 instep sts. Needle No. 3: Pick up 15 sts along other side of heel piece, K across remaining 8 sts. The decreases of instep which follows, usually continues until the same number of sts, as were needed for the ankle is the total on the 3 needles again (60 sts).

To Shape Instep (F 73b, c, d):
Round 1: Needle No. 1: K. Needle No. 2: Work in pattern st. Needle No. 3: K.
Round 2: Needle No. 1: K to within last 3 sts, K 2 tog, K 1. Needle No. 2: Work in pattern st. Needle No. 3: K 1, slip 1, K 1, p.s.s.o., K to end of needle.

Repeat these last 2 rounds until there are 60 sts on 3 needles.

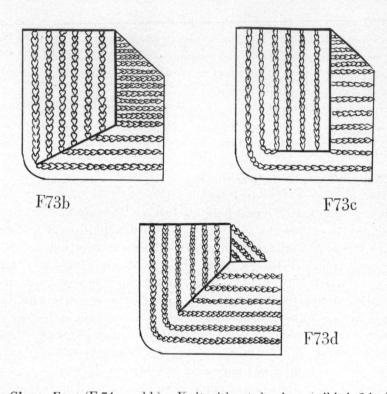

F73b

F73c

F73d

To Shape Foot (F 74a and b): Knit without shaping until it is 2 inches less than desired length (measure from back of heel). For example, if size is 10½, foot should measure 8½ inches before shaping for toe. The "toeing off" usually requires 2 inches.

To Shape Dutch Heel (F 73c):
Repeat between **'s of French Heel.

Turn heel as follows:
Row 1: K 19 sts, slip 1, K 1, p.s.s.o., turn.
* *Row 2:* Slip 1, P 9, P 2 tog, turn.

Row 3: Slip 1, K 9, slip 1, K 1, p.s.s.o., turn. Repeat from * until 14 sts remain on needle. P to end of needle, turn. K 7 sts and leave on needle.

Needle No. 1: K 7 (the remaining half of heel sts) and, with same needle pick up 16 sts or required number of sts along side of heel piece. Needle No. 2: Work in pattern st across 30 sts of the instep. Needle No. 3: Pick up 16 or required number of sts along other side of heel piece and K across remaining 7 sts. Shape instep same as above.

To Shape Auto Heel (F 73d):

Leave 30 sts on Needle No. 2 for instep. Work back and forth on 30 sts for heel as follows: Slip 1, P 28 sts. Turn, slip 1, K 27 sts. Turn, slip 1, P 26 sts. Turn. Continue working in stockinette st in this manner, always slipping the first st and always knitting or purling 1 *less* st until 11 sts remain unknitted on each side of small center group of 8 sts, ending with a P row. Turn and K back along 8 center sts just purled. Then pick up strand between last st just knit and first unknit st. Place it on left-hand needle, and K this loop with first unknit st. Turn and purl back along center 9 sts; pick up strand between last st just purled and first unpurled st. Place it on left-hand needle and P this loop with first unpurled st. Turn and repeat this process always having 1 *more* st until all sts are knit again, ending with a P row. Knit half the number of sts (15) on heel and leave these sts on needle. K next 15 sts and pick up 4 sts along side of heel and place on this needle (Needle No. 1). K across 30 sts of the instep (Needle No. 2). With third needle, pick up 4 sts along other side of heel and K across remaining 15 sts of heel (Needle No. 3).

Round 1: K around 3 needles.
Round 2: Needle No. 1: K to within last 3 sts, K 2 tog, K 1. Needle No. 2: K. Needle No. 3: K 1, slip 1, K 1, p.s.s.o., K to end. Repeat these 2 rounds 3 times (60 sts on all 3 needles).

The toe may be shaped by the "rounded toe" method (F 74a) as described for decreasing the top of a mitten (pg 233), or in the more common "flat-toe" (F 74b) method.

To Shape Flat Toe (F 74b):

Round 1: Needle No. 1: K to within last 3 sts. K 2 tog, K 1. Needle No. 2: K 1, slip 1, K 1, p.s.s.o., K to within last 3 sts, K 2 tog, K 1. Needle No. 3: K 1, slip 1, K 1, p.s.s.o., K to end. *Round 2:* K. Repeat these 2 rounds until there are 10 sts on needle No. 2.

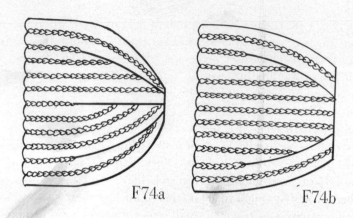

F74a   F74b

Before weaving sts always arrange sts so that the number of sts on needle No. 2 is equal to the total number of sts on Needles Nos. 1 and 3. Place sts on Needles Nos. 1 and 3 on one needle. Break yarn, allowing about 3 ins. Kitchener Stitch as described in F 21a and b.

Socks with Replaceable Heel and Toe (F 75):

Note: Every sock with a Dutch or French Heel can be worked in this manner.

Follow instructions for the particular sock desired until the turning of the heel has been completed. Cut 3 strands of contrasting yarn each approximately 24 ins. in length. With one strand, leaving an end 8 ins. long K across remaining heel sts. Using second strand of yarn, again leaving an end 8 ins. long, pick up the specified number of sts. Do not K across instep sts. Using third strand of yarn, again leaving an end 8 ins. long, with Needle No. 3, pick up the specified number of sts. Now with original strand of yarn work across half the number of heel sts and slip these sts onto Needle No. 3. With Needle No. 1 work across remaining half of heel sts and the sts picked up with contrasting yarn. With Needle No. 2, work across instep sts. With Needle No. 3 work across second group of sts picked up with contrasting yarn and first half of heel sts. Now follow instructions for the shaping of the instep, foot and toe as explained for the particular sock you are making. Weave sts together with contrasting yarn (F 21a and b).

Note: Pull out strand of contrasting yarn from each side of heel gusset. Pick up these sts and bind off. Using main color, weave these sts to heel. *To replace heel:* Open seams at heel and pull out contrasting yarn, thus releasing heel and sole sts. Pick up sole sts and rip out heel to the beg. *Note:* If yarn snags, cut heel 2 rows from the beg and only rip the remaining 2 rows. Pick up heel sts on needle and follow directions for heel. With contrasting yarn weave heel and sole sts tog. Sew openings at sides of heel with original color.
To replace toe: Pull out contrasting yarn. Rip back to beyond hole.
Note: If yarn snags, cut sock 2 rounds beyond hole. Pick up sts and arrange in proper manner on 3 needles. Join yarn and reknit, following original instructions.

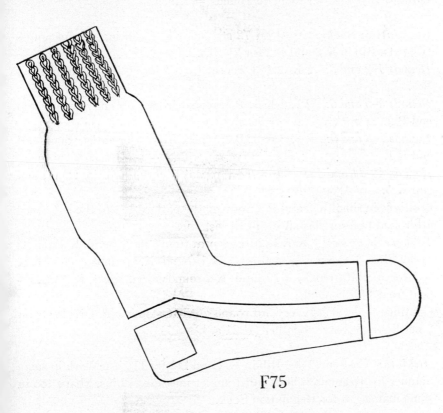

F75

Spiral anklets and regulation socks

Men's, 10–11   Women's, 9–10

Materials Required:

For Regulation Socks: 3 oz. fingering yarn 3 (women), 4 ply (men)

For Anklets: 2 oz. fingering yarn 3 (women), or 4 (men), ply
One set d.p. knitting needles No. 2 (Standard)

Gauge: 8½ sts = 1 inch; 12 rounds = 1 inch

Regulation Socks: Cast on 72 sts. Join (F 6b), being careful not to twist sts. Rib in K 2 and P 2 for 2½ ins.
Rounds 1–2 and 3: * K 3, P 3, repeat from * for entire round and end P 3.
Rounds 4–5 and 6: P 1, * K 3, P 3, repeat from * for entire round and end P 2.
Rounds 7–8 and 9: P 2, * K 3, P 3, repeat from * for entire round and end P 1.
Rounds 10–11 and 12: * P 3, K 3, repeat from * for entire round and end K 3.
Continue in rib of K 3 and P 3, moving the pattern 1 st to the left every 4th round to form bias-effect, until sock measures 20 ins.
To shape round toe: * K 7, K 2 tog, repeat from * for 1 round. K 2 rounds even. * K 6, K 2 tog, repeat from * for 1 round. K 2 rounds even, * K 5, K 2 tog, repeat from * for 1 round. K 2 rounds even. * K 4, K 2 tog, repeat from * for 1 round.
Continue to dec 8 sts every 3rd round until 16 sts remain. Divide sts on 2 needles and weave together (F 21 a, b).

Anklets: Cast on 72 sts. Rib in K 2 and P 2 for 1½ ins. Work in same manner for Regulation Sock until anklet measures 12 ins. Shape toe in same manner as for Regulation Sock.

226

Sizes: 7–8, 9–10, 11–12

Materials Required: 3 or 4 ply fingering yarn: 1 oz each of blue, white black and red for diamonds and diagonals.

For anklets (socks on table in Color Plate A): For all sizes, 2 oz. of yellow for background.

For regulation socks: For all sizes, for background 2 oz. of 3 ply in yellow, 3 oz. of 4 ply fingering yarn.
1 pair straight knitting needles No. 1 (Standard); 1 pair straight No. 2 (Standard); 1 set d.p. No. 1 (Standard).

Gauge: 8½ sts = 1 inch; 12 rows = 1 inch

Note 1: The colors (F 76) will be referred to as follows:

Chart F 76 is for size 9–10.
Yellow.................. (space on chart F 76)..................M
Blue.................... (· on chart F 76)....................A
White................... (— on chart F 76)....................B
Black................... (∧ on chart F 76)....................C
Red.................... (X on chart F 76)....................D

Wind 10 yarn bobbins, 2 full bobbins each in M, A and B; and 2 bobbins each of 2 yds. in C and D.
Note 2: If you are in doubt in regard to your stitch gauge, use a smaller needle or the number of sts for the smaller size, if you are a loose knitter: and vice-versa if you are a tight knitter. See Stitch Gauge pg. 162.
Note 3: *Knee-length socks* can be made by using the same number of sts as quoted for the regulation sock but using a size larger needle for the first 2 diamond-lengths or to the calf of the leg, then follow instructions as they are planned. A change in size can be made by changing the size of needles (pg 162).

	Sizes:	7–8	9–10	11–12

Regulation Sock:

On No. 2 straight needles with M, cast on (F 4)..........sts — 56 | 64 | 72

Rib (F 12) in K 2 and P 2 for 3½ inches. Dec (F 15) 1 st at both ends of next row. Start diamonds as follows:

	7–8	9–10	11–12
Row 1: K with A 2 sts; with M......................sts	11	13	15
With C 1 st; with D 1 st; with M......................sts	11	13	15
with B 2 sts; tie in second ball of M, with M.............sts	11	13	15
with D 1 st; with C 1 st; with M......................sts	11	13	15

with A 2 sts. Always twist yarns around each other once when changing colors (F 37), to prevent making holes.

	7–8	9–10	11–12
Row 2: P with A 3 sts; with M.........................sts	9	11	13
with C 1 st; with M 2 sts; with D 1 st; with M...........sts	9	11	13
with B 4 sts; with M.................................sts	9	11	13
with D 1 st; with M 2 sts; with C 1 st; with M...........sts	9	11	13

with A 3 sts.

	7–8	9–10	11–12
Row 3: K with A 4 sts; with M.........................sts	7	9	11
with C 1 st; with M 4 sts; with D 1 st; with M...........sts	7	9	11
with B 6 sts; with M.................................sts	7	9	11
with D 1 st; with M 4 sts; with C 1 st; with M...........sts	7	9	11

with A 4 sts.

Continue in stockinette st in this way, knitting or purling 1 more st on each half of A half diamonds and 1 more st on each side of B diamond, moving the C diagonals 1 st toward the outside and the D diagonals 1 st toward the center every row until sts are on the needle as follows:

	7–8	9–10	11–12
Work with A...sts	7	8	9
with M 1 st; with C 1 st; with M......................sts	10	12	14
with D 1 st; with M 1 st; with B......................sts	12	14	16
with M 1 st; with D 1 st; with M......................sts	10	12	14
with C 1 st; with M 1 st; with A......................sts	7	8	9

Next row: For first cross of diagonals with diamonds, continue as follows:

	7–8	9–10	11–12
Work with A...sts	7	8	9
with C 1 st; with M.................................sts	12	14	16
with D 1 st; with B.................................sts	12	14	16
with D 1 st; with M.................................sts	12	14	16
with C 1 st; with A.................................sts	7	8	9

Following row: Work with A.........................sts — (see below)

	7–8	9–10	11–12
Following row: Work with A.........................sts	6	7	8
with C 1 st; with A 2 sts; with M......................sts	10	12	14
with B 2 sts; with D 1 st; with B......................sts	10	12	14
with D 1 st; with B 2 sts; with M......................sts	10	12	14
with A 2 st; with C 1 st; with A......................sts	6	7	8

Continue in pattern until sts are on the needles as follows:

	7–8	9–10	11–12
Work with A 2 sts, with C 1 st; with A.................sts	10	12	14
with M 2 sts; with B.................................sts	10	12	14
with D 1 st; with B 2 sts; with D 1 st; with B...........sts	10	12	14

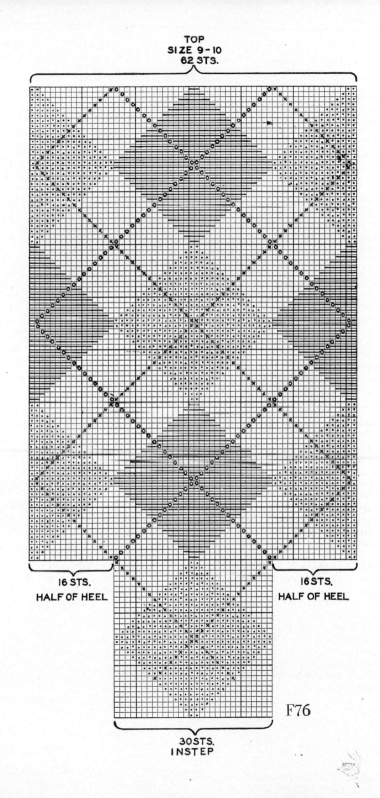

TOP
SIZE 9-10
62 STS.

16 STS.
HALF OF HEEL

16 STS.
HALF OF HEEL

F76

30 STS.
INSTEP

	Sizes:	7–8	9–10	11–12
with M 2 sts; with A............................sts with C 1 st; with A 2 sts.		10	12	14
Next row: Work with A 1 st; with C 1 st; with A.........sts		12	14	16
with B..sts		12	14	16
with D 2 sts; with B..............................sts		12	14	16
with A..sts with C 1 st; with A 1 st.		12	14	16
Following row: Work with A 2 sts; with C 1 st; with A.....sts		10	12	14
with M 2 sts; with B..............................sts		10	12	14
With D 1 st; with B 2 sts; with D 1 st; with B...........sts		10	12	14
with M 2 sts; with A..............................sts with C 1 st; with A 2 sts.		10	12	14
Continue in pattern until sts are on needle as follows: Work with A......................................sts		7	8	9
with C 1 st; with M...............................sts		12	14	16
with D 1 st; with B...............................sts		12	14	16
with D 1 st; with M...............................sts		12	14	16
with C 1 st; with A...............................sts		7	8	9
Next row: Work with A............................sts		6	7	8
with M 2 sts; with C 1 st; with M.....................sts		10	12	14
with D 1 st; with M 2 sts; with B.....................sts		10	12	14
with M 2 sts; with D 1 st; with M.....................sts		10	12	14
with C 1 st; with M 2 sts; with A.....................sts		6	7	8
Following row: Work with A.........................sts		5	6	7
with M 4 sts; with C 1 st; with M.....................sts		8	10	12
with D 1 st; with M 4 sts; with B.....................sts		8	10	12
with M 4 sts; with D 1 st; with M.....................sts		8	10	12
with C 1 st; with M 4 sts; with A.....................sts		5	6	7
Continue in pattern to just before the end of A and B dia- monds, when sts are on the needle as follows: Work with A 3 sts; with M..........................sts		8	10	12
with C 1 st; with M 4 sts; with D 1 st; with M...........sts		8	10	12
with B 4 sts; with M..............................sts		8	10	12
with D 1 sts; with M 4 sts; with C 1 st; with M...........sts with A 3 sts.		8	10	12
Next row: Work with A 2 sts; with M..................sts		10	12	14
with C 1 st; with M 2 sts; with D 1 st; with M...........sts		10	12	14
with B 2 sts; with M..............................sts		10	12	14
with D 1 st; with M 2 sts; with C 1 st; with M...........sts with A 2 sts.		10	12	14
Break off A and B bobbins. Tie on B at each end and A at center of next row. *Next Row:* Work with B 2 sts; with M..sts		11	13	15
with C 1 st; with D 1 st; with M.....................:...sts		11	13	15
with A 2 sts; with M..............................sts		11	13	15
with D 1 st; with C 1 st; with M.....................sts with B 2 sts.		11	13	15

	Sizes:	7–8	9–10	11–12

Following row: Work with B 3 sts; with M . . . . .sts . . . 9 . . . 11 . . . 13

with D 1 st; with M 2 sts; with C 1 st; with M . . . . .sts . . . 9 . . . 11 . . . 13

with A 4 sts; with M . . . . .sts . . . 9 . . . 11 . . . 13

with C 1 st; with M 2 sts; with D 1 st; with M . . . . .sts . . . 9 . . . 11 . . . 13

with B 3 sts.

Continue in this manner until there are 3 complete diamonds at seam of sock and the sts are on the needle as on Row 1. Break off A balls at each end and B ball at center, and the C and D threads nearest the ends of the needle.

Slip center . . . . .sts . . . 26 . . . 30 . . . 34

on st holder for instep. Shape heel on first and last . . . . .sts . . . 14 . . . 16 . . . 18

as follows: Slip these sts on needle and join. Be sure that seam or joining of heel sts from each end of the needle is in the center of your work. With M work even in stockinette st or double heel (pg. 221) for . . . . .ins . . . 2 . . . 2¼ . . . 2½

ending with a P row.

Turn heel as follows: K . . . . .sts . . . 16 . . . 18 . . . 20

K 2 tog, K 1, turn.

Row 1: Slip 1, P 5, P 2 tog, P 1, turn.

Row 2: Slip 1, K 6, K 2 tog, K 1, turn.

Row 3: Slip 1, P 7, P 2 tog, P 1, turn.

Continue in this manner, always having 1 more st before dec until there remain . . . . .sts . . . 16 . . . 18 . . . 20

on needle. With K side of work facing you, pick up . . . . . . .sts . . . 14 . . . 16 . . . 18

along side of heel piece. P back and pick up (F 18) . . . . .sts . . . 14 . . . 16 . . . 18

on other side of heel piece. Shape instep as follows: K 1, K 2 tog, K to within last 3 sts, K 2 tog, K 1. P back.

Repeat these last 2 rows until . . . . .sts . . . 26 . . . 30 . . . 34

remain on needle. Work even until foot measures . . . . .ins . . . 6 . . . 8 . . . 10

(measure from back of heel, allowing 2 ins. for toeing off).

Drop heel sts temporarily and pick up . . . . .sts . . . 26 . . . 30 . . . 34

of instep. Continue in pattern until you have completed 5 or 6 diamonds. Piece should fit with ease the heel-to-toe piece just completed; if not, work even with M until it does fit tightly rather than loosely, this heel and sole piece. Divide heel sts in half and slip each half onto d.p. needles. With instep needle referred to as Needle No. 2 and the heel needle to the right of instep needle, as Needle No. 1, and the heel needle to the left as Needle No. 3, work round and round to shape toe as follows:

Round 1: K across all needles.

Round 2: Needle No. 1: K to within last 3 sts, K 2 tog, K 1. Needle No. 2: K 1, slip 1, K 1, p.s.s.o., K to within last 3 sts, K 2 tog, K 1. Needle No. 3: K 1, slip 1, K 1, p.s.s.o., K to end of needle. Repeat these last 2 rounds until . . . . .sts . . . 8 . . . 10 . . . 12

remain on Needle No. 2. Slip sts of Needles No. 1 and No. 3 on one needle and weave sts tog, (F 21a and b).

Anklets (Color Plate A):

On No. 1 straight needles with M cast on . . . . .sts . . . 56 . . . 64 . . . 72

231

Rib in K 2 and P 2 for 1½ inches. Dec 1 st at both ends of next row. Change to No. 2 needles and work in pattern in same manner as for regulation sock until 1 diamond has been completed. Shape heel and sole in same manner as for Regulation Sock. Continue in pattern on instep sts for 2 or 3 diamonds as desired. Work even until piece is desired length (pg. 222). Shape toe in same manner as for Regulation Sock.

Finishing:
Join seams and block to size.

Mittens and gloves

The essential factors in planning mittens and gloves are, as in all knitting, the measurements and stitch gauge. The measurements required are the width or circumference of the hand at the base of the fingers, and the length of the hand from the tip of the middle finger to the center back wrist. Since the wrist measurement is usually 1 inch smaller than the knuckle measurement, the difference is allowed for by ribbing for at least 2 inches on a smaller needle than those used for the body of the mitten or glove. For the beginner and for one who is uncertain of her stitch gauge (pg 162), it is advisable to use a rib stitch throughout the entire mitten or glove. The rib stitch, as you know, is elastic, and the same ribbed mitten or glove will fit two or three different sizes. The thumb, too, is planned and a gusset is begun usually 3 or 4 rounds above the ribbing.

Mittens (F 77):
  For example: In planning your mitten this is the method used:
Stitch gauge on No. 4 needles: 6 sts = 1 inch, 10 rows = 1 inch.
Width of hand measured around knuckles = 7 inches.
Depth of hand from tip of middle finger to wrist = 7 inches.
Girth of thumb at base is usually ⅓ less than the width given for the
  hand. Approximately 3 inches (3 × 6 = 18 sts).
  Therefore, the number of sts required is 42 (7″ × 6). Proceed as follows:

On No. 2 d.p. needles cast on 42 sts (14 sts on each of 3 needles). Join (F 6b), being careful not to twist sts, and rib in K 2 and P 2 for 3 inches. Change to No. 4 needles and K even for 4 rounds. Next round begin thumb gusset for right hand as follows:

Round 1: Needle No. 1: K 1, inc. in next st, K 2, inc. in next st, K to end of round.

Round 2: Knit.

Note: If yarn is light weight and more than 10 rounds are required to equal 1 inch, work 2 even rounds between increase-rounds, instead of one as explained here.

Round 3: Needle No. 1: K 1, inc. in next st, K 4, inc. in next st, K to end of round.

Round 4: Knit.

Round 5: Needle No. 1: K 1, inc. in next st, K 6, inc. in next st, K to end of round. Continue to increase in this manner every alternate round, thus having 2 more sts between increases, until there are 12 sts (10 sts plus 2 inc. sts each side) for base of thumb (approximately ⅔ the number of sts required for entire width of thumb).

Next round: K 1, slip 12 sts onto holder, and cast on 6 sts to replace these sts. K even on 46 sts until mitten measures 5 inches from top of ribbing (2-inch allowance for shaping top of mitten).

Next round dec at even intervals to 42 sts (must be an even multiple of 6). Now decrease 6 times in every alternate round at even intervals (every 3rd round for light-weight yarn) about 5 times.

For example: Shape top of mitten as follows:

Round 1: * K 5, K 2 tog, repeat from * for entire round.

Round 2 and all even rounds: Knit.

Round 3: * K 4, K 2 tog, repeat from * for entire round.

Round 5: * K 3, K 2 tog, repeat from * for entire round.

Round 7: * K 2, K 2 tog, repeat from * for entire round.

Round 9: * K 1, K 2 tog, repeat from * for entire round.

Break yarn, allowing about 2 inches; run through 12 sts and fasten off; or weave sts tog (F 21a and b).

Thumb: Slip 12 sts from holder on needle, pick up 6 sts from the base of the 6 cast-on sts.

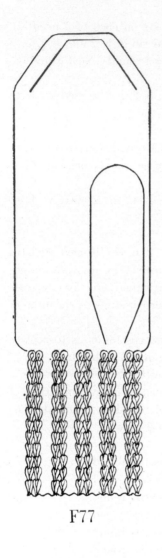

F77

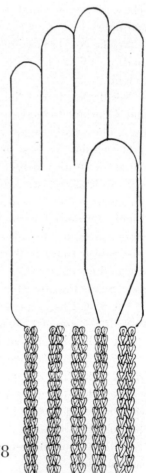

F78

234

Note: To prevent holes it is sometimes advisable to pick up an extra st at each corner and to dec directly above it on next round if decreasing is essential for size. Arrange 18 sts on 3 needles and knit even for desired length of thumb—2 inches for a size 7 mitten. Next round dec at even intervals to 16 sts (must be a multiple of 4).

Now dec 4 times in every alternate round at even intervals.

Round 1: * K 2, K 2 tog, repeat from * for entire round.

Round 2 and all even rounds: Knit.

Round 3: * K 1, K 2 tog, repeat from * for entire round.

Round 5: K 2 tog for entire round.

Break yarn, run through sts and fasten off; or weave sts tog (F 21a and b).

The left-hand mitten can be made in exactly the same manner. However, if a pattern stitch or the "flat-toe" shaping (F 74b, pg 223), at the top of the mitten is used, the thumb gusset is begun at the end of the round, instead of the beginning.

For example:

Round 1: K to within last 5 sts of the end of the round. Then inc. in the next st, K 2, inc. in next st, K 1.

Round 2 and all even rounds: Knit.

Round 3: K to within last 7 sts, then inc. in next st, K 4, inc. in next st, K 1.

Continue in this manner until desired number of sts has been added for gusset.

Gloves (F 78):

It is simply the fingers that make the difference between the mittens and the gloves. Therefore the same calculations are made up to the beginning of fingers which are usually commenced 1 to $1\frac{1}{4}$ inches above the completion of the thumb gusset. The easiest rule to follow for the correct position of the thumb is simply this: On the right hand the st directly above the first inc. st on the right side of the thumb gusset is the center st of the outside of the first finger. On the left hand the st directly above the last inc. st on the left side is the center st of the outside of the first finger. At this st divide the sts in half, keeping one half of the sts on a holder for the front of the hand and the other half of the sts on a second holder for the back of the hand. Now divide the back and front sts into four equal parts. If the sts are not an even multiple of 4, consider the "extra sts" as part of the first finger; and if the sts are an even multiple of 4, the "extra sts" needed to give the first 3 fingers the same number of sts will be supplied by casting on the "extra sts" to bridge the gap between the front and back sts.

Proceed as follows:

First or Index Finger: Slip one-quarter of the sts of the front and back onto needles, cast on 2 sts to bridge gap between front and back (cast on 4 sts if there were no "extra sts"). Divide sts evenly on 3 needles and knit even for desired length—3 inches for size 7 glove. Shape top of finger in same manner as top of thumb of mitten (pg 235).

Second Finger: Slip one-quarter of the sts of the front and back onto needles, cast on 2 sts for the gusset on one side, and pick up 2 sts from the 2 (or 4) cast-on sts of the index finger. Shape in same manner as index finger, making it ¼ inch longer.

Third Finger: Work in the same manner as second finger and make it same length as index finger.

Little Finger: Pick up remaining sts from holders, also pick up 2 sts from previous gusset. Shape in same manner as index finger, making it ¼ inch shorter.

Thumb: Work in same manner as mitten thumb (pg 233).

CHAPTER 7

CROCHETING

CROCHETING

➜➤➤ CROCHETING is the twin sister of knitting and it takes its name from the French spelling of the word, hook-croché. As in knitting, it is an interlocking of loops, yet unlike knitting the loops are formed with a single needle or hook. To many, the manipulation of one needle makes it easier to crochet than to knit, and because a single stitch in crochet is an interlacing or overlapping of several strands of thread, it is more frequently used for articles for the home than for wearing apparel.

As in all phases of needlework the joy of crocheting lies in creating. The amateur may begin by following the instructions of a single motif crocheted in fine thread for a dinner cloth or liturgical runner and design a modern luncheon set as shown in the photograph G 34. The applications of the use of these three motifs is only a glimpse into the technical side of "beauty unlimited," as well as an interesting presentation of the importance of stitch gauge. This photograph tells very clearly what a change in hook and thread will do. It urges you graphically to begin your home course in designing by following the instructions in this book as to stitches. Dare to use straw for the "round motif" and be pleasantly surprised.

Instructions for Crocheted Afghan (Color Plate G, see pg 242).

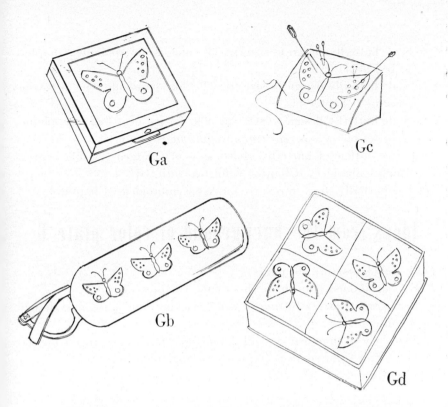

Ga

Gc

Gb

Gd

Design your own from color plate G

With a bit of ingenuity, you can design from a crocheted afghan.

1. Use butterfly charts for needlepoint (Chapter 10) designs in petit-point for compact cover (Ga), eyeglass case cover (Gb); in gros point for bag, pillows, pictures, etc.
2. Make petit point pin cushion (Gc) from butterfly charts for needle-point designs (Chapter 10).
3. Use the butterfly charts for needlepoint (Chapter 10) designs in petit-point for cigarette case (Gd).
4. Use butterfly design for textile painting and sequin embroidery (Chapter 14) for evening bag (Ge).
5. Combine textile painting with sequin embroidery (Chapter 14), using butterfly design for slippers (Gf) and blouse (Gg).

6. Scale butterfly design to size (pg 339) and use for appliqué (Chapter 5) bedspread (Gh).
7. Scale butterfly design to size (pg 339) for lampshade (Gi) in textile painting (Chapter 14).
8. Scale butterfly design to size (pg 339) for garment bag in appliqué (Gj); for pillow (Gk) in trapunto quilting (Chapter 5).
9. Trace outline of butterfly chart, as is or enlarged (pg 339), using simple embroidery (Chapter 3) for tea-cloth (Gl).
10. Use butterfly chart in reverse for Assisi embroidery (Chapter 4).

Ideas from the background of color plate G

For helpful hints, turn the pages.
1. For curtain and lampshade directions (Chapter 13).
2. For instructions for tufting or candlewicking similar to chair design (Chapter 5).
3. Trace and enlarge leaf design of wallpaper for hooked rug (Chapter 11), simple embroidery (Chapter 3) or appliqué (Chapter 5).

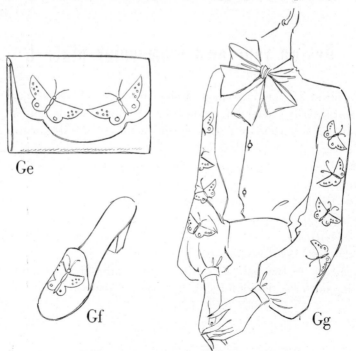

Ge

Gf

Gg

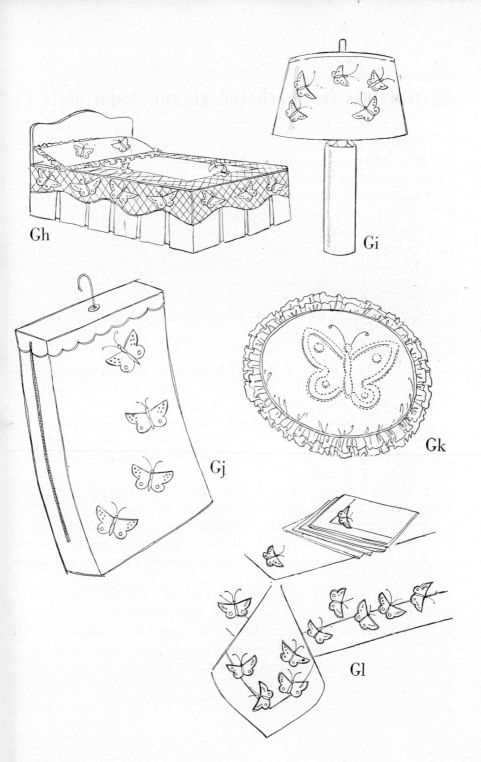

Gh

Gi

Gj

Gk

Gl

Instructions for crocheted afghan (color plate G)

Materials Required:

32 oz. 4-fold Germantown in light grey

34 oz. 4-fold Germantown in dark grey

1 oz. each 4-ply fingering yarn in lavendar (A), light blue (B), medium blue (C), dark rose (D), kelly green (E), white (F), yellow (G), light green (H), light rose (I).

2 oz. 4-ply fingering in black

1 bone afghan crochet hook, No. 5 (standard)

1 blunt-end tapestry needle

Gauge: $5\frac{1}{2}$ stitches = 1 inch; 4 rows = 1 inch (Stitch Gauge, pg 162).

Directions:

1. To crochet a square: With No. 5 bone crochet hook and Germantown yarn, chain 60. Work in afghan stitch (G 22a, b, c) for 96 rows. Piece should measure 11 inches square. With same color yarn, work 1 row of single crochet (G 3a) around entire square, placing 3 sc in each corner (G 27) to mitre and making certain to have the same number of stitches on each side—approximately 60 stitches on each side of square. Fasten off.
2. Make 17 squares in dark grey and 18 squares in light grey.
3. Press each square with a damp cloth and moderate iron.
4. Following chart Gn and Go, cross stitch (C 37) one butterfly in each dark grey square in position shown in Chart Gm. Embroider in outline stitch (C 4) the antennae of each butterfly in black. Cross stitch spots in black.
5. Repeat step 3 for each embroidered square.
6. Join squares (Gm) with a slip stitch (G 11) in dark grey Germantown.
7. Work 6 rows of single crochet (G 3a) around entire afghan, placing 3 sc in each corner (G 27) to mitre.
8. Press border with damp cloth and moderate iron.

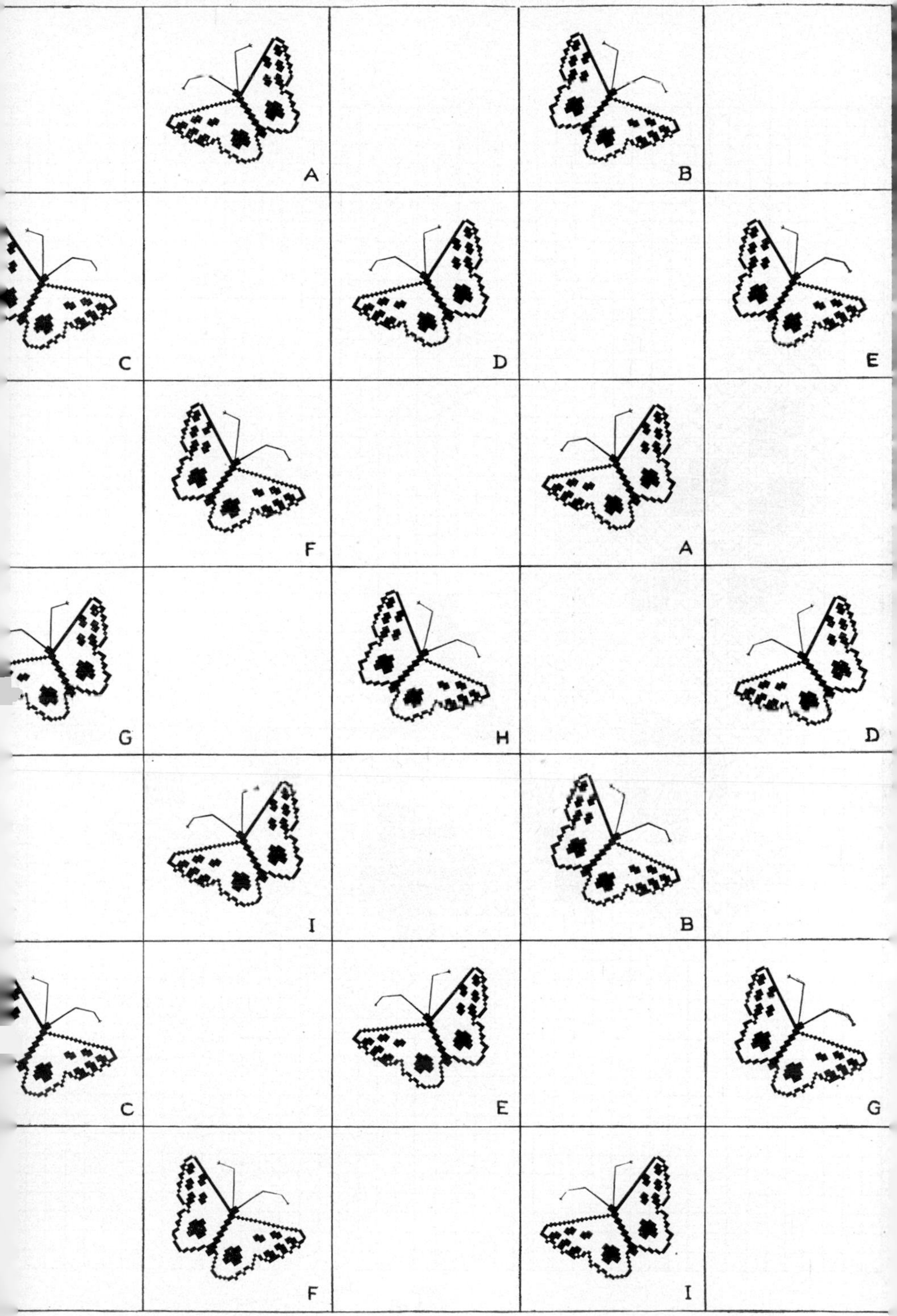

A   B

C   D   E

F   A

G   H   D

I   B

C   E   G

F   I

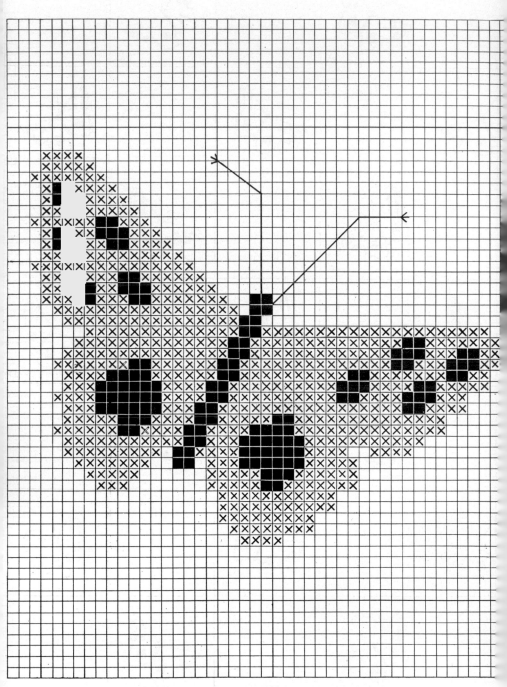

Gn

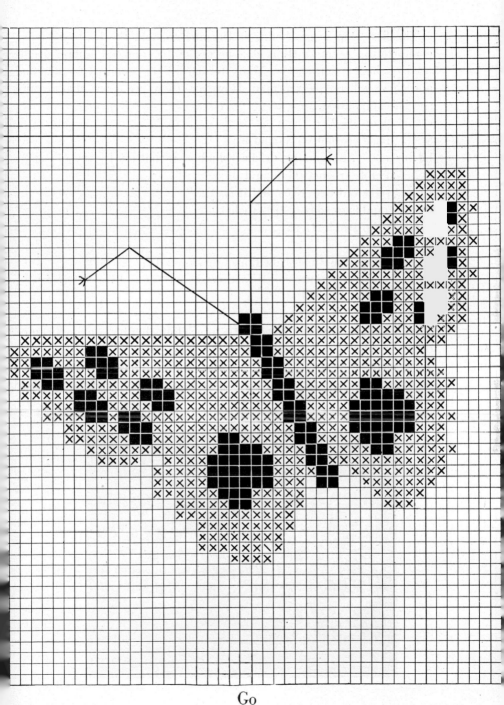

Go

The first step in crocheting is learning to hold the hook and yarn comfortably. As in knitting, it is necessary to know the abbreviations used on instruction sheets. Many terms are the same as for knitting and these will not be repeated. However, there are a few that require special explanation.

ch. . . .chain (G 2)

sc. . . .single crochet (G 3a and b)

hdc or sdc. . . .half double or short double crochet (G 4)

dc. . . .double crochet (G 5a and b)

tc. . . .treble crochet (G 6a and b)

dtc. . . .double or long treble crochet

sl st. . . .slip stitch (G 11)

sk. . . .skip

sp. . . .space (sometimes called open mesh—G 13)

bl. . . .block (sometimes called solid mesh—G 14a and b)

p. . . .picot (G 12)

Stitch Gauge: As explained in the preceding chapter, the importance of stitch gauge can never be over-emphasized. Read carefully page 162. To measure your stitch gauge in crochet, make a chain at least 4 inches in length and work in the desired pattern stitch for at least 3 inches. As in knitting, block piece and calculate the number of stitches to one

G1

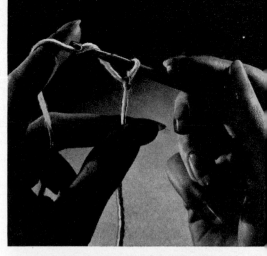

inch and the number of rows to one inch that *you* crochet with the hook and yarn to be used in crocheting a specific article. To impress you with the importance of the gauge, two motifs are shown (G 1). The same instructions were used for both motifs. Merely change of thread and hook produced the difference (for instructions see page 267).

Chain Stitch: Make a slip knot (F 4a) and place loop on hook which is held in right hand. * Wrap yarn around hook (G 2) and draw yarn through loop on hook, permitting first loop to drop off. Repeat from * for desired number of chain stitches.

Single Crochet: Make a chain (G 2) desired length. Insert hook into second chain stitch from hook, * y.o., and draw yarn through stitch (2 loops on hook), y.o., and draw yarn through both loops on hook. Repeat from * in each chain stitch. Row 2: Turn, ch 1. * Insert hook in top of next st, going through both strands of stitch unless otherwise stated, y.o., and draw yarn through stitch (2 loops on hook) (G 3a), y.o., and draw through both loops on hook. Repeat from * across row. Repeat Row 2 (G 3b).

247

G3a

G3b

Half or Short Double Crochet: Make a chain (G 2) desired length.
* Y.o., insert hook in third ch from hook and draw up loop (3 loops on
hook), y.o., and draw yarn through 3 loops. Repeat from * in each chain.
Row 2: Turn, ch 2, * y.o., insert hook in top of next st, going through
both strands unless otherwise stated, y.o., and draw yarn through stitch
(3 loops on hook),·y.o., (G 4), and draw through 3 loops. Repeat from *
across row. Repeat Row 2.

Double Crochet: Make a chain (G 2) desired length. * Y.o. and insert
hook in the fourth ch from hook and draw up a loop (3 loops on hook),
y.o. and draw through 2 loops (2 loops on hook), y.o. and draw through
last 2 loops. Repeat from * in each chain. Row 2: Turn, ch 3, * y.o.,
insert hook through top of next st, going through both strands of the
stitch, unless otherwise stated, ·y.o. and draw through st (3 loops on
hook), y.o. and draw through 2 loops (2 loops on hook), y.o. (G 5a) and
draw through last 2 loops. •Repeat from * across row. Repeat Row 2
(G 5b).

Treble Crochet: Make a chain (G 2) desired length. * Y.o. twice, insert hook in fifth ch from hook, and draw up a loop (4 loops on hook);
y.o. and draw through 2 loops (3 loops on hook); y.o. and draw through 2
loops (2 loops on hook); y.o. and draw through last 2 loops. Repeat from
* in each chain. Row 2: Turn, ch 4, * y.o. twice, insert in next st going
through both strands of the stitch, unless otherwise stated, and draw up
loop (4 loops on hook); y.o. (G 6a) and draw through 2 loops (3 loops on
hook); y.o. (G 6b) and draw through 2 loops (2 loops on hook); y.o. and
draw through last 2 loops. Repeat from * across row. Repeat Row 2.
A *long treble*, as well as various types of a treble crochet, can be made by
wrapping the yarn over the needle as many times as desired and then
drawing y.o. through 2 loops at a time, until one loop remains on hook.

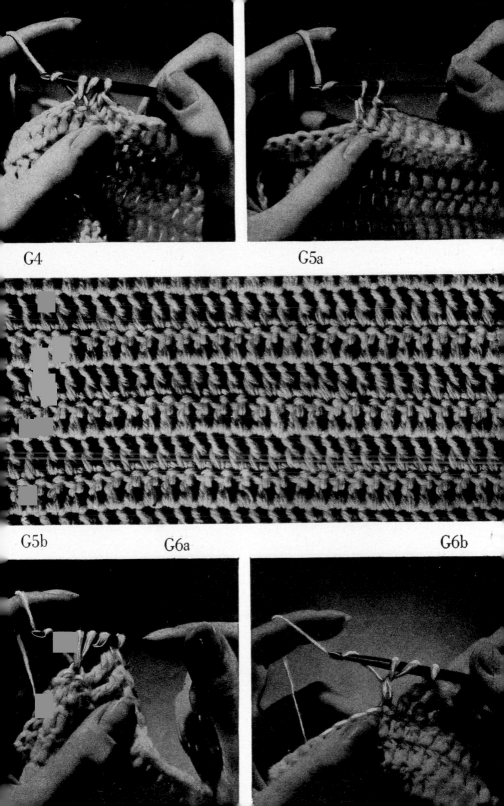

G4

G5a

G5b

G6a

G6b

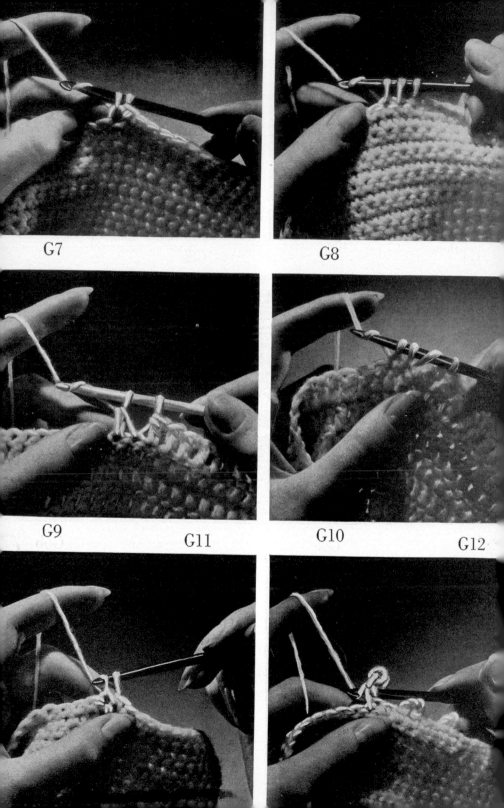

G7

G8

G9

G10

G11

G12

To Increase a Single Crochet: Work 2 stitches in 1 stitch (G 7). This principle applies to the increasing of all stitches (dc, tc, etc.).

To Decrease a Single Crochet: Draw up a loop through each of the next 2 stitches (3 loops on hook), y.o., and draw through 3 loops (G 8).

To Decrease a Double Crochet: Draw up loop through each of next 2 sts, finish as usual (G 5a, b), drawing through two loops at a time (G 9).

To Decrease a Treble Crochet: Wrap yarn around needle one less time than usual and pick up "missing loop" by drawing loop through each of next 2 sts (G 10). Finish stitch in usual manner (G 6a and b).

Slip Stitch: Make a chain (G 2) desired length. Insert hook into second ch on hook, y.o., and draw through ch and loop at same time. Repeat in each chain. Row 2: Turn, ch 1, * insert through top of next st, y.o. and draw through top of st and loop at same time (G 11). Repeat from * across row. Repeat Row 2. This stitch is used to form a tight edge.

Picot: There are 2 methods. Method 1: Sc (G 3a and b) in foundation, ch 3 or 4, depending on length of picot desired, and slip stitch (G 11) in top of sc (G 12). Method 2: Work a sc, ch 3 or 4 for picot and sc again in same space. Work as many sc's between picots as desired.

Space or Open Mesh: Make the chain (G 2) foundation and 5 extra chains to turn. Row 1: 1 dc (G 5a and b) in 6th ch from hook, * ch 2, skip 2 ch, 1 dc in next ch. Repeat from * across row and end with 1 dc in last ch. Row 2: Ch 5 to turn, * 1 dc in dc of previous row, ch 2, skip 2 ch of previous row. Repeat from * across row and end with 1 dc in 3rd ch of group of 5 ch of previous row. Repeat Row 2 (G 13).

251

G13

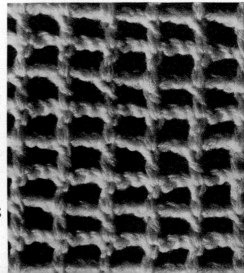

Block or Solid Mesh: 4 double crochets (G 5a and b) form a block or solid mesh (G 14a) and 3 double crochet are required for each additional block or solid mesh. For example, 2 adjoining blocks are formed of 7 dc and 3 adjoining blocks are formed of 10 dc (G 14b). Spaces and blocks or open mesh and solid mesh are used in filet crochet.

Lacet Stitch: Make foundation chain (G 2) and 8 extra chains. 1 sc (G 3a and b) in 9th st from hook, * ch 3, skip 2 ch, 1 dc (G 5a and b) in next st, ch 3, skip 2 ch, 1 sc in next ch, repeat from * across row and end with 1 dc in last ch. Cut off unwanted chain-length. Row 2: Ch 8, 1 dc in 2nd dc * ch 5, 1 dc in next dc, repeat from * across row and end 1 dc in 6th ch of original group. Row 3: Ch 5, * 1 sc in 3rd ch, ch 3, skip 2 ch, 1 dc in next dc, ch 3, repeat from * across row and end with 1 dc in 6th ch of original group of 8 ch. Repeat Rows 2 and 3 throughout (G 15). The lacet or small V-shaped stitch is usually combined with spaces and blocks.

Star Stitch: Make a foundation chain (G 2). Row 1: Skip 1 ch and draw up a loop in each of next 5 sts, y.o. and draw through 6 loops on hook, ch 1, * draw a loop through the eye formed by ch just made, draw a loop through back of last loop of star just made, draw a loop through same ch where last loop of previous star was made, draw a loop through each of next 2 ch sts, y.o., and draw through the 6 loops on hook, ch 1. Repeat from * across row and end ch 1. Cut off unwanted chain length. Row 2: Ch 4 and turn. Skip first ch, draw up a loop in each of next 3 chains, draw a loop through side of first star, draw a loop through eye of next star, y.o. and draw through 6 loops on hook, * ch 1, draw a loop through eye formed by ch just made, draw a loop through back of last loop of star just made, draw a loop through same ch where last loop of previous star was made, draw a loop through side of star of previous row, draw a loop through eye of next star, y.o. (G 16a) and draw through 6 loops on hook, ch 1, repeat from * across row and end ch 1. Repeat Row 2 throughout for pattern stitch (G 16b).

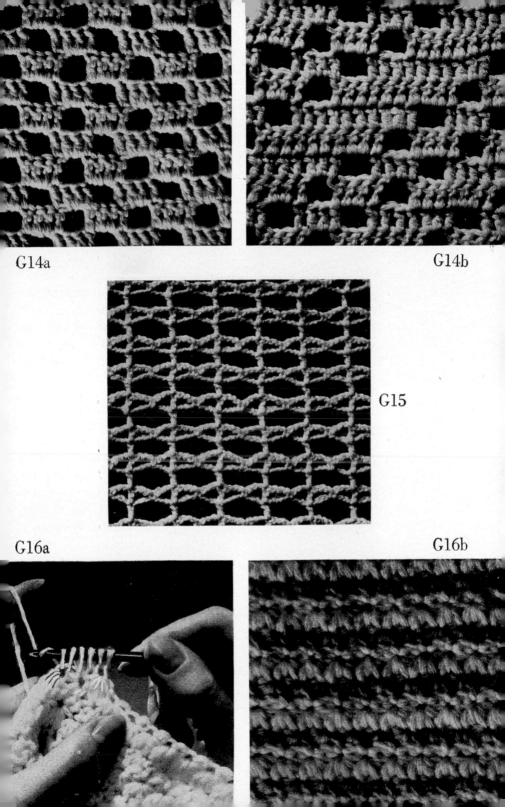

G14a

G14b

G15

G16a

G16b

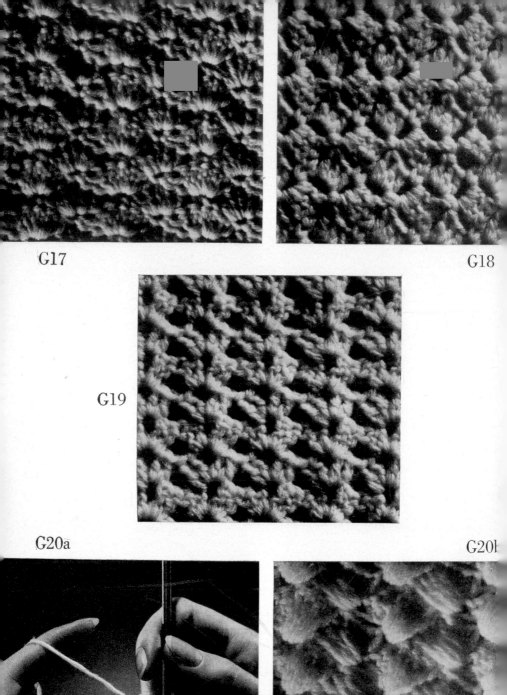

G17

G18

G19

G20a

G20b

Shell Pattern: Make the foundation chain (G 2) and 3 extra chains to turn. Row 1: Turn, 4 dc (G 5a and b) in the 4th ch., * skip 2 ch, 1 sc in next ch., skip 2 ch, 5 dc in next ch. Repeat from *, and end with 1 sc. Cut off unwanted chain length. Row 2: Ch 3, turn. 4 dc in first sc. * 1 sc in 3rd dc of previous row, 5 dc in next sc of previous row. Repeat from * across row and end with 1 sc in 3rd dc of last group. Repeat Row 2 throughout, thus working 5 dc in each sc of the previous row and 1 sc in the center dc of the group of 5 dc of the previous row. Shells may be made with as many dc in a group as desired (G 17).

Brick or Crazy Shell: Make the foundation chain (G 2) and 3 extra chains to turn. Row 1: 3 dc (G 5a and b) in 4th ch from hook, * skip 3 ch, 1 sc in next ch, ch 3, 3 dc in same ch. Repeat from * across row, and end with 1 sc. Row 2: Ch 3 and turn. 3 dc in sc of previous row, * 1 sc in the space made by ch-3 of previous row, ch 3 and 3 dc in same (ch-3 of previous row). Repeat from * across row and end with 1 sc in last ch-3 of previous row. Repeat Row 2 throughout (G 18).

Shawl Stitch: Make the foundation chain (G 2) and 3 extra chains to turn. Row 1: 1 dc (G 5a and b) in the 4th ch, ch 2, 2 dc in same ch (4th). * Skip 3 ch, 2 dc in next ch, ch 2 and 2 dc in same ch. Repeat from * across row. Row 2: Ch 3 and turn, 1 dc into space made by ch-2 of previous row, ch 2, 2 dc in same space, * 2 dc in next space made by ch-2 of previous row, ch 2 and 2 dc in same space. Repeat from * across row. Repeat Row 2 throughout (G 19).

Fancy Puff: Make the foundation chain (G 2) and 3 extra chains to turn. Row 1: Work 8 dc (G 5a and b) in 4th ch from hook. * Skip 4 ch and work 1 sc (G 5a and b) into next ch. Skip 4 ch and work 8 dc in next ch. Repeat from * across row and end with 4 dc. Row 2: Turn without making a chain. 4 dc in first sc, now work 4 dc in the last dc of the group of 4 dc of row below, thus going over and almost concealing the 4 dc just completed, * 1 sc between the 4th and 5th dc of next group of 8 dc, 4 dc in the next sc, now work 4 dc in the last dc of the previous group of 8 dc of row below (G 20a), thus going over and almost concealing the 4 dc

G21a

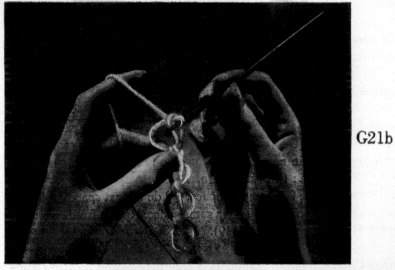

G21b

G21c

just completed. Repeat from * across row and end with 1 sc between the 4th and 5th dc of last group of 8 dc and 4 dc in the last dc of this group. Repeat Row 2 for pattern stitch (G 20b).

Knot Stitch: Row 1: Make a ch (G 2), then * draw up loop ¼ in˙ (G 21a). Work 1 sc through back strand of elongated loop just made (G 21b and c). Repeat from * an even number of times for desired length. This forms the foundation row. Row 2: Make 2 extra elongated loops (4 loops in all) to turn. Skip 4 loops and work 1 sc in center of 4th sc or knot of Row 1. * Draw loop up ¼ in., work 1 sc in back strand of same loop, draw a second loop up ¼ in, work 1 sc in back strand of this loop, skip 1 knot and work 1 sc in 2nd knot (G 21d). Repeat from * across row and end with 1 sc in last knot. Row 3: Make 2 elongated loops to turn, * work 1 sc through first loose knot of previous row, draw loop up ¼ in, 1 sc in back strand of same loop, draw a 2nd loop up ¼ in, 1 sc in back strand of this loop, skip heavy knot of previous row. Repeat from * across row and end with 1 sc in last loose knot. Repeat Row 3 throughout (G 21e).

G21d

G21e

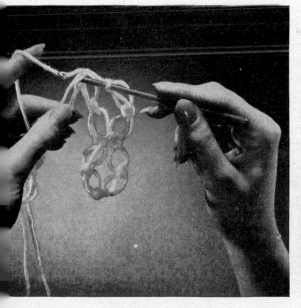

Afghan Stitch: Make a foundation chain (G 2) and 1 extra ch to turn. Row 1: Draw a loop through each ch and leave all loops on hook (G 22a). At the end, there should be the same number of loops on the hook as there were foundation chains. Row 2: Y.o. and draw through first loop on hook, * y.o. and draw through 2 loops on hook (G 22b). Repeat from * until there is only 1 loop on hook. Row 3: Draw a loop through each upright stitch. At the end, there should be as many loops as on Row 1. Repeat Rows 2 and 3 for pattern st (G 22c).

Embossed Afghan: Make a foundation chain (G 2) with multiple of 4 chains plus one extra. Row 1: Draw up 1 loop in each ch (G 22a). Row 2: Take loops off as follows: Draw yarn through 1 loop, * draw yarn through 4 loops, draw yarn through 2 loops. Repeat from * across row. Row 3: * Draw up 1 loop between single upright st and the group of 3 sts, draw up 1 loop on top of the group of 3 sts, draw up 1 loop between the group of 3 sts and next single st, draw up 1 loop in the single upright st (5 loops on hook). Repeat from * across row. There should be as many loops on needle as there were on Row 1. Repeat Rows 2 and 3 for pattern st (G 23).

Cable Afghan: Make foundation chain (G 2) a multiple of 10 chains plus 2 extra. Row 1: Draw up 1 loop in each chain (G 22a), leaving loops on hook. Row 2: Y.o. and draw through 1 loop, * y.o. and draw through 2 loops (G 22b). Repeat from * across row, leaving last loop on hook. Row 3: Bring yarn forward and hold below next upright st, draw up a loop through upright st (afghan purl st). Work a P st in each of next 2 sts—3 P sts in all. * Draw up loop by inserting hook through center of next st and underneath the ch (afghan knit st). Work an afghan K st in each of next 5 sts—6 K sts in all. Work an afghan P st in each of next 4 sts. Repeat from * across row and end with 3 P sts. Row 4: Same as Row 2. Row 5: Same as Row 3. Row 6: Y.o. and draw through 1 loop, (y.o. and draw through 2 loops) twice—3 P sts taken off. * Cable on next 6 K sts as follows: Slip hook out of last loop on hook and 6 K loops; twist them by slipping hook through first 3 K loops (G 24a), then the last 3 K loops and finally the first loop. Take off these sts and the next 4 P sts in usual manner (Row 2). Repeat from * across row. Repeat Rows 3, 4, 5 and 6 for pattern st (G 24b).

G22a

G23

G22b

G22c

G24a

G24b

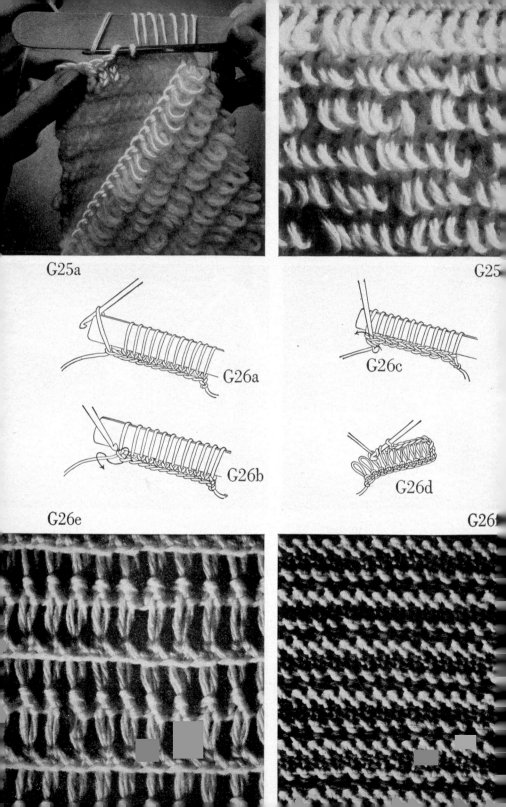

G25a

G25

G26a

G26b

G26c

G26d

G26e

G26

Loop Stitch: Cut piece of cardboard ¼, ½ or ¾ inch wide and 3 inches in length. A tongue-depressor or mesh stick can be used as a gauge. Make a chain (G 2) desired length. Row 1: Work 1 sc (G 3a and b) in each stitch. Row 2: * Hold cardboard in back of work, insert hook in next sc, wind yarn around cardboard from back to front, yarn over hook (G 25a) and draw loop through st, yarn over hook and draw through first loop, y.o. and draw through 2 loops on hook. Repeat from * to form each loop. Work 1 loop in each st. Repeat Rows 1 and 2 for pattern st (G 25b).

Attached Loop Stitch: Row 1: Ch (G 2) 2, slip loop from hook onto cardboard or tongue-depressor (G 26a). Remove hook and insert it in first ch, * ch 2, slip loop from hook and insert hook in second last ch (G 26b and c). Repeat from * for desired length. Remove the cardboard whenever necessary or permit the stitches to fall off the far end. End with ch 3 or the number of chains required to measure the same length as the width of the cardboard. Remove the cardboard. Row 2: Work 1 sc (G 3a and b) in each loop (G 26d). Row 3: Repeat Row 2 of the loop stitch above. Repeat Rows 2 and 3 for pattern st (G 26e). This stitch is usually used as the foundation for interesting woven effects—merely weave (N 4a and b) contrasting yarn in and out each strand of loops (G 26f). However, it is most effective when made with fine cotton and stiffened with starch or gum arabic for lace mats and doilies. To increase or to form an outside corner in the attached loop stitch, work 3 or 5 loops in the corner stitch (G 26g). To decrease, or to form an inside corner in the attached loop stitch, draw yarn through 3 or 5 corner stitches, depending upon the type of yarn and the corner desired (G 26h).

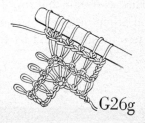

G26g

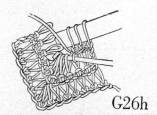

G26h

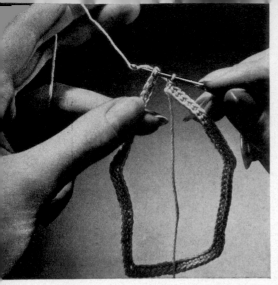

G27   G28   G2

Turning Corners—Simple Corner: Make a chain (G 2) foundation, counting the number of chains and making sure that they can be divided evenly into the number of sides that there will be on the article. If the article is four-sided, then the number of chains must be divisible by four, if it is five-sided, then the number of chains must be evenly divided by 5. Row 2: Work 1 sc (G 3a and b) in every ch and at the ch that will be at corner, work 3 sc if the corner is on a 4-sided article; or 2 sc if there are more than 4 sides. Join into a ring if desired (G 27).

Pattern Corner: When the first row of work is completed, continue with the pattern making sure to work a sufficient number of stitches or chains at corners to allow the lace to turn round the previous rows without making a frill and without being so tight that the edges will curl. In G 28, at the corner 3 dc (G 5a and b) are worked in 2nd row in corner, then the usual ch 2 and finally a second group of 3 dc in same st. The method used in any particular lace pattern must be found by trial.

262

G30

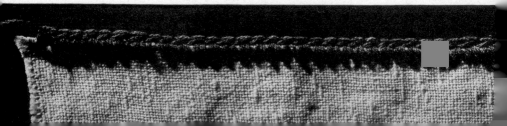

Corner Worked Across Width: This corner presents a more difficult problem. A simple example is illustrated here to make the working clearer. The fact that the pattern is symmetrical makes the turning of the corner easier than if another type of pattern were used. Also, the lace has not a shaped edge to confuse the work still further. When the length of lace has reached a measurement that will include the width of the lace as well as the length of the side of article to be decorated, and when a convenient point in the pattern has been reached, the work is turned and the next row worked along the side of the lace.

The work will now proceed into sides of dc and chain stitches instead of into tops and loops of the stitches. Take extra care with the tension of the work in this first row, and then continue in the usual way (G 29). Corners in more complicated patterns are turned by the same principle.

Straight Edgings: When the crocheted edging is worked straight along the thread of the material, a guiding line for the depth of the stitches can be made by drawing out one thread of the material. This will also make easier the insertion of the hook. Prepare the edge of the material by tacking the hem to the wrong side. Then consider the depth of the stitching and draw out a thread at that depth on right side. Proceed to work in sc (G 3a and b), which is the best stitch for an edge with only a single turn of material. Space the stitches to a suitable number of threads (G 30).

Edgings with Picot: Make a foundation chain (G 2), turn and work 1 row of sc (G 3a and b). Row 2: Turn, ch 5 and work 1 dc (G 5a and b) into 3rd sc from hook. Continue working spaces as follows: * Ch 2, skip 2 sc of previous row, 1 dc in next st. Repeat from * across row and end with 1 dc in last sc. Row 3: Ch 3 and turn, work 1 sc into first space from hook. * Ch 5, then work 1 sl st (G 11) in 3rd ch from hook, ch 2, and work 1 sc in center of next space. Repeat from * across row and end with 1 sc in last space (G 31).

263

G31

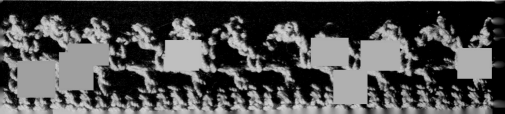

Changing Color in Crochet: When the second color continues in the same direction and on the same line as the first color, commence the sc and dc as usual and at the second step of the last sc or dc pick up the second color (G 32) and pull it through the loop or loops on the hook. Drop first color, leaving the thread to hang until it is picked up in next row. Work across row. If, however, the first color is to be eliminated entirely, lay first color along top of previous row and work over it for 3 stitches. Then cut thread. The strand which is left at the back of the work must be loose enough to prevent the work from puckering.

Planning, Blocking and Finishing the Garment: The same method and care must be taken in planning and completing a crocheted garment as was explained for the knit garment (page 208).

Designing a Crocheted Doily: Crochet patterns are usually designed on paper that has been ruled with lines marking the height and width of the stitches to be used. Therefore, the size of these stitches must be known first. Before commencing to design, experiment with various threads and hooks, making a 3 inch block of solid work to arrive at the best texture of work for the purpose in hand. From the chosen specimen, measure the height of 1 stitch and the distance from the center of 1 stitch to the center of the next. This will give the stitch gauge of the planned article. Take a piece of paper, rule horizontal lines the height of a row apart and vertical lines across the paper the width of the stitches apart. Graph paper can be bought ready-ruled, but the measurements of the ruling are not always suitable for crochet designs. As crochet designs are seldom very large, the extra time taken in preparing the paper oneself is well worthwhile and the exact size of the finished work gauged fairly accurately. The designs are made by filling in with soft pencil those sections that will be solidly worked; single stitches and lengths of chains are indicated by a single line, and lacets or V-shaped strands by 2 curving diagonal lines. To find out the number of foundation chains to make, count the number of stitches that would be required to make the first row of pattern solidly and add three chains to turn. Or, make a long chain, crochet across the foundation chain for desired width or length and cut off excess. Simple symbols are used to indicate the kind of stitch to employ when copying a design from a chart. Blocks of solid work are shown as solid blocks on the drawing and spaces are left as blanks on the paper. The shapes made by the stitches can be taken as the form of the symbol; e.g.: picots may be shown as small circles and loops of chains as semi-circles; and drawn as near to their relative size as possible. Sometimes the shape of the stitches will suggest the symbols, as the scallop symbol describing a loop and corded edge. In designing doilies, one may combine the chart with the written explanation (G 33 and G 34).

G33

Design your own

Solid Square: Ch (G 2) 9, dc (G 5a and b) in first st, (ch 5, dc in same st) twice, ch 5, sl st (G 11) in next 3rd st of first ch-9. Work round and round. Round 2: (Ch 1, 7 dc in 3d st of next ch-5 loop, ch 1, sc (G 3a and b) in next dc) 4 times. Round 3: Ch 5, 4 tc in same st with last sc, (ch 5, sc in 4th dc of next shell, ch 5, 5 tc in sc between shells) repeat around. Join final ch-5 with a sl st in 1st ch-5. Round 4: Sl st in next 2 tc, * ch 7, (2 tc, 3 double tc and 2 tc) in first loop of sc between shells, ch 7, sc in 3d tc of next shell. Repeat from * 3 times. Round 5: Ch 3, * 5 dc in next space, ch 6, sl st in last dc for a picot, 2 dc in same space, dc in both loops of next 3 sts, (1 dc, a ch-6 picot (G 12), 3 dc, a ch-9 picot, 3 dc and a ch-6 picot) all in one loop of next (corner) st, dc in both loops of next 3 sts, (2 dc, a ch-6 picot and 5 dc) all in next space, 1 dc in sc, a ch-6 picot. Repeat from * around. Sl st in first ch-3, a ch-6 picot and fasten off.

Make and join squares by the corner picots and the 5 picots on each side. To join corner picots, in place of a ch-9 corner picot, make a ch-4, sl st in first loop of center st of a ch-9 corner picot on another square, ch 4, sl st back in last dc to complete picot. Join the corners of the next 2 adjoining squares to this same single corner st on corner picot of first square, and make all corner joinings of other squares in same way. To join side picot, instead of a ch-6 picot, ch 3, sl st in corresponding picot on side of another square, ch 3, sl st back in last dc to complete picot (G 34).

Lacy Square: Ch (G 2) 36, making 19th st very slightly longer so that it can be easily seen, tc in this long st, (ch 7, tc in next 6th st) twice, ch 5, tc in next 6th (end) st. Row 2: Ch 15, then turn, sk last 2 tc, sc (G 3a and b) in 4th st of next ch-7 loop, ch 7, sc in 4th st of next 7-ch loop, ch 9, tc in 6th st of end ch. Row 3: Ch 15, turn, dc (G 5a and b) in 6th st of ch-9 loop, (dc, ch 7, dc) in 4th st of next ch-7 loop, dc in 4th st of next loop, ch 9, tc in next 6th st of same loop. Row 4: Ch 11, turn, tc in 6th st of ch-9 loop, (ch 5, tc in 4th st of next loop) twice, ch 5, tc in next 6th st. Row 5: Ch 5, dc through center of bar of last tc, * ch 2, dc in next row, (ch 2, dc in center of next space, ch 2, dc in next row) twice, (ch 2, dc in

next 3d st) twice to corner, ch 5, dc in same corner st, (ch 2, dc in next
3d st) 8 times, * ch 5, dc in same corner st, ch 2, dc in center of next tc.
Repeat from * to *. Ch 5, sl st in 3d st of first ch-5. Row 6: Ch 1, turn,
* 3 sc in corner space, ch 9, sl st in last sc for a picot, 2 sc in same corner
space, sc in next dc, ch 6, sl st in last sc for a picot, ** (2 sc in next sp, 1 sc
in dc) twice, a ch-6 picot (G 12). Repeat from ** 3 times. Repeat from *
around. Sl st (G 11) in first ch-1, a ch-6 picot and fasten off (G 34).

Round Motif: Wind thread 12 times around handles of 4 crochet
hooks held together, slip off and cover ring with 24 sc (G 3a and b),
sl st in first sc. Row 2: Ch (G 2) 1, * sc in next 2 sc, (ch 6, sc in 5th ch st
from hook for a picot) 4 times, ch 14, remove hook, insert it back in 2d
ch st after last picot, catch 1 picot and pull through, ch 1, 1 sc, 1 hdc
(G 4) and 2 dc (G 5a and b) in ring, * ch 3, sl st in last dc for a picot,

** (3 dc in ring, ch 5, sl st in last dc for a picot) 3 times, 5 dc, 1 hdc and 1 sc in balance of ring, sl st (G 11) at base of ring, (ch 5, sc in 5th ch st from hook for a picot, sc between next 2 picots) 3 times, ch 5, picot (G 12), sc between next picot and center ring. Repeat from * to *. Ch 1, sl st back in 5th st up side of last petal, ch 1, sl st back in last dc. Repeat from ** around center ring (12 petals). Fasten off. Tack first and last petals together (G 34 and 1).

To fasten a round motif in a large opening: Attach thread to joining of squares at center of 1 side of opening, * (ch 6, sc in 5th ch st from hook for a picot) 3 times, ch 2, sl st in center picot of 1 petal on round motif, (ch 6, picot) 3 times, ch 2, sc back in next 3d (center) picot on next solid square, (ch 6, picot) 3 times, ch 2, 1 double treble in corner of large opening, (ch 6, picot) twice, ch 2, sl st in next petal on round motif, (ch 6, picot) twice, ch 2, sl st back in double treble, (ch 6, picot) 3 times, ch 2, sc in next 3d (center) picot on next solid square, (ch 6, picot) 3 times, ch 2, sl st in next petal on round motif, (ch 6, picot) 3 times, ch 2, sc back in joining of solid squares (center of side of opening). Repeat from * 3 times. Fasten off. Repeat in each large opening.

Stretch and pin crochet right-side-down in true shape on a large padded board or table, stretching until design is opened out. Steam and press dry through a damp cloth.

CHAPTER 8

HAIRPIN LACE, NETTING AND NET EMBROIDERY

HAIRPIN LACE, NETTING AND NET EMBROIDERY

>>>> THE ancient arts of netting, net-embroidery and hairpin lace lend themselves to many adaptations. The ornate insertion (H 3) made on a self-made hairpin with heavy yarn is attractive as a strip for an afghan when it is combined with broad strips in simple afghan stitch (G 22). This same idea can be used, replacing the hairpin lace insertion with a strip formed of 2 or 3 rows of netting (H 4) or with net embroidery on a machine-made net (H 15 and 17).

Netting is so ancient a handicraft that one cannot say authoritatively when it was first practiced. In Persia, Italy and France where the finest silk and linen netting was embroidered with gold and silver or embroidered to resemble cutwork and filet crochet, the netting needle was made of steel with pincer-like ends and the gauge rounded and of uniform thickness throughout its length. The size of the needle and gauge depends upon the size of the loop desired and the fineness of the thread. The stitches always take the same form, either round or oblong. Today the netting needle and gauge used for fine work are approximately 7 inches in length and 1 inch in width. For coarse work a large needle and gauge are used. Both can be cut or whittled from any thin, hard wood, or from tongue depressors.

Authorities differ greatly on the actual method of netting. Experienced fishermen never use a gauge; they pull the cord taut by hand; turn their work at the end of a row and continue to work right-handed, while others work entirely with the left hand. To many, especially beginners, it is easier to use a gauge to make the meshes uniform; to pull the cord taut with the netting needle and to anchor the beginning corners of the net and never turn it. The completed net, however, will be satisfactory whichever method is used, provided the knots forming each mesh do not slip.

Instructions for Net Hammock (**Color Plate H,** *see pg 274*).

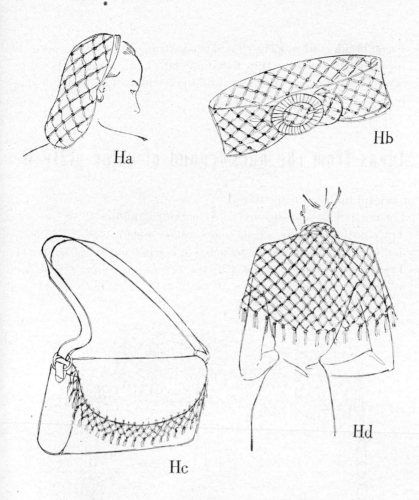

Ha

Hb

Hc

Hd

Design your own from color plate H

With a bit of ingenuity, you can design from a net hammock.
1. Scale the mesh of net to size (H 4a to k) and make snood (Ha), belt (Hb), and shawl (Hd).
2. Scale mesh to size (H 4a to k) and combine with leather or fabric for sport bag (Hc and Color Plate L).
3. Using heavy cord or fine thread, make net (H 4) and fringes (Chapter 14) for canopy bed (He) or tablecloth, as for hammock (pg 274).

4. Using braid, cord, wool or thread, make fringe (H 4 and Chapter 14) for chair (Hf), pillow (Hg), footstool (Hh) and draperies (Hi).
5. Scale mesh of net to size (H 4) and make child's toy, beach or shopping bag (Hj).

Ideas from the background of color plate H

For helpful hints, turn the pages.
1. For box pillow, and slip cover instructions (Chapter 13).
2. Trace outline of horse's head and rooster; scale to size (Chapter 10) and use for child's hooked, crocheted or needlepoint rug (Chapter 11).
3. Trace and scale to size (pg 339) the greens, entire or in part, in a modern arrangement for rugs (Chapter 11), place mats (G 34) and chair seat-covers (Chapter 13).

He

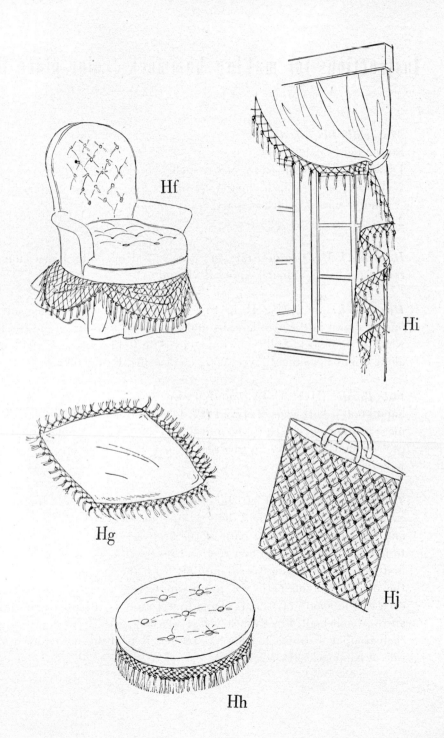

Hf

Hi

Hg

Hj

Hh

Instructions for making hammock (color plate H)

Materials Required:
Strong lightweight cord
1 Gauge 1¾ inches for a mesh 1¾ inches square.
2 chestnut bars ¾ inch square, 39 inches long with 25 ¼ inch holes
counter-sunk 1¼ inches apart.
2 metal rings

Hammock Measurements: 46" wide x 72" long. Note: Join each new reel of cord with a double knot (E 7b and c).

Hammock: Following H 4a to f, use 2 strands of cord instead of one as shown in the photographs and chain 100, forming 50 meshes for width of hammock. Still following steps H 4g to k, work back and forth along original chain until piece is 72 inches long. Fasten off.

Side Border (Hk): Cut a strand of cord 28 inches long. Make an over-hand knot at both ends of strand. Fold strand in half and join to border mesh as shown in sketch N 16a and b. Join 11 of these double-strands to each mesh of side edge. Tie one reel of cord at each end of side edge for weaving.

To weave: Take reel at left end of side edge and weave over and under each strand (N 4b) to right side. Drop this reel. Pick up second reel and following the weaving path of the first reel, weave over and under to left side. Now pick up first reel and reverse the weaving-path of the first row. Repeat this last weaving-path with the second reel. Alternate the double weaving-paths for approximately 5 inches. Trim reels at each end to length of strands. Take first 4 strands of border and make an overhand knot directly below last weaving path. Continue to knot each group of 4 strands to complete border. Repeat this border for other side of hammock (Hk).

Clews (Hl): Cut 25 strands, each 2½ yards in length. Fold each strand in half and join to metal ring as shown in sketch N 16a and b. Anchor metal ring to stationary post. In same manner as for border, weave first double strand on right to left side, draw through first hole at left end of wooden bar and knot temporarily. Weave first double strand on left to right side; draw through first hole at right end of wooden bar and knot temporarily. Continue in this manner, eliminating a double strand at each end until each double strand has been drawn through a hole in the wooden bar. Repeat this procedure for second bar. Beginning at the left end of the first bar, draw first double strand through first 2 meshes at one end of the hammock. Re-thread double strand through first hole and overhand knot to itself, allowing 6 inches for fringe. Repeat for each hole of first bar. Repeat this procedure to attach bar at opposite end of hammock.

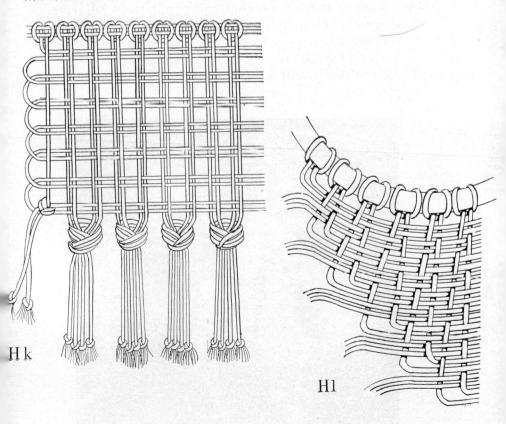

H k

H l

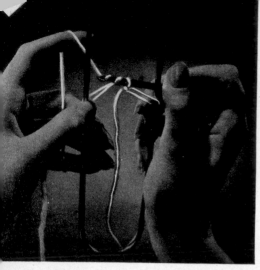

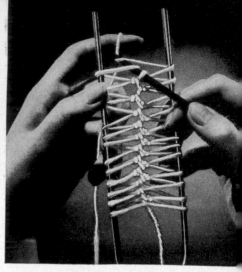

Hla

Hlb

Hairpin Lace or Hairpin Crochet: Originally made with very fine thread and an ordinary straight hairpin. A hairpin fork or staple can easily be made by bending a piece of wire any desired width; the manufactured forks of today are usually 1½, 2 and 3 inches in width. The work itself is done with a crochet hook. In the following photographs, heavy

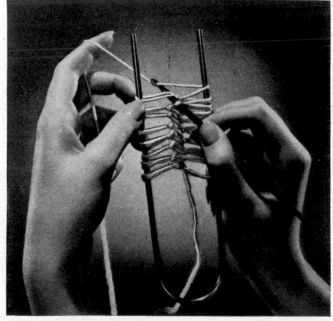

Hlc

yarn was used to show more clearly the formation of the stitch. These same edges can be used with fine thread for lace-edgings and insertions.

To Make Lace Strips: With crochet hook, make a very loose chain (G 2); drop off hook. Holding hairpin fork with point upward, insert prongs of fork upward into loop. Draw loop until knot is in center between prongs. With thread and fork in left hand and with crochet hook in right hand, draw a loop through knot and a second loop around original loop over prongs—2 loops on crochet hook—yarn over crochet hook (H 1a) and complete single crochet stitch (G 3a and b). * With yarn in front, turn hairpin fork counter clockwise or from left to right, thus making a loop over right prong. Hook is always held in position shown. Insert crochet hook up through front strand of large loop on left prong, draw loop through (H 1b) and complete single crochet. Repeat from * until fork is full. Remove all loops from fork. Re-insert prongs of fork into last 4 or 5 loops and continue until desired length. To fasten off pull strands through last loop. Variations of this stitch can be made by picking up both strands of large loop on left prong (H 1c); and by working a single crochet first through loop on left prong and also through loop on right prong. Lace thus formed is then ready to be used as insertion or as edging and must be finished with an edge in crochet.

Simple Insertion: Merely join each loop with a slip stitch (G 11) or a single crochet stitch (H 2, G 3). For an ornate insertion, join 3 loops with a slip stitch (G 11) and work 1 slip stitch between each cluster (H 3).

277

H2

H3

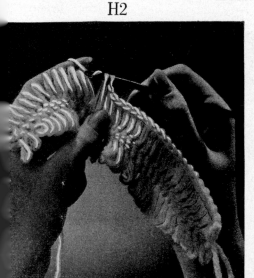

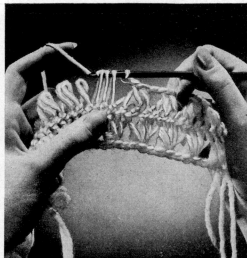

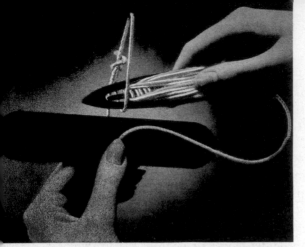

H4a

Netting

Common terms used in netting instructions:

1. Clove Hitch: To knot as shown in H 4g, h and H 11.
2. Reeve: To pass the end of a rope through an eye or an opening.
3. Seize: To bind one rope to another, a rope to a spar, etc. as shown in H 10c.
4. Small Stuff: Any small cord or line.

Netting: Begin on a foundation loop of heavy thread or twine from 4 to 8 inches in length. This foundation or anchor loop is made by doubling a length of thread and knotting the ends. This loop is then anchored around nearest stationary object and must reach to person's work. As work increases, the length of the loop is shortened. 1. Fasten twine to spine and wind over spine, alternating from front to back.

278

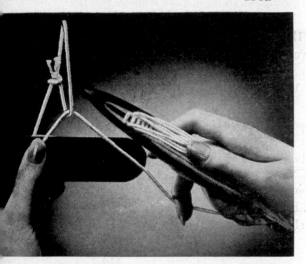

H4b

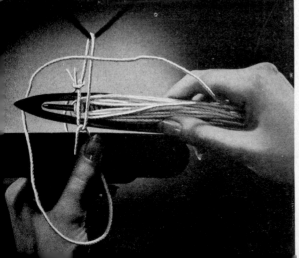

H4c

Turn the needle over and repeat. Continue until the needle has been filled leaving ¼ inch at tip of spine free. From the loose end of the twine on the needle, make a loop twice as wide as the gauge. Tie this loop around anchor loop. Place the knot of loop in the middle of the left side and hold gauge in left hand (H 4a). The gauge is used to measure the space of the mesh. Holding needle in right hand, pass through loop from right to left (H 4a). 2. Holding the twine firmly with thumb, to the bottom of gauge at first loop, loop twine down and around to the right (H 4b). 3. Pass needle under first two strands and over third and fourth strands (H 4c). H 4d shows the knot before being pulled hard and tight as in H 4e. 4. Do not remove the thumb from below knot until the knot has been made tight by pulling toward right (H 4e).

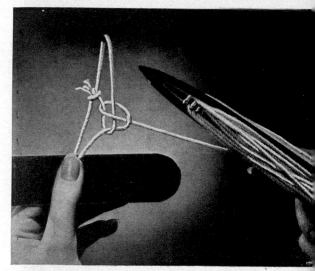

H4d

H4e

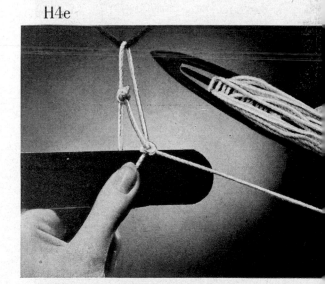

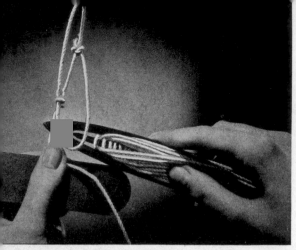

H4f

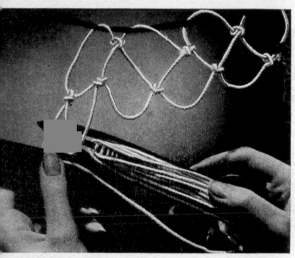

H4g

5. Remove the gauge and place the new knot on the left (H 4f). Finish knot as in H 4a, b, c, d and e. Repeat until the desired number of meshes have been made. The first row in netting looks like a string of knotted loops. The number of meshes to be set up depends on the size of the net desired. Always be sure that all the loops are the same size, thus forming an even line. 6. Before beginning the second row, thread a heavy cord through the first row of meshes (H 4g). This is now the new anchor loop and should also be shortened as work increases. Cut first anchor loop and tie to help in locating starting mesh with this cord (see dark loop to right in H 4g). 7. Now work across or horizontally instead of down (H 4h). Start a knot at the first mesh to the left (H 4g). 8. Finish the knot as in H 4a, b, c, d

280

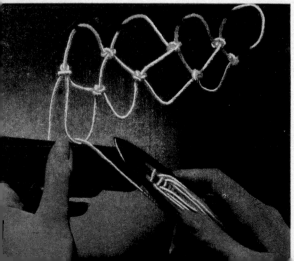

H4h

and e. Continue working across to right (H 4h) until row is completed. 9. When you have completed the row of meshes, change the needle to the left hand and the gauge to the right hand (H 4i). Working this row from right to left, start a new knot at the mesh indicated by the needle (H 4i). 10. Hold the twine firmly with the thumb at the bottom of the loop (H 4j) and reverse the steps shown in (H 4c). 11. Complete the knot by pulling the twine tightly down toward the left (H 4k). Continue working to the left until row is completed. Repeat alternate right and left rows until desired length of netting is completed. If preferred, omit steps H 4i, j and k and work always from left to right.

To Reduce a Mesh at the End of a Row: Do not net last mesh.

281

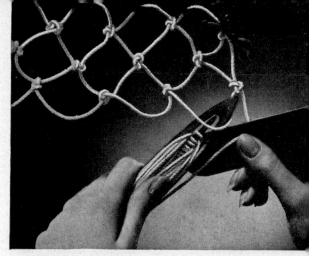

H4i

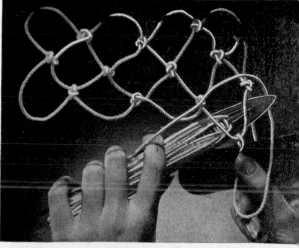

H4j

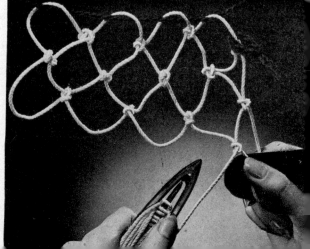

H4k

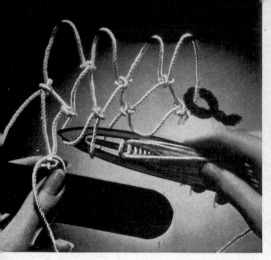
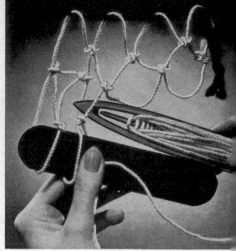

H5   H6

To Reduce a Mesh in the Middle of a Row: Net two meshes at a
time by sliding needle through two loops instead of one and complete
knot (H 5).

To Increase a Mesh: Make two knots in the same loop (H 6).

To Make a Square of Netting With Closed Loops or An Even Edge:
Begin with 2 or 3 knots and increase by making 2 knots in the last loop in
each of the following rows. This increases one mesh on every row. Continue in this manner until piece measures one mesh more than desired.
Work 1 row with this extra loop; then reduce 1 mesh by knotting two
loops together at the end of each row until two loops remain. Knot last
2 loops together.

*To Make a Square of Netting With Open Loops or An Uneven
Edge:* Begin the square in the middle. Chain the desired number of
meshes; then reduce one mesh in each row by merely skipping the last
mesh. Continue in this manner until two loops remain. Knot last 2 loops
together. To complete square, fasten thread at the beginning and work in
same manner as for first row.

Materials Required For Fish Landing Net (H 7): Strong, lightweight cord, 1 gauge ¾ inch wide or tongue depressor.

282

Directions: Chain 80 meshes (H 4a to f). When a chain is spread out there will be two rows, each row ½ the number of meshes chained. Set up 40 meshes on contrasting string and fasten to anchor. Net mesh to desired depth usually 24 meshes deep. Taper off bottom by reducing number of meshes.

To reduce: Net two meshes at a time by sliding needle through two loops instead of one and finish knot (H 5) in the following order:
1. Reduce one in first row (near the middle).
2. Take off every third mesh in second row.
3. Take off every second mesh in succeeding rows.

Tie last few meshes together with cord. If a more pointed net is desired (such as a *butterfly net*), take off fewer meshes in a row. This will taper off the net more gradually to form a point.

To Join Sides With Knotting:
1. Lay outer edges of mesh parallel.
2. Place middle of cord for knotting at top of net with equal length sidecords hanging free.
3. Knot each side cord to adjoining mesh of net.
4. Knot cords together.
5. Continue steps 3 and 4, trying to keep knotting meshes same size as netting meshes to bottom of net.

Finally, clove hitch (H 11) to frame.

Note: If a hoop is used for frame, meshes can be worked directly on the hoop as follows:
1. Set up desired number of loops on hoop with evenly spaced clove hitches (H 11).
2. Net from loops as above.

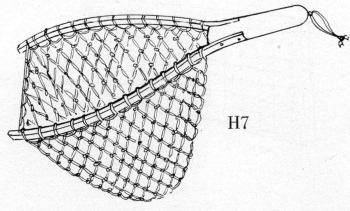

H7

Materials Required For Lawn Tennis Net (H 8): Strong, light-weight cord, 1 gauge 1¾'' wide for mesh 1¾'' square.

Net Measurements: The tennis net is made with square meshes. 36 ft. wide x 3 ft. high, Single Court; Double 40 ft. wide x 3 ft. high.

A. To Net Square Mesh: Start with loop tied to a stationary anchor. Row 1: Net 2 meshes in loop. Row 2: Net 1 mesh in first loop of Row 1. Net 2 meshes in second loop. Continue to net 1 mesh in each loop until end of row, then net 2 meshes in last loop (H 9a). Continue in this manner (H 9b) until there are 3 feet of meshes in the row. (This represents the height of the completed net.)

B. To Square Up Lower Corner and to Begin to Add Necessary Width to Net: 1. At end of next row, slide netting needle through 2 last meshes and make 1 knot (decrease, H 5). 2. At end of following row, net 2 meshes in last loop (increase, H 6). Repeat steps 1 and 2 until there are 36 feet of meshes in row, or more if longer net is desired. Continue to slide needle through last 2 meshes and make 1 knot (H 5) at end of every row until 2 meshes remain. Tie last 2 meshes with cord.
C. Sew piece of canvas or duck folded two or three times, to make a 5 inch wide binding, along top of net. Reeve heavy rope or small galvanized wire-cable through binding. Make eyelets at ends of binding for cords to hold binding taut. Punch hole at end of binding. Sew around hole a few times to strengthen. Sew above strengthening and through eyelet (H 10a and b). Seize heavy rope (H 10c) to bottom of net with clove hitches (H 11). For additional strength the net may be taped on the sides and along the bottom. The top of the net should be 3 feet 6 inches from ground at posts.

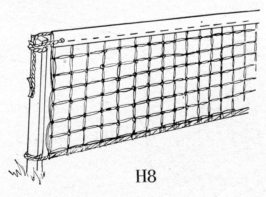

H8

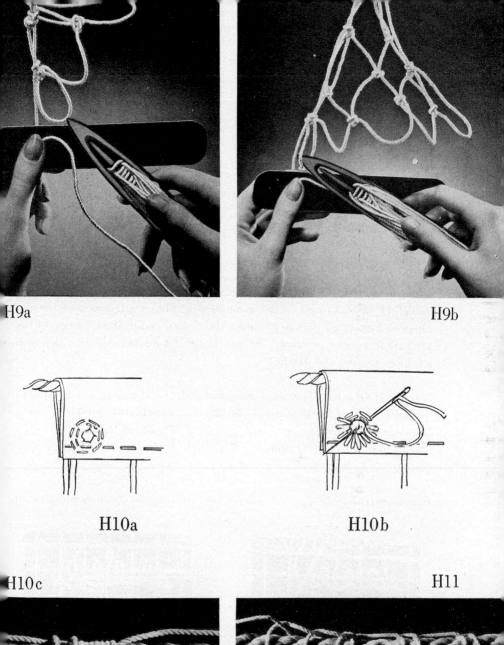

H9a   H9b

H10a   H10b

H10c   H11

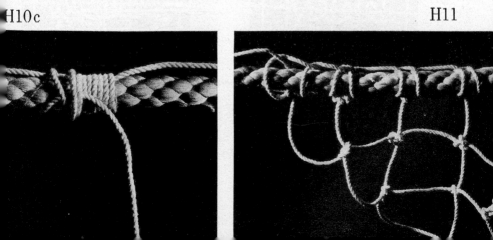

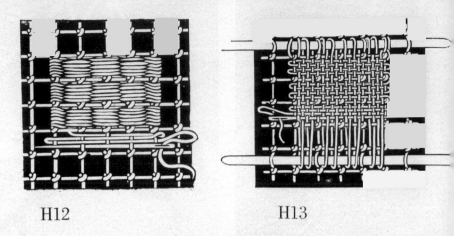

H12   H13

Net Embroidery: Merely the weaving of motifs and borders on hand-made (H 4a to k) and machine-made net. The construction of the net plays an important part in planning the design and in the selection of the kind of thread to be used. The net is the foundation upon which you works in a variety of stitches.

Darning Stitch: The most popular and the simplest stitch. Weave thread back and forth over net (H 12). The number of times one works back and forth in a given square or group of squares depends upon the thread used for darning and the effect desired. Even narrow lightweight ribbon has been used effectively for infant's wear and home furnishings.

Linen Stitch: In the old embroideries the linen stitch is most often

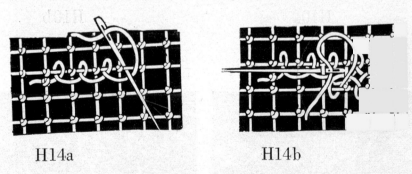

H14a   H14b

used. The thread is woven usually twice, over and under the threads of the net as required by the design. The design thus formed is then completed by weaving over and under the threads of the net and the threads just laid, as in the darning stitch (H 12). If a woven square of several meshes is to be covered by the linen stitch, it is advisable for the first darning to place a coarse knitting needle or mesh stick over the first and last row (H 13). This keeps all threads the same length and prevents the first row from becoming shorter when the second darning is worked.

Simple or Straight Loop Stitch: Basically a blanket-stitch in which the needle passes downward under the bar and in front of the thread (H 14a). The length of the loop must be at least half the height of the bars of the net. On the return row, make a stitch over the vertical bar of the net, then over the loop and under the bar which is under the loop (H 14b).

To Copy or Trace a Design: Sketch or trace the design or motif on transparent paper, preferably tracing paper; baste paper to hand-made or machine-made net and with a fine blunt-end needle, follow the outline of the design with a small running stitch, taking each stitch in and out of the mesh in a darning movement. Keep the outline stitches as continuous and unbroken as possible and never use a knot. Keep the thread pulled

H15

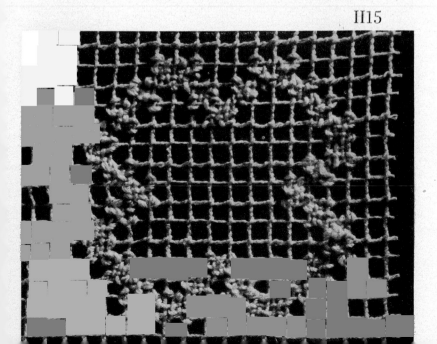

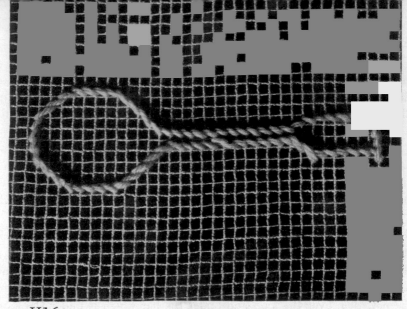

H16

just tight enough to form a clear and definite outline, without puckering. Finally, cut away tracing paper. Any and all of the stitches described above as the darning stitch (H 15), as well as applications of the embroidery stitches, described in Chapters 3 and 4, especially the stem (H 16), the feather (H 17), herringbone, cross, lazy-daisy and chevron stitches are worked over the net as the design indicates or as the individual desires.

H17

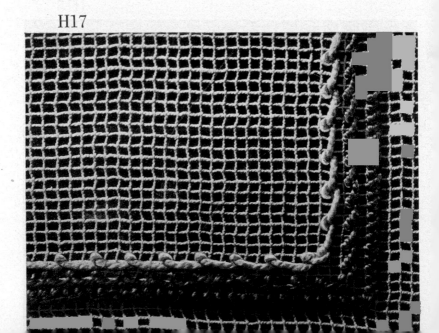

CHAPTER 9

TATTING

TATTING

➤➤➤ TATTING is a series of knots and loops which are drawn up in circles or semi-circles. The tatting shuttle is composed of two blad shaped like an ellipse, pointed at the ends and joined together by a b in the middle. For fine work the tatting shuttle should measure 2½ to inches in length, and ¾ to 1 inch in width. For coarse work, a longer a broader shuttle is used. The two ends of the blades should be sufficient close together to prevent the thread from escaping too freely; this especially important when working with two shuttles, or a ball and shu tle. Some shuttles are made with a hook at one end to pull the thre through picots in joining. However, for a beginner the one without a ho is easier to manage as the hook impedes one's progress and is in the w at times. It is just as easy to use a crochet hook or pin to pull the thre through in joining. When learning to tat, it is advisable to use a thre that is coarse enough to see all the stitches. All qualities and types thread can be used but it must be a sufficiently twisted one.

Jiffy tatting is the newest angle of this old art. It is to tatters, wh jiffy knitting is to knitters. In jiffy tatting, one strays from the famil and dares to tat with lightweight cord, fine wire and an oversized shutt Simple picot rings are made singly in the same manner as a crochet or knit motif for a bedspread, then joined to form whatever is desir

In blocking tatted pieces that require stiffening as place mats, bri headpiece, etc. use starch or gum arabic. To enhance its beauty, alwa remold the original contour of the motif exaggerating the roundness all rings and picots.

Instructions for Tatted Place Mat (Color Plate I see pg 295).

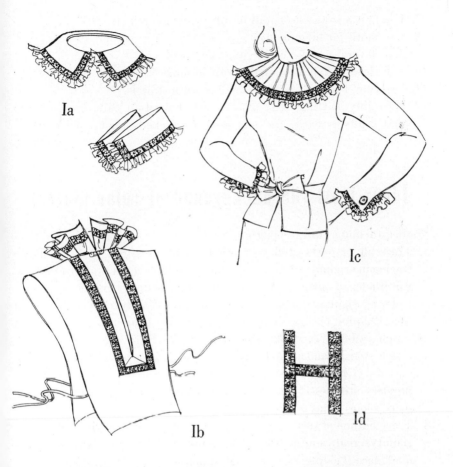

Ia

Ic

Ib

Id

Design your own from color plate I

With a bit of ingenuity, you can design from a tatted place mat.

1. Use motif (Ik) for collar and cuff set (Ia) and dickey (Ib).
2. Use Rows 1 to 6 as an insertion in a blouse (Ic).
3. Use small center motif for initials (Id) and complete names.
4. Use first 4 rows for bridal headpiece (Ie).
5. Use motif for napkins and place mats (If).
6. Use motif for babies' and children's dresses (Ig), and bonnet (Ij).

7. Use first 3 rows as a small motif for handkerchiefs (Ih).
8. Use motif for lingerie (Ii).
9. Join several motifs for evening-skirt peplum.
10. Use Rows 1 to 3 as a small motif in lingerie.
11. Use Row 1 and Rows 2 as small motif in towels.
12. New Jiffy Tatting—Use heavy cord or wool and a large shuttle to make jiffy squares for shopping bags, bedspreads, place mats.

Ideas from the background of color plate I

For helpful hints, turn the pages.
1. Trace all or parts of flower arrangement in center of table; baste tracing in original size on blouse, handkerchiefs, lingerie, baby clothes. Embroider in outline, satin or encroaching stitch (Chapter 3).
2. Enlarge original tracing, entire or in part (Chapter 10) and design a rug (Chapter 11), needlepoint (Chapter 10) chair-top or pictures in simple embroidery (Color Plate C).
3. Cut a stencil, and paint tulips and leaves in a variety of colors on material (Chapter 14, textile painting). If desired, decorate with embroidery stitches (Chapter 3), beads and sequins (Chapter 14) for scarf, blouse, and handbag.
4. Trace outline of tatted place mat and leaf-plate; and with a bit of ingenuity, create another place mat of material combined with machine-made lace (Chapter 1); with net appliqué (Chapter 5).

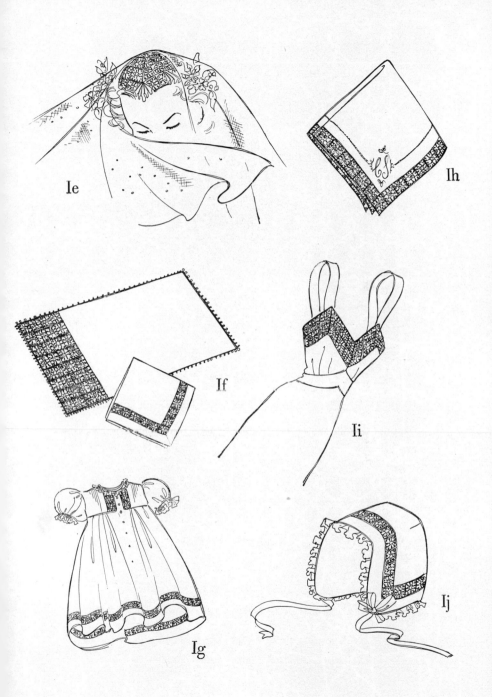

Ie

Ih

If

Ii

Ig

Ij

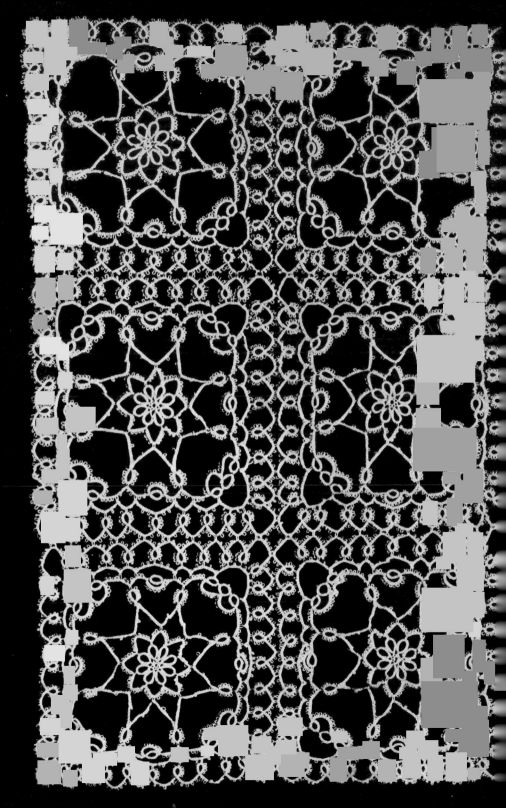

nstructions for tatted place mat (color plate I)

Materials Required:
ball of Six Cord Mercerized Crochet, Size 30.

Center . . . R (I 2) of 1 ds (I 1a to f), 7 sm p's (I 3) sep by 1 ds, 1 ds, cl.
'ie threads in square knot just far enough from r to form 8th p. *Round 1:*
ℓ of 5 ds, sm p, 9 ds, p, 9 ds, sm p, 5 ds, cl. Fasten to same sm p from
/hich r was started. * Carry thread to next sm p on center and fasten.
ℓ of 5 ds, join to sm p of preceding r, 9 ds, p, 9 ds, sm p, 5 ds, cl and
ısten to same sm p on center. Repeat from * 6 more times, joining
ʌe 8th r by the last sm p to the first sm p of the first r. Tie and cut.
Round 2: Fasten ball and shuttle threads to p of first r of preceding
ʌd. * Ch of 2 ds, 9 p's sep by 2 ds, 2 ds. Fasten to p of next r. Repeat
·om * around, fastening 8th ch to p from which first ch started. Tie
ʌd cut. *Round 3:* Tie ball and shuttle threads together. R of 2 ds,
1 p's sep by 2 ds, 2 ds, cl—a p ring made. Rw, make a ch of 3 ds, p,
7 ds, p, 7 ds, join to 5th p of next ch of preceding rnd, (7 ds, p) twice,
ds. Rw and make another p ring. Rw, ch of 3 ds, join to last p of
·eccding ch and repeat from * around, joining last p of last ch to
·rst p of first ch and fastening last ch at base of first r. *Round 4:* Tie
 all and shuttle threads together. R of 7 ds, sm p, 7 ds, p, 7 ds, sm p,
ds, cl. Rw, ch of 2 ds, 9 p's sep by 2 ds, 2 ds. * Rw, sm r of 10 ds, join
ɔ second sm p of preceding r, 5 ds, sm p, 5 ds, cl. Rw, ch of 2 ds, 7 p's
·ep by 2 ds, 2 ds, fasten to 6th p on next r on preceding rnd. Ch of 2 ds,
p's sep by 2 ds, 2 ds. R of 10 ds, sm p, 10 ds, cl. Rw, ch of 2 ds, 8 p's
·ep by 2 ds, 2 ds, fasten to sm p of preceding r. Rw, ch of 2 ds, 5 p's sep ·
y 2 ds, 2 ds, fasten to 6th p of next r on preceding rnd. Ch of 2 ds, 7 p's
·ep by 2 ds, 2 ds. Sm r of (5 ds, sm p) twice, 10 ds, cl. Rw, ch of 2 ds, 9

p's sep by 2 ds, 2 ds. Rw, r of 7 ds, join to second sm p on preceding r, 7 ds, p, 7 ds, sm p, 7 ds, cl. Rw, ch of 2 ds, join to last p on preceding ch, 2 ds, 8 p's sep by 2 ds, 2 ds. Repeat from * around, joining the second sm p of the last r to the first sm p of the first r, also joining the last p of the last ch to the first p of the first ch and fasten the last ch at base of first r. Tie and cut. *Round 5:* Fasten ball and shuttle threads to first sm p of last r of preceding rnd. Ch of 2 ds, sm p, * 4 ds, 9 p's sep by 4 ds, 4 ds, sm p, 2 ds. Fasten to sm p of next sm r on preceding rnd. Ch of 2 ds, join to last sm p of preceding ch, 4 ds, 3 p's sep by 4 ds, 4 ds, sm p, 2 ds. Fasten to 5th p of next ch on preceding rnd. Ch of 2 ds, join to sm p of preceding ch, 4 ds, p, 4 ds, sm p, 2 ds. Fasten to 3rd p of next ch on preceding rnd. Ch of 2 ds, join to sm p of preceding ch, 4 ds, 5 p's sep by 4 ds, 4 ds, sm p, 2 ds. Fasten to 3rd p of next ch on preceding rnd. Ch of 2 ds, join to sm p of preceding ch, 4 ds, p, 4 ds, sm p, 2 ds. Fasten to 3rd p of next ch on preceding rnd. Ch of 2 ds, join to sm p of preceding ch, 4 ds, 3 p's sep by 4 ds, 4 ds, sm p, 2 ds, fasten to sm p of next sm corner r. Ch of 22 ds, join to sm p of preceding ch and repeat from * around. Joining the last sm p of last ch to the first sm p of the first ch and fasten the last ch to the sm p from which this rnd started. *Round 6:* Tie ball and shuttle threads together. ** r of 2 ds, 4 p's sep by 2 ds, 2 ds, join to second p of corner ch on preceding rnd, 2 ds, 4 p's sep 2 ds, 2 ds, cl. Rw, ch of 3 ds, 5 p's sep by 3 ds, 3 ds. Rw, r of 2 ds, 4 p's sep by 2 ds, 2 ds, join to 4th p of same ch, 2 ds, 4 p's sep by 2 ds, 2 ds, cl. Rw, ch of 3 ds, 11 p's sep by 3 ds, 3 ds. Rw, make another r like those just made and join it to the 6th p of the same ch. Rw, ch of 3 ds, 5 p's sep by 3 ds, 3 ds. Rw, make another r and join it to the 8th p of the same ch. * Rw, ch of 3 ds, 5 p's sep by 3 ds, 3 ds. Rw, make another r and join it to the 8th p of the same next ch on the preceding rnd. Repeat from * 4 more times. Rw, ch of 3 ds, 5 p's sep by 3 ds, 3 ds, and repeat from ** around square, fastening the last ch at the base of the first r. Tie and cut.

Make 6 square motifs. To form mat: At outside corners, join 8th and 9th p's of ch of 11 p's sep by 3 ds (I 1a to f) of preceding motif; continue along sides to join center or 3rd p of ch of 5 p's sep by 3 ds of preceding motif; at center corner, join 3rd and 4th, 8th and 9th p's of ch of 11 p's sep by 3 ds of preceding motif. Repeat. Starch and press. (Ik).

Abbreviations and glossary

As in knitting and crocheting, a knowledge of the abbreviations and terms used in the instructions, is essential.

r....ring (I 2)—When the desired number of stitches is made, draw up the shuttle thread so that the first and last stitches touch, making a circle or ring. When "r" appears at the beginning of directions, always get thread in a position around the fingers of the left hand to start the ring.

lr....large ring

sm r....small ring

d or ds....double stitch—a combination of two half stitches (I 1a to f).

p....picot—a loop between stitches (I 3).

lp....long picot—a long loop between stitches (I 3).

s p or sm p....small picot—a very small loop between stitches.

sep....separated

cl....close (I 2).

rw....reverse work

sp....space

ch....chain—a series of double stitches made with the shuttle on the ball thread (I 5b).

* (asterisk)—Repeat the instructions following the asterisk as many more times as specified in addition to the original.

"Joining to a p"—Counted as the first half of the following "ds" (I 4).

Single Knot or Josephine Knot—A ring made of single stitches or just the first half of a double stitch. The knots are drawn up very closely to form a circle.

Scallops—A series of double stitches drawn into a semi-circle leaving a single thread across the bottom.

Winding the Shuttle—Fasten the thread by a knot to the little bobbin inside the tatting shuttle and wind thread evenly around bobbin. Never allow thread to project beyond the edge.

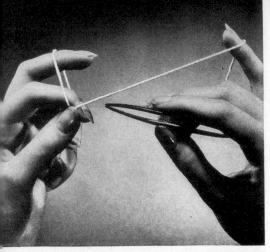

1a

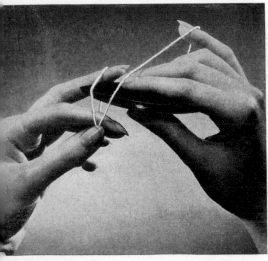

1b

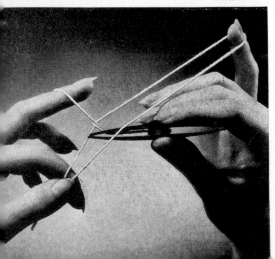

1c

How to Hold Thread:

1. Unwind shuttle leaving an end 14 to 18 inches in length. With left hand, grasp the free end of thread between thumb and forefinger.
2. Spread the middle, ring and little fingers and bring thread around to make a circle, holding it securely between thumb and forefinger.
3. Bend the little finger to catch the thread against the palm and extend the middle finger to catch the loose part of the circle.
4. With right hand, grasp flat sides of shuttle between thumb and forefinger in an horizontal position, having thread come from back of bobbin. Note position of pointed end of shuttle.

Double Stitch—(This is the basic stitch). First half of this stitch is made by:

1. Holding thread and shuttle as described, have the shuttle thread cross fingers on palm side, then across all fingers on outside of hand, extending little finger slightly to support the thread (I 1a)
2. Without turning or releasing the shuttle, slide it first under (I 1b and then over thread held between middle and forefinger o

298

left hand (I 1c).

3. Drop middle finger of left hand.
4. Draw shuttle thread taut, thus forming a loop with thread that is around the left hand (I 1d).
5. Extend dropped finger of left hand, thus sliding the stitch down the taut shuttle thread and making a tight stitch between thumb and forefinger. This completes first half of a double stitch.

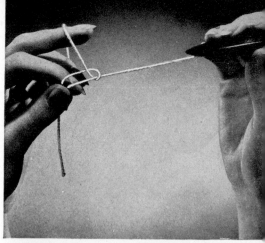

Note: Practice this step until you do it with ease. When you pull the shuttle, the shuttle thread should slide easily through the stitches (I 1d).

In the second half of the double stitch:

1. The shuttle thread may or may not be wound around right hand as for first half of double stitch. Experienced tatters prefer to merely hold the shuttle in an horizontal position.
2. Slide the shuttle first over and then under the thread between middle and forefinger of left hand (I 1e) and complete stitch as for first half of double stitch. This completes one double stitch (ds)(I 1f—slightly exaggerated). Practise until you can make ds with ease, then try making a ring (I 2) and a picot (I 3).

I1d

I1e

I1f

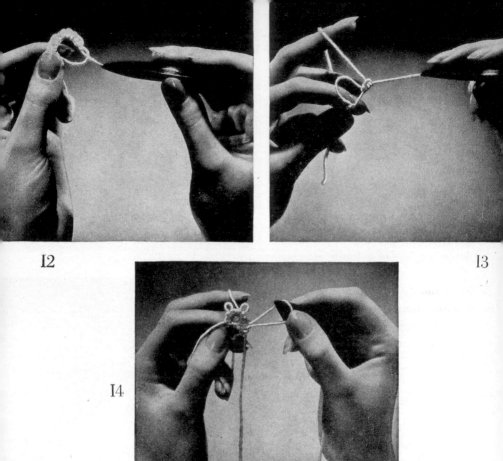

12   13

14

15a   15b

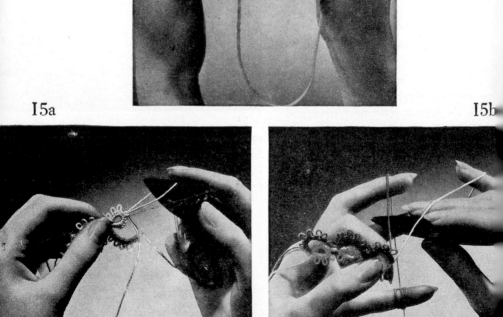

To Make a Ring: Draw the thread on the shuttle or the loop-thread up closely so that the first and last stitches touch (I 2).

To Make a Picot: Make first half of a ds, but as you slide it into position, stop about ¼ inch from preceding ds. Make second half of ds as before, then slide entire ds close to preceding ds. A picot followed by a ds is made (I 3).

Note: A picot refers only to the loop and does not include the ds which fastens the loop.

To Join Rings: Before commencing second ring, be sure to leave a free-strand about ¼ of the circumference of the completed ring; e.g.
   1. Make 3 ds of 2nd r about ¼ of an inch away from first r. A space is made. 2. Insert pointed end of shuttle through last p of first r, catch thread encircling left hand and draw out loop (I 4). 3. Pull shuttle through this loop and draw shuttle thread taut. This joins 2nd r to first r and counts as the first half of next ds. 4. Complete ds and remainder of r as for first r.

Use Two Shuttles or a Ball and Shuttle:
1. When scallops or rings are not to be joined at the base by a thread.
2. When you wish to conceal the passage of the thread to another group of stitches. 3. When two colors are used in making rings (I 5a and b).

   Rings are made only with the shuttle and chains are made with the shuttle on the ball-thread (I 5b). When using two shuttles, or a ball and shuttle, tie thread ends together. The thread with which you are not working is passed over 2nd finger of left hand and wound around little finger (I 5b). This leaves shuttle or ball hanging. Hold shuttle with which you are working in right hand and proceed as if using only one shuttle. 4. When rings and chains appear in the same design, it is necessary to use two working threads (a shuttle thread and a ball thread). To make a chain after a ring, reverse work (rw), so that base of ring is held between thumb, but instead of making a complete circle, have it across back of fingers only, then wind it twice around little finger to control tension. Make stitches close together and drop ball thread. Reverse work and pick up shuttle thread to make another ring (I 5b).

The Edge Shown is Worked as Follows: Tie ball and shuttle threads together. * With light thread, make 2 ds, 4 p's separated by 2 ds, 9 ds, close (I 5a). Rw. With dark thread, work over light thread and make ch of 3 ds, 5 p's separated by 2 ds, 3 ds. Join to fourth p of ring (I 4). Drop dark thread and rw. Repeat from * for desired length.

Materials Required For Edging (I 6):
1 ball Tatting Cotton Size 70.
A rolled edge handkerchief.
Tie ball and shuttle threads together. R (I 2) of 4 ds (I 1a to f), 5 p's (I 3) sep by 3 ds, 4 ds, cl. * Rw, ch of 4 ds, 5 p's sep by 3 ds, 4 ds. Rw, 1r of 4 ds, 6 p's sep by 3 ds, join to second p made on previous r, 4 ds, cl. R of 4 ds, 4 p's sep by 3 ds, join to end p of previous lr, 4 ds, cl. Repeat from * for length desired, ending with lr. Sew edging to handkerchief. Sew end r's together to keep continuity of pattern.

Materials Required For Tatted Appliqué Corner and Edging (I 7):
1 ball each of green and white Tatting Cotton, Size 70.
A rolled edge handkerchief.

Edging . . . Tie ball and shuttle threads together. With green, (r (I 2) of 6 ds (I 1a to f), p (I 3) and 6 ds) 5 times. * Rw, ch of 6 ds, 3 p's sep by 3 ds, 6 ds, p, 6 ds; skip one r of the 5-r group, join to p of next r, 4 ds.

Rw, lr of 3 ds, 5 p's sep by 3 ds, 3 ds, cl. Rw, ch of 4 ds, p and 6 ds, join to p of previous ch, 6 ds, 3 p's sep by 3 ds, 6 ds. Rw, r of 6 ds, p and 6 ds, cl. r of 6 ds, join to free p of previous ch, 6 ds, cl, (r of 6 ds, p and 6 ds, cl) 3 times. Repeat from * for length desired. Tie and cut.

Corner Spray . . . Flower (Make 6) . . . With white make (r of 15 ds, cl.) 4 times. Tie and cut.

Leaf . . . (Make 5) . . . With green make (r (I 2) of 6 ds (I 1a to f), p (I 3) and 6 ds, cl) twice. Tie and cut. Form branches of spray with green and tack in place. Place flowers and leaves in position and sew in place. Sew edging to handkerchief.

Materials Required For Edging (I 8):
1 ball of shaded yellows in Size 70 Tatting Cotton.
A rolled edge handkerchief.
R (I 2) of 4 ds (I 1a to f), 3 p's (I 3) sep by 3 ds, 4 ds, cl. Rw, sp of ⅛″, sm r of 4 ds, p and 4 ds; cl. Rw, sp of ⅛″, r of 4 ds, join to last p of first r, * (3 ds, p) twice; 4 ds, cl. Rw, sp of ⅛″, lr of 4 ds, join to p of sm r, 3 ds, 4 p's sep by 3 ds, 4 ds, cl. Rw, sp of ⅛″, r of 4 ds, join to adjacent p of previous r (3 ds, p) twice, 4 ds, cl. Rw, sp of ⅛″, sm r of 4 ds, join to end p of lr, 4 ds, cl. Rw, sp of ⅛″, r of 4 ds, join to adjacent p of previous r, (3 ds, p) twice; 4 ds, cl. Rw, sp of ⅛″, sm r of 4 ds, p and 4 ds, cl. Rw, sp of ⅛″, r of 4 ds, join to adjacent p of previous r. Repeat from * for length desired. Tie and cut. Sew edging to handkerchief.

I8

19

Materials Required For Round Motif and Edging (I 9):
1 ball of shaded yellows in Size 70 Tatting Cotton.
A rolled edge handkerchief.

Corner Motif . . . *Round 1:* R (I 2) of 1 ds (I 1a to f), 12 p's sep by 1 ds, cl. Tie and cut. *Round 2:* R of 3 ds, p, 2 ds, 7 p's sep by 1 ds, 2 ds, p, 3 ds, cl. Rw, sp of ⅛ inch, sm r of 4 ds, join to first p of first rnd, * 4 ds, cl. Rw, sp of ⅛ inch, r of 3 ds, join to end of p of previous r, 2 ds, 7 p's sep by 1 ds, 2 ds, p, 3 ds, cl. Rw, sp of ⅛ inch, sm r of 4 ds, join to next p of first rnd. Repeat from * around, ending with sp of ⅛ inch, join to base of first r. Tie and cut. *Round 3:* Tie ball and shuttle threads together. * Ch of 4 ds, p and 4 ds, join to center p of the 9-p group on r of previous rnd, 4 ds, p, 4 ds. Rw, lr of 3 ds, p, 2 ds, 7 p's sep by 2 ds, 2 ds, p, 3 ds, cl. Rw. Repeat from * around, ending with lr, join to first ch. Tie and cut. *Round 4:* Tie ball and shuttle threads together. Ch of 3 ds, 12 p's sep by 2 ds, 3 ds. Rw, r of 4 ds, join to end p of lr on previous rnd, * 3 ds, 5 p's sep by 2 ds, 3 ds, join to end p of next lr on previous rnd, 4 ds, cl. Rw, ch of 3 ds, 12 p's sep by 2 ds, 3 ds. Rw, r of 4 ds, join to other end p of same lr as last r was joined. Repeat from * around. Join. Tie and cut.

Edging . . . R of 4 ds, 5 p's sep by 3 ds, 4 ds, cl. * Rw, ch of 11 ds. Rw, r of 4 ds, join to end of p of previous r, 3 ds, 4 p's sep by 3 ds, 4 ds, cl. Repeat from * for length desired. Tie and cut. Sew motif to corner handkerchief, cutting out linen. Sew on edging, having end r's touch corner motif.

Materials Required For Edging (I 10):
1 ball of white mercerized Crochet Cotton, size 30.
1 Shuttle and 1 Ball, Rick-Rack.
R (I 2), 6 d (I 1a to f), join in base between points of rick-rack, 6 d, cl r, turn. * Ch, 3 d, p (I 3), 3 d, join in next point of rick-rack, 3 d, p, 3 d, turn. R, 6 d, join in next base between points of rick-rack, 6 d, cl r, turn, repeat from * for length desired. Work across opposite side in same manner.

Materials Required For Edging (I 11):
1 ball of white mercerized Crochet Cotton, size 30.
1 Shuttle and 1 Ball, Rick-Rack.
Join thread in point of rick-rack, ch, 5 d (I 1a to f), turn. * R (I 2), 1 d, 5 p sep by 1 d, 1 d, cl r, turn. Ch, 5 d, join to next point of rick-rack, 5 d, turn. Repeat from * for desired length. Working across opposite side, join thread in first point of rick-rack, ch, 1 d, p, 5 d, turn. * R, 1 d, 2 p sep by 1 d, 1 d, join to base between points of rick-rack, 1 d, 2 p sep by 1 d, 1 d, cl r, turn. Ch, 5 d, p, 1 d, join to next point of rick-rack, 1 d, p, 5 d, turn. Repeat from * for length desired.

I10

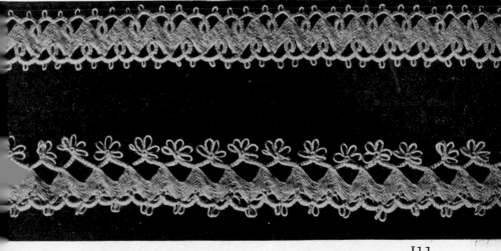

I11

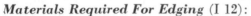

Materials Required For Edging (I 12):

1 ball of white mercerized Crochet Cotton, size 30.

1 Shuttle and 1 Ball, Rick-Rack.

Row 1: R (I 2), 6 d (I 1a to f), p (I 3), 6 d, cl r, turn. Ch, 6 d, join to point of rick-rack, 6 d, turn. R, 6 d, join to p of first r, 6 d, cl r. * R, 6 d, p, 6 d, cl r, turn. Ch, 6 d, join to next point of rick-rack, 6 d, turn. R, 6 d, join to p of last r made, 6 d, cl r. Repeat from * for length desired. Working across opposite side of rick-rack, R, 6 d, join on side of rick-rack near point, 6 d, cl r. R, 6 d, join on opposite side near next point of rick-rack, 6 d, cl r, turn. Ch, 6 d, p, 6 d, turn. Repeat from beginning across row.

Row 2: R, 6 d, join to p of ch of previous row, 6 d, cl r, turn. * Ch, 6 d, p, 6 d, turn. R, 6 d, join to picot of same ch, 6 d, cl r. R, 6 d, join to p of next ch, 6 d, cl r, turn. Repeat from * across row.

Materials Required For Edging (I 13):

1 ball white mercerized Crochet Cotton, size 30.

1 Shuttle and 1 Ball, Rick-Rack.

R (I 2), 2 d (I 1a to f), p (I 3), 3 d, join to point of rick-rack, 3 d, p, 2 d, cl r. * R, 2 d, join to last p of last r made, 3 d, join in base between points of rick-rack, 3 d, p, 2 d, cl r. R, 2 d, join to last p of last r made, 3 d, join to next point of rick-rack, 3 d, p, 2 d, cl r, turn. Ch, 3 d, 5 p sep by 3 d, 3 d, turn. R, 2 d, p, 3 d, join to same point of rick-rack as last r made, 3 d, p, 2 d, cl r. Repeat from * for length desired. Work other side in same manner.

CHAPTER 10

NEEDLEPOINT

NEEDLEPOINT

➤➤➤ NEEDLEPOINT or needlework tapestry is an ancient art, a development in embroidery from the designs of the great tapestries of the past, which were woven on royal looms. Today we include under the name of needlepoint or tapestry, any kind of embroidery that is worked on counted threads and any type of embroidery in which the stitches completely cover the material on which the work is done. Needlework tapestry is worked on either a single or double thread canvas. Both types of canvas are made in fine, medium and coarse sizes. The stitches used in needlepoint are simplicity itself and lend themselves to great variety. The tapestry or worsted needle used for this work is usually long, strong and blunt with an oval eye wide enough to thread easily. The exact size of the needle to be used depends upon the size of the canvas and the thread. Needlepoint canvas is sold with a stamped design, underlaid (tramé) or the design can be worked from a chart. In tramé pieces, a thread is laid between the narrowly-spaced threads of the double thread canvas and the stitches made over the "underlaid" threads (J 6). Needlework tapestries are usually made in petit point or gros point stitches or a combination of both. In pieces combining petit point and gros point stitches, all petit point sections are worked first. Some pieces are made entirely in the cross stitch. The Gobelin stitch in its many variations, though sometimes used for whole pieces, is more often seen only in backgrounds. In all stitches, when beginning work, leave an end at least 1 inch long on wrong side and "catch in" by stitches as you continue. At the end of the thread, run needle through several stitches on wrong side to fasten. The thread or yarn should never be longer than thirty inches or it tends to work thin and tangle. If the yarn "curls" while working, allow the thread and needle to hang a moment to allow the yarn to untwist. This also gives a smoother surface to the finished piece.

Instructions for Needlepoint Hassock (Color Plate J, pg. 311).

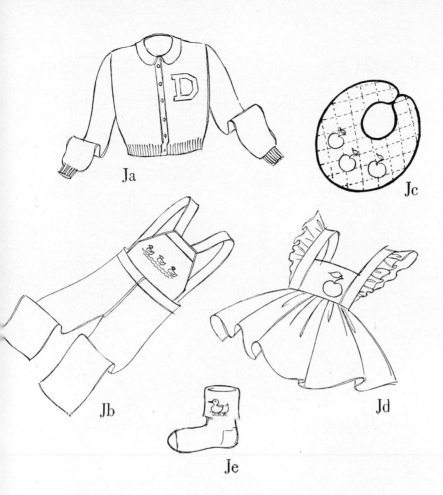

Design your own from color plate J

With a bit of ingenuity, you can design from a needlepoint hassock.

1. Use charts for duplicate stitch (Chapter 6) on child's sweater (Ja), mittens, or anklet cuffs (Je).

2. Trace and enlarge, design (pg 339) for simple embroidery (Chapter 3) or appliqué (Chapter 5) overalls (Jb), baby's bib (Jc) and pinafore (Jd).

3. Work hassock design on petit-point canvas for chair seat (Jf), pincushion (Jg).

4. Use drum design for appliqué (Chap. 5) pillow (Jh–Chapter 14).

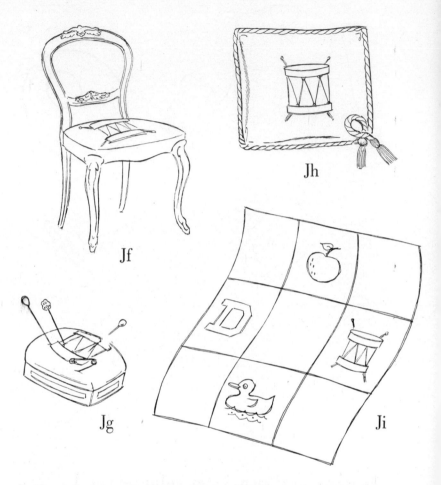

Jh

Jf

Jg

Ji

5. Use 4 designs as is for rug (K 19, Chapter 11).
6. For a series of different size blocks, use canvas of different mesh. For example, if rug canvas of original is 4 stitches to one inch, use canvas with 5 meshes to one inch or 8 meshes to one inch.
7. Trace and enlarge motifs singly or in groups for appliqué drapery set.
8. Use drum design for knitting box or lamp.
9. Combine 4 designs with solid squares in black of needlepoint, felt, or rug patches (Ji and Chapter 11).

Ideas from the background of color plate J

For helpful hints, turn the pages.

1. Trace and enlarge (pg 339) horse's head for furniture and accessories in child's room (see ideas for designs from Color Plate J).
2. Use alphabet letters (Jj) for monograms or names in outline, chain, feather, cross-stitches (Chapter 3) or duplicate stitch (Chapter 6). Or, make simple crochet chain and following outline of letters, overcast to sweaters, blankets, mittens, etc.

Instructions for hassock (color plate J)

Materials Required:
1½ yards 40-inch rug canvas (4 meshes = 1 inch)
Rug yarn—7 oz. each grey, red, yellow, blue and white; 2 oz. black
1 blunt-end tapestry rug needle.

1. Allowing 1 inch for seams, mark off on canvas the number of meshes required for 2 adjacent squares—letter D (Jm) and duck (Jn); etter A (Jj) and apple (Jk).
2. Allowing 1 inch for seams, mark on canvas number of meshels required for top, drum (Jl).
3. Using the half-cross stitch (J 5a and b), work figures and letters of hassock, following charts (Jj, to n—see color key, pg 317).
4. Using the half-cross stitch (J 5a and b), work background of Jn in blue; Jl in yellow; Jk in white and Jj in red.
5. Embroider all accent lines on charts Jl and n in outline stitch (C 4).
6. Block pieces (page 338).
7. Join one side seam, leaving one side seam open.
8. Join top piece to side pieces.
9. Join open side seam to complete block.
10. Use this needlepoint piece as a slipcover for an old hassock or make a hassock to fit the finished needlepoint piece.

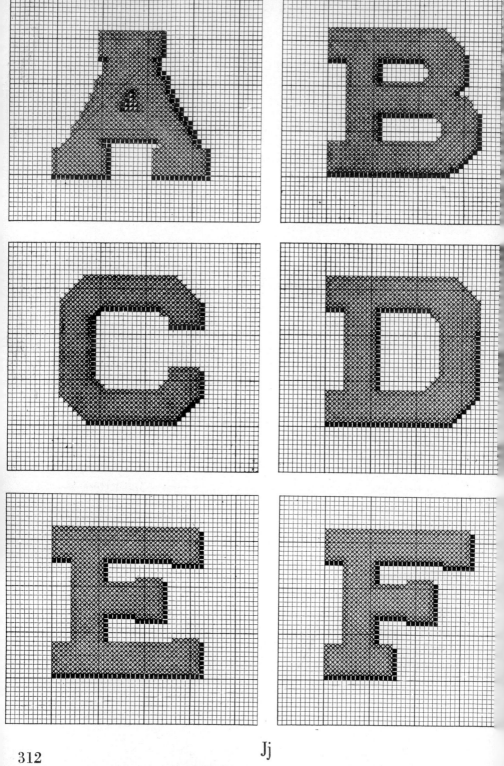

Jj

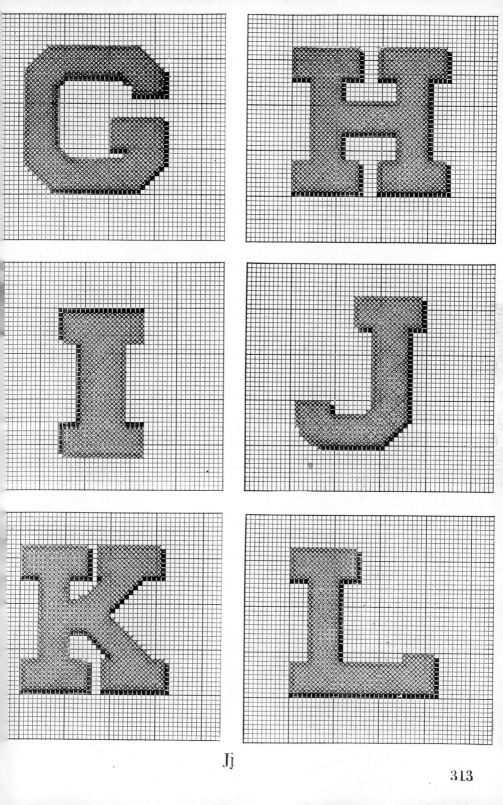

Jj

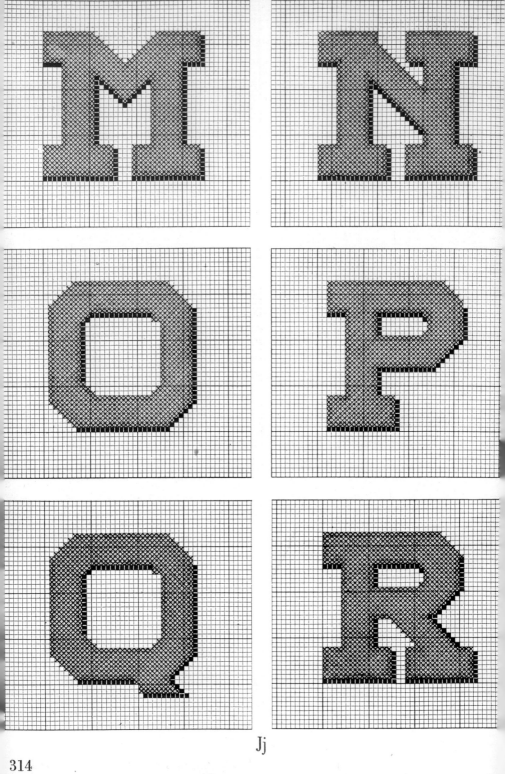

Jj

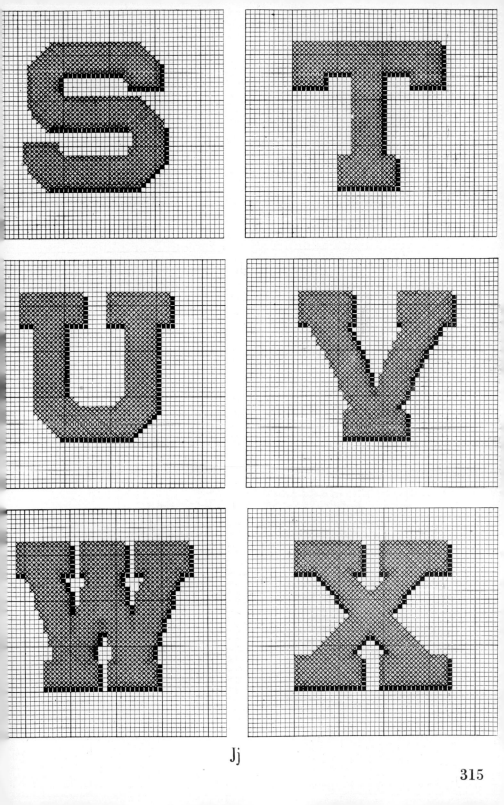

Jj

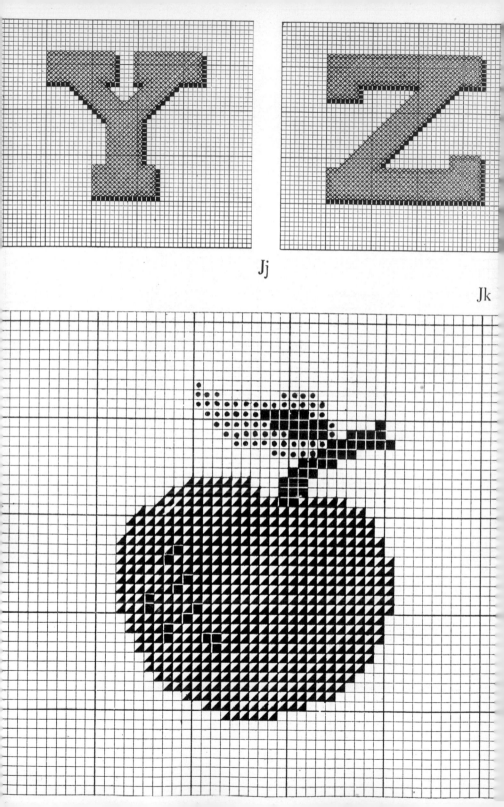

Jj

Jk

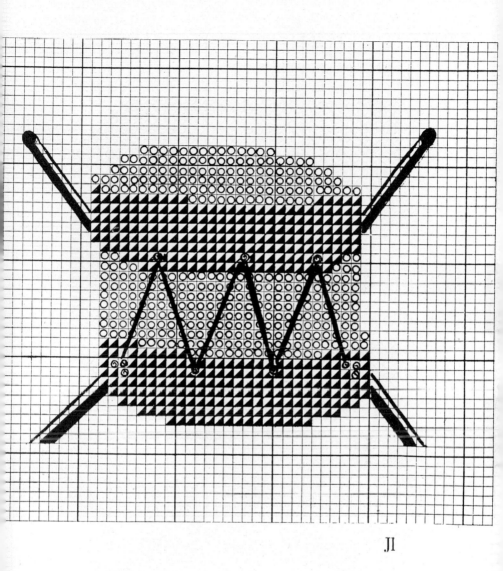

JI

COLOR KEY

O = WHITE
◢   RED
■   BLACK
X   YELLOW
–   GREY

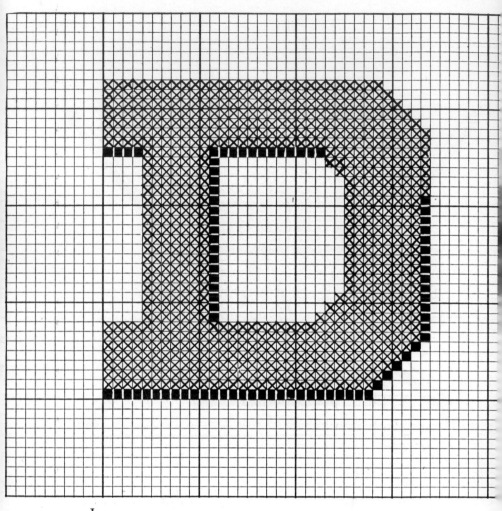

Jm

Jn

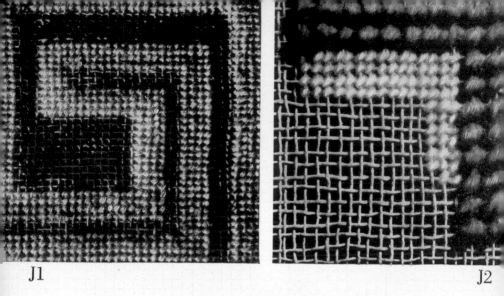

J1   J2

Note: To cover 1 square inch of canvas it requires approximately 1 yard of yarn for the half cross stitch (J 5a and b); 1¼ yds. for the gros point (J 3a, b, c) and 1¼ yds. for the petit point stitch (J 1).

Petit Point, Tent or Continental Stitch: This stitch produces a small slanting stitch on the front and a longer slanting one at the back (J 3a). At the end of a row, the work is turned upside down and a small upright stitch is made in order to bring the needle into position for the next row, as every line is worked from right to left. It is usually worked on single thread canvas (J 1). However, if parts of the design planned for double thread canvas are to be worked in the petit point stitch, the stitch itself is always worked over just the single thread of the canvas. To aid

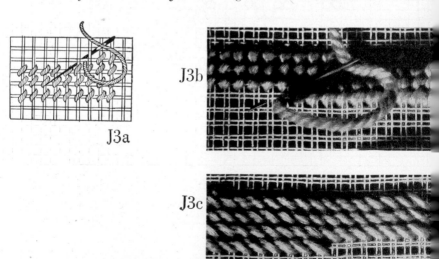

J3b

J3a

J3c

320

yourself in keeping an even stitch for the petit point section, it is advisable to wet the desired section and to separate the horizontal and vertical double threads of the canvas, forcing the threads into even rows (J 2).

Gros Point Stitch: As its name implies, it is a larger edition of petit point. It is worked in the same manner as petit point but over 2 threads in height and width, usually on double thread canvas (J 3a, b and c). This stitch may be used for charts Jj to m.

Bias Tent or Basket-Weave Stitch: Basically the petit point stitch worked diagonally over a large space. The work is done in diagonal rows, alternately up and down, beginning at the upper right-hand corner of the canvas. In the upward working of this stitch, the needle passes horizontally under two single threads or two rows of double threads of canvas every time an upward stitch is made (J 4a); and in the downward working, the needle passes vertically under two single threads or two rows of canvas each time a downward stitch is made (J 4b). This stitch forms a basketlike weave on the wrong side (J 4c). It can be applied to the gros point or petit point stitches.

J4a

J4b

J4c

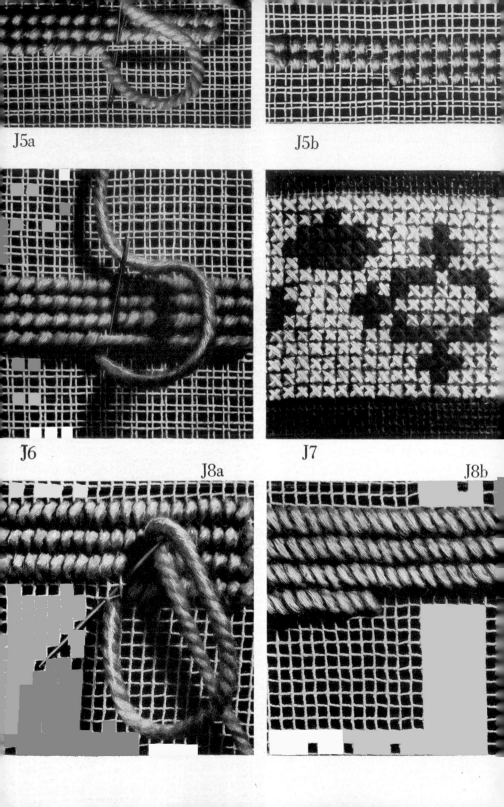

J5a

J5b

J6

J7

J8a

J8b

Half-Cross Stitch: Draw needle through square of canvas at lower left-hand corner. Insert needle into next square above and draw it through square directly below. This forms the first slanting stitch (J 5a). Continue in this manner, always moving over one square to the right and keeping needle in vertical position which forms a straight stitch on wrong side (J 5b). When row is finished, turn work upside down. Thread and work is then in position to work toward right. Practically all stamped, or tramé (underlaid) pieces are worked in the half-cross stitch as it takes approximately ¼ less thread than the gros point stitch. If design is to be underlaid, bring needle and thread up through canvas from right-hand side. Carry it across top between narrow row to left side (J 6). Now work in half stitch (J 5a and b).

Cross Stitch: Worked in two rows; the first half in the same manner as the half-cross stitch (J 5a and b) from left to right and the second half or return row in the same manner, but this time from right to left, thus crossing the stitch of the previous row (J 7).

Gobelin Stitch: Commonly used for backgrounds and worked over more threads in height than in width (J 8a and b).

Straight Gobelin: This is worked in horizontal rows. The needle is passed vertically over 2 single threads of canvas, thus forming a slanting stitch on the wrong side.

Oblique Gobelin Stitch: Worked over 1 vertical and 2 horizontal threads of canvas (J 8a and b). In working stitch on double thread canvas, it is advisable to use a thick needle to force apart the "double threads" and to avoid the fraying of the thread as it is drawn through. This stitch can also be worked on double thread canvas by working over two vertical and four horizontal threads of canvas.

Long and Short Oblique Stitch: This stitch is worked in vertical rows. Row 1: Starting at the upper left-hand corner, bring needle up in the first square in the fourth row. Pass needle down in fourth square of

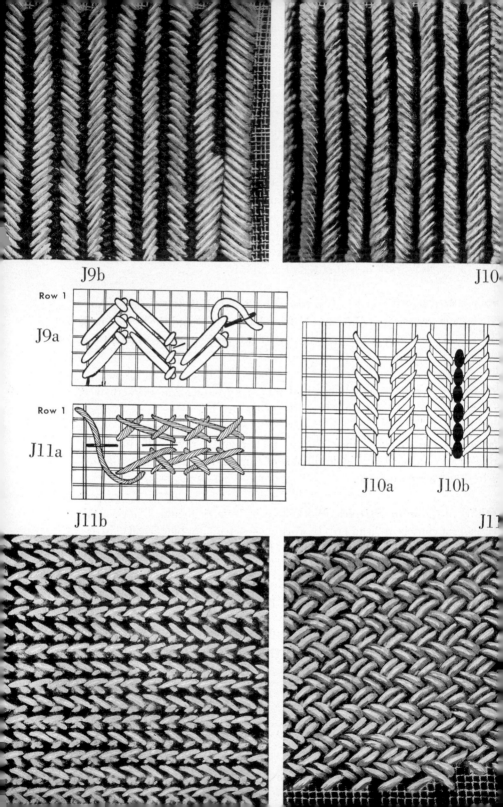

J9b

J10

Row 1

J9a

Row 1

J11a

J10a   J10b

J11b

J11

the first row. Bring needle up in third square of the first row and pass needle down through fourth square of second row (J 9a). A variation of this stitch is effective when the long oblique stitches are worked in one color and the short oblique stitches in a contrasting color. First work all the long stitches and then all the short stitches (J 9b).

Long Oblique Stitch with Running Stitch: This stitch, too, is worked in vertical rows. The oblique stitches may be worked by skipping 2 squares as explained above, or only 1 square (J 10a). The rows in which the long oblique stitches meet are then filled with a running stitch worked from top to bottom, and then bottom to top to give the effect of a backstitch (J 10b and c).

Greek or Herringbone Stitch: As the name indicates, it is a herringbone stitch worked on canvas in horizontal rows. Row 1: Working from left to right, bring needle up in the third square of the third row and pass needle down through the fifth square of the first row. Bring needle up in the third square of the first row and down through the seventh square of the third row. Bring needle up in fifth square of third row, down in seventh square of first row; up in fifth square of first row and down in ninth square of third row. Repeat. Row 2: Working from right to left, bring needle up in the last square of fifth row. Pass needle down in third last square of third row. Bring needle up in first square of third row and down in fifth square of the fifth row (J 11a). Repeat (J 11b).

Double Herringbone Stitch: This stitch is worked on single thread canvas and is an outgrowth of the Greek stitch. Row 1: Bring the needle up in the third square of the fourth row and down in the seventh square of the first row for the short stitch. For the long stitch, pass needle up in the fifth square of the first row and down in the ninth square of the third row. Bring needle up in seventh square of fourth row and down in eleventh square of first row. Pass needle up in the ninth square of first row and down in thirteenth square of third row. Repeat. The second row overlaps the first row by working from right to left from the sixth row to the third row (J 11c).

Row 1

J12a

Fern or Fishbone Stitch: This stitch is worked in vertical rows. Row 1: Starting at the upper left-hand corner, bring needle up in first square of first row and down in third square of third row. Pass needle up in second square of third row and down in fourth square of first row. Bring needle up in first square of second row, down in third square of fourth row; then pass needle up in second square of fourth row and down in fourth square of second row (J 12a). Repeat (J 12b).

Knit or Chain Stitch: This stitch is equally effective on single or double thread canvas. It is worked in vertical rows from bottom to top, similar to the duplicate stitch in knitting (F 1a to d). Beginning at the lower left-hand corner, bring needle up in third square of bottom row and down in fifth square of fifth row. Pass needle up in first square of fifth row and down in third square of bottom row. Bring needle up in third square of third row (2 rows above completed stitch) and down in fifth square of seventh row (2 rows above top of completed stitch); then up in first square of seventh row and down in third square of third row. Repeat (J 13).

J12b

J1.

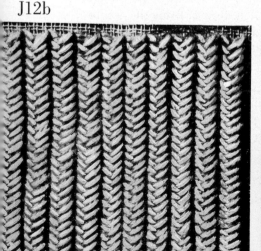

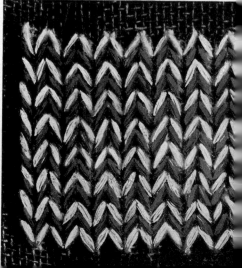

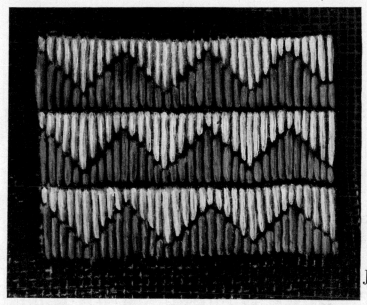

J14a

Bargello or Florentine Stitch: Worked from left to right in upright stitches over any given number of threads. It is usually worked on single thread canvas and is counted from a chart. Most designs are so planned that when one row is completed, practically all the counting is finished. Variations of this long and short stitch are shown in following charts and photographs.

Simple Long and Short Stitch (J 14a and b):
For the beginner who enjoys the satin stitch on single-thread canvas.

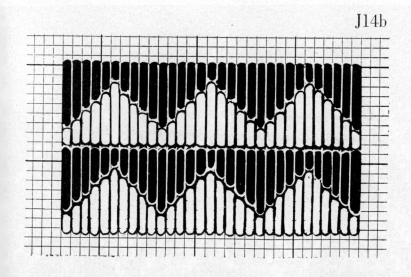

J14b

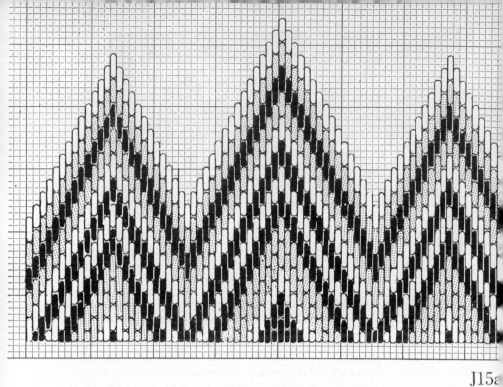

J15a

Saw Tooth Design (J 15a and b):
Rows of stitches of equal length that give the appearance of an intricate design.

J15b

J16a

Skyscraper Design (J 16a and b):
Particularly effective when used for piano-bench cover or a knitting bag,
in three colors as shown, or in a multi-color design.

J16b

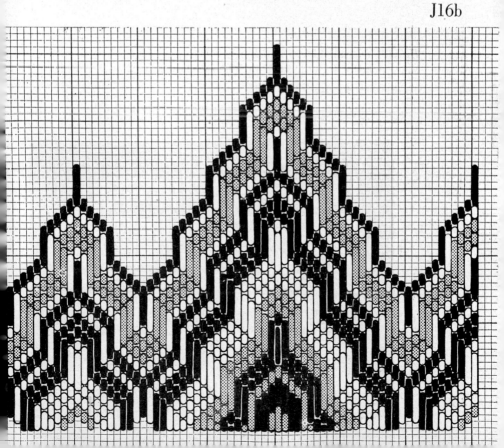

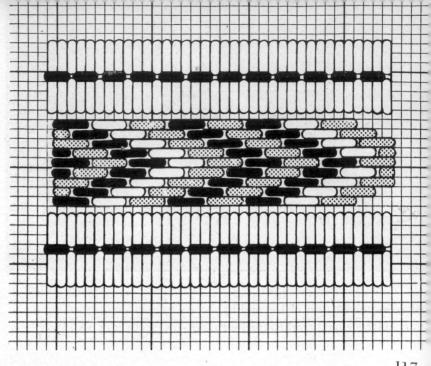

J17a

Border Design (J 17a and b):
For the needlewoman who appreciates a contrast in line. Can be used as an all-over design.

J17b

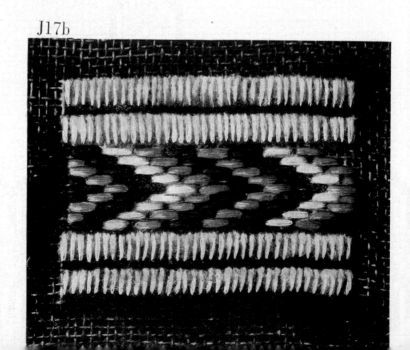

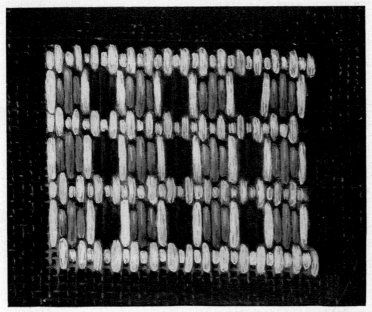

J18a

Shadow Design (J 18a and b):
Subtly effective in its repetition.

J18b

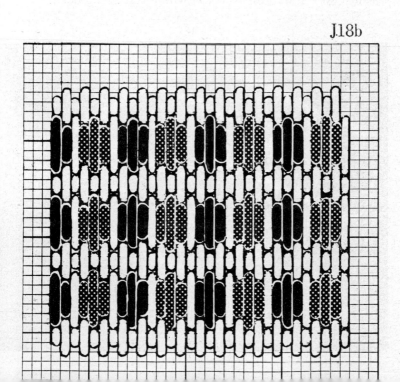

331

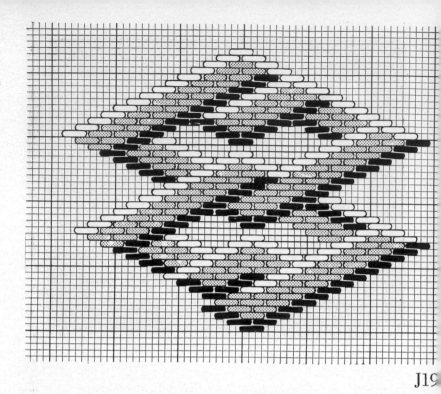

Interlocking Diamonds (J 19a and b):
Usually worked in brilliant colors with a soft background.

J19b

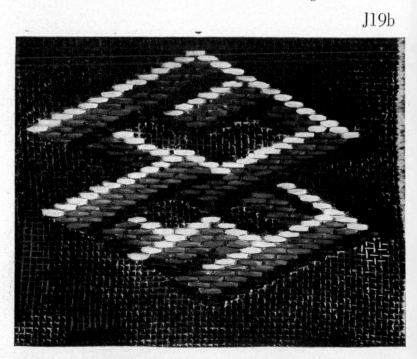

J20a

Checkerboard Design (J 20a and b):
Used ordinarily for a chair seat cover, yet lends itself to a rug for a boy's room when worked on coarse double-thread canvas.

J20b

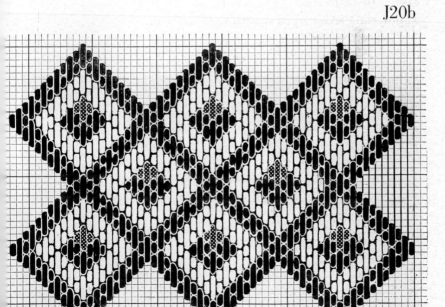

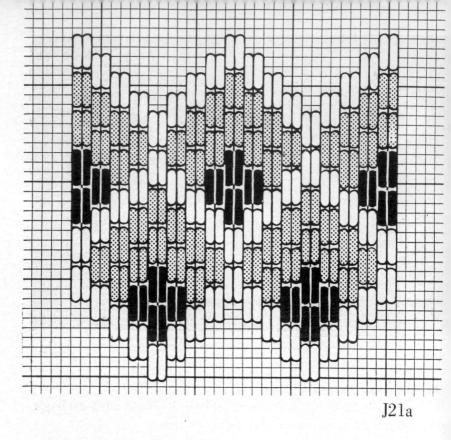

J21a

Coffee Bean Design (J 21a and b):
Appropriate and attractive with modern decor.

J21b

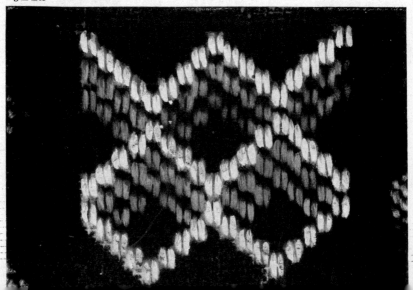

J22a

Simple Diamond (J 22a and b):
Zigzag rows of stitches that produce tiny diamonds.

J22b

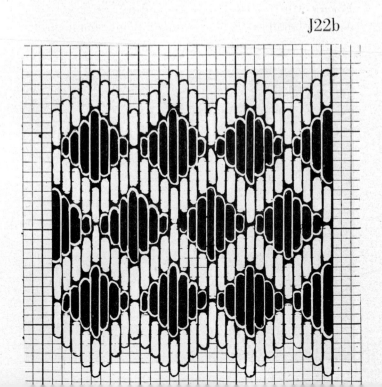

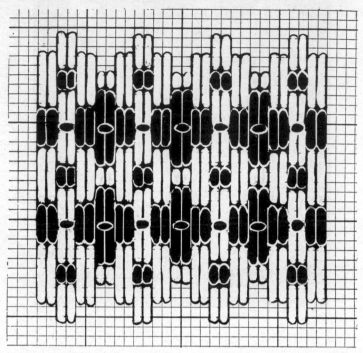

J23a

Forget-Me-Not Design (J 23a and b):
A play of double stitches creating a dainty floral effect.

J23b

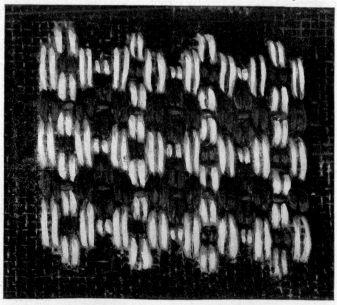

J24a

Mitred Design (J 24a and b):
Popularly used as a corner motif or an all-over design.

J24b

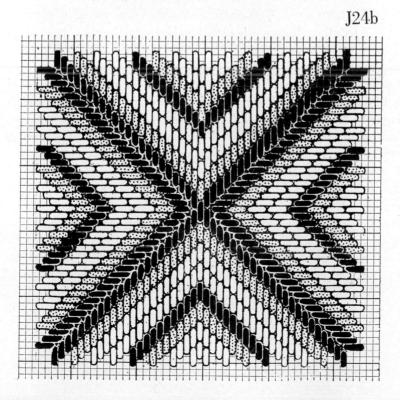

Blocking: When a piece of needlepoint is completed, it is necessary to stretch the piece. Sponge piece very well on wrong side until the wool and canvas are very wet; or roll it in a very damp Turkish towel and leave it there until the entire piece is quite damp. Stretch the piece into shape and tack it face down on a board with rust-proof thumbtacks, the tacks to be no more than ¾ of an inch apart. Allow the piece to dry thoroughly before removing it. This will take from one to three days depending on the weather conditions. It is not necessary to press the piece but should this be desired, after it is thoroughly dry, cover it wrong side up with a damp smooth towel and steam it with a hot iron. Do not permit iron to touch the piece of needlepoint.

Mounting Finished Work: Great care should be taken in mounting the finished piece, particularly if the piece is for furniture. Needlepoint pieces are priceless and whenever possible, should be blocked and mounted by an experienced craftsman. Pillows (Chapter 13) ordinarily are hemmed and joined to a back of heavy fabric. Picture panels, wall hangings and bell pulls should be faced with tape and backed with heavy sateen. Small rings are sewed at intervals across the top and the hanging suspended from a rod. Wall pictures should be framed in the same manner as a painting. Rugs are hemmed or faced with a tape (K 6) or lined with felt or sailcloth.

Designing Your Own Needlepoint: It is delightful to create a design that is representative of one's own personality. If you are an artist, it is simple to draw the design on heavy paper, trace it onto the canvas and then paint with tempera colors. However, if you are not an artist, you may still like to create a design of your own by using a group of motifs gleaned from an endless source of inspiration; as wall paper, dress fabrics, rugs, paintings, etc. In this case, if the motif is the size desired, merely trace the design of the original piece, pin tracing paper to canvas and transfer design to the canvas by pressing through the outline with a very sharp and heavy pencil or over carbon paper (Nj). Finally go over pencil markings with drawing ink, using a fine brush. When the ink is dry, use tempera or textile paints for the motif, or merely crayon the original tracing as a guide. Now, draw from your store of stitches. A most interesting texture can be produced by combining stitches as you wish, or as called for by the lines of the design itself.

To Enlarge a Design: If, on the contrary, the design is not the size desired, trace the original design, rule this tracing of the original design into small equal squares, approximately 1 inch in size. Calculate the desired size and mark this size on another piece of tracing paper. Divide the overall size into the *same number* of equal squares as on the original tracing. Now whatever is seen in each square of the original tracing, draw into each corresponding square of the new tracing (Kj) then transfer to canvas as explained above. This same principle can be used if a design is to be made smaller.

Use of Graph Paper and Graph Charts: The simplest and most common method used in copying and creating designs for needlepoint is that of "blocking" or "counting" the design on graph paper. In this

J25

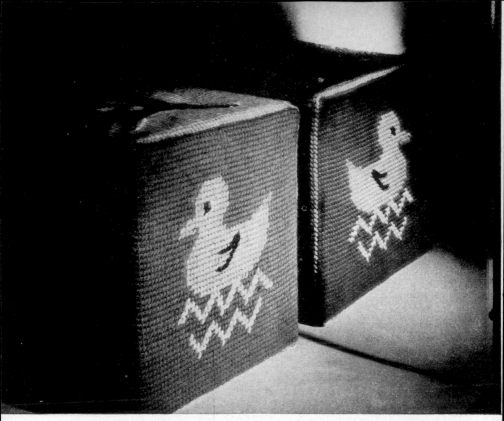

method, each mesh of canvas is represented by a square or block on the graph paper. The design is first outlined on the graph paper and then the blocks are crayoned or painted in the desired colors. In many instances, especially on instruction sheets, symbols are used to represent the different colors (see charts for hassock at beginning of chapter).

To enlarge or diminish a design from a graph paper chart, choose the proper size canvas to obtain the desired finished piece of needlepoint Copy a small figure from a petit point piece or chart and use it for a rug by merely using a coarse canvas and counting the squares of the original piece (J 25). Use the same figure for a pillow or chair seat by working the design on a different size canvas—double-thread or over two strands of single-thread. *To reverse the position of a design*, place the finished article (J 26) or the graph in front of a mirror and count the stitches in the reflection. Or merely trace the design on tracing paper; turn traced design to wrong side and go over traced lines from upper side. The retraced design gives you the original design in reverse.

CHAPTER 11

RUG MAKING

RUG MAKING

>>> RUG making in one form or another has been a universal pastime since time immemorial. Rugs have been woven, braided, hooked, worked on coarse needlepoint canvas, made of pompons stitched on burlap, and in so great a variety of ways that it is impossible to explain each type in detail.

Rug making is within the grasp of everyone, even a kindergarten child. What could be simpler than a three-strand braid that is no more than the method used to plait hair? A fore-knowledge of sewing is helpful in joining the braided pieces, but not essential. Even crocheting need not be known to begin to hook a rug with a crochet hook or the many needlepoint stitches to make a needlepoint rug. It's fun to design while learning. There is no better and easier way to learn than to take some oddments and a needle; and from scraps make a rug for others to admire.

Instructions for Hooked Rug (Color Plate K, pg 346).

Ka

Kc

Kb

Design your own from color plate K

With a bit of ingenuity, you can design from a hooked rug.

1. Scale to size (pg 339) twig-and-leaf motif on heavy fabric for chair
(Ka) and draperies (Kb). Work in crewel embroidery (Chapter 4).

2. Scale to size (pg 339) corner design for household linens (Kc), bag
(Ke) and blouse (Kh) and embroider in satin stitch (C 39).

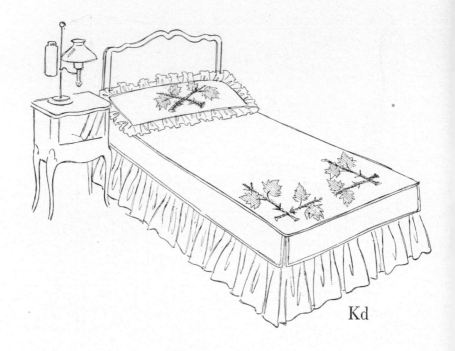

Kd

3. Scale to size center design for appliqué spread (Color Plate E and Kd).
4. Scale to size leaf design for sweater motif (Kf) in outline stitch (C 4) or duplicate stitch (F 1a to d).
5. Scale to size center scroll and leaves for scarf (Kg) in textile painting (Chapter 14).
6. Scale to size leaf design for dickey blouse (Ki) in textile painting (Chapter 14).
7. Use design, entire or in part, in simple embroidery (Chapter 3) for household linens, accessories, and wearing apparel.
8. Scale to size (pg 339) design of appliqué spread (Kd) for a hooked, crocheted or needlepoint rug.
9. Scale to size (pg 339) design of textile painted scarf (Kg) for a needlepoint chair (Chapters 10).

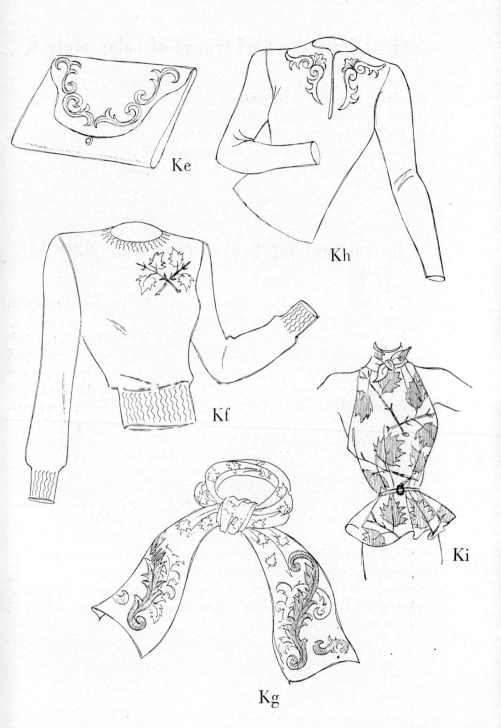

Ke

Kh

Kf

Ki

Kg

Ideas from the background of color plate K

For helpful hints, turn the pages.
1. For pillow instructions (Chapter 13).
2. For knitting instructions (Chapter 6).
3. For textile painting instructions (Chapter 14).
4. Use print design in pillows and on cover of dish for Fair-Isle knitting (Chapter 6).

Instructions for hooked rug (color plate K)

1. Scale and trace to size (Chapter 10, pg. 339) the design shown in chart Kj. Each square equals 6 inches.
2. Hook with crochet hook (K 3) or automatic needle (K 4); or tuft with or without a gauge (K 21a and b) in three shades of green gold and four shades of rust for the leaves; three shades of leaf-green and three shades of cocoa-brown for the scrolls and a Gobelin-blue for the background as shown in Color Plate K, or in colors of your own choosing.
3. Block (pg 352) and line (pg 353).

Hooked rugs

Of all types, the hooked rug is the most popular, and is easy as well as inexpensive to make. Though there are yarns especially treated for rug making, many of the hooked rugs are made of old materials. Woolen yarns and fabrics are best, but cotton, linen, silk, and rayon fabrics as well as stockings may be used.

Kj

Preparing the Oddments: Cutting the cloth is very important. Stockings must be cut spirally (K 1). Use your judgment about the width, adjusting it to the type of material and the effect you wish to achieve. This means a little experimenting. It is a good idea to cut up a lot of material and roll it into balls, one color to a ball, so that when you get to the hooking you will not have to stop to cut. Short lengths can be sorted by color and kept in envelopes or boxes.

When using old yarns or materials, you will find that some colors will not fit into the color scheme and must be re-dyed. Remove the original color with a color remover and re-dye yarns or materials in whatever shades are required. Materials are usually dyed in the piece. Strips or small bits should be tied in a piece of cheesecloth before dyeing. A variety of shades can be obtained by taking some pieces out of the dye from time to time; or by using materials that differ in tone and color.

Materials: The foundation for hooking is of burlap, monk's cloth or gunny sacks. If gunny sacks are used, they should be washed, boiled, and dipped in hot starch to which a pinch of powdered Arabic (from a drug store) has been added and dissolved. Iron while damp, on one side

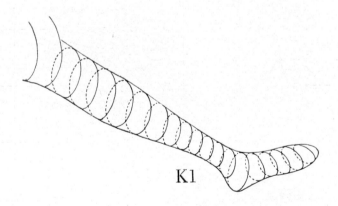

K1

K2

only, to give a glossy surface on which to draw the design. The hook may be the old-fashioned type of crochet hook with a slender handle or one of the many automatic types. With the plain or crochet hook you work from the right side of the rug (K 3). With the automatic hook, you work from the wrong side (K 4). Though it is possible to work without a frame, for best results it is advisable to use a frame. The most popular frame is the easel type which is supported on legs, stands about 30 inches high and tilts at an angle. It has roller bars top and bottom with which to adjust the work. Place foundation on frame and tack securely in place, stretching tightly to get a perfectly taut surface. Thread automatic needle.

Hooking

Hooking is merely drawing the yarn or strip up through the foundation with the hook. It is possible to create an embossed effect by working the design in loops slightly longer than the loops of the background (K 2).

K3

With the Plain or Crochet Hook: Work from the right side of the rug. Hold the yarn or strip of cloth between the thumb and forefinger of the left hand, underneath the foundation, and the hook lightly in right hand. Insert hook through foundation, and then catch end of yarn and pull through foundation. Skip a few threads of material and insert hook through again; pull up gently and leave a loop (K 3). The usual length of the loops is $\frac{1}{4}$ to $\frac{3}{8}$ inch, or as desired. Only practice can give the knack of holding the yarn or strip in left hand taut but not pulled. Always pull both ends of each strip or yarn through to right side and trim even with loops. This is for neatness and strength. The outline of the pattern should be hooked first. This should be done carefully. Then the design filled in, bringing the loops close together, but not crowded. Last, work background, taking special care that all corners are filled in. When you change to a strip of another color or shade, mingle the two in a broken line, placing the end of one line a little above the end of the

K4

receding one. Mottled backgrounds are made by using several shades
f the same color.

ith the Automatic Hook: Work from the wrong side of the rug and
se the hook to push rather than pull loops through foundation. First be
ire that yarn or strip runs freely through needle and that it does not
itch. Always insert needle vertically, bringing end of yarn on the right
r underside of foundation. Withdraw needle just clear of the material.
ever lift needle above foundation; slide and insert again (K 4). This
me a loop will be formed on the right or underside of rug. If needle
accidentally raised too high, pull yarn back as it was before and make
itch over again. It is better not to clip the loops of hooked rugs made of
d cloth, as they are more attractive and wear better with loops uncut.
the loops of a yarn rug are cut, the clipping is done with sharp scissors
hile the rug is still in the frame (K 5).

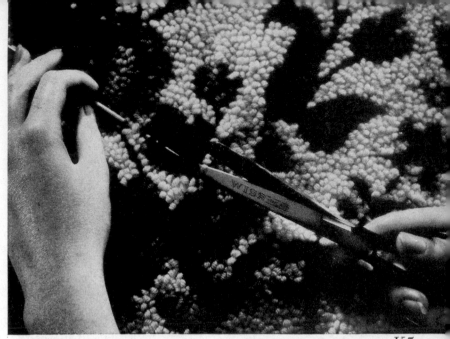

K5

To Clip: Turn the frame so that the right side of the work is on top.
It is advisable to run a double-pointed steel needle through the loops and
to pull the loops up firmly from the foundation before cutting. Remove
steel needle. For cutting, use long, narrow, sharp scissors. Slide one point
of scissors in through the loops and cut about one inch of loops at a time
(K 5). When working the next row of loops, push clipped loops back with
the hand so that no strand will be caught in the descending hook.

Blocking: With a sponge or piece of Turkish toweling wrung out of
hot water, go over the entire top or looped side of the rug enough to
dampen it. Place the rug face down on a smooth surface which has been
covered with clean paper. Put the rug in shape but do not stretch tightly.
Walk on it as much as possible. This sets and flattens the stitches and
keeps them in place.

If you have left the edges of the rug unfinished, leave enough unhooked
foundation all around so that you will have about 3 inches to turn under
and hem securely. Or, you can turn a narrow edge and bind with strong
fabric or carpet binding (K 6). If liquid rug sizing is available, spread a

even coat over the entire back; allow sizing to dry thoroughly, then line.

To Line Rug: Cut the lining 1½ inches more than the width and length of the rug all around. Place the lining flat on the table. Place the rug on the lining, having the 1½ inches project on all sides. Baste the rug onto the lining about 2 inches in from the edge all around. Turn the rug over so that the lining is on top. Use strong thread, make large stitches and catch-stitch (A 9) the lining onto the back of the rug. Remove basting.

Braided rugs

Braided Rugs are somewhat easier to make than hooked rugs. It is most important that the strips which go into any one braid and the braids which go into any one rug, all be of the same size and thickness. Thicker braids in the center will cause the rug to "cup," while thinner braids in the center will cause it to "ripple." Cut or tear material into strips from 1 to 3 inches wide. The weight of the material and the width of the strips will determine the texture of the rug. Lighter weight fabrics must be cut wider than heavier materials and may even be used double if

K6

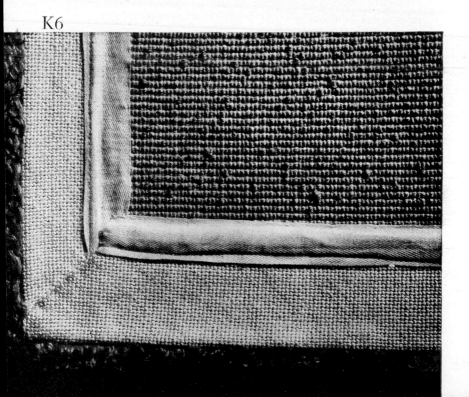

necessary. While the bigger braid makes the rug grow faster, it is believed that braids of ¾ to 1 inch in width make the best looking rugs.

Prepare and dye materials in same manner as for hooked rugs. Ends of strips should be cut diagonally (K 7a), brought together and sewed firmly on wrong side (K 7b). Press seams open (K 7c). Fold edges in, at least ½ inch (K 7d), and then fold strip down center, with raw edges on the inside (K 7e). Experienced rug-makers are able to fold as they braid but for a novice it might be helpful to run the turned-under edges together with long, blind stitches. Cottons can be creased with an iron. Strips ready for braiding may be wound into balls (K 8) or around a rolled magazine.

While braiding is simple to do, it must be done correctly if the rug is to hold its shape. When you begin the braid, tack or pin the strands together (K 9). Keep your tension firm and steady for a smooth, tightly woven braid. It also helps if the braid is weighted down or attached to something so that it is possible to stretch the braid slightly as you work. A straight pin put through the center and moved forward as the work progresses, also helps to keep braids tight. Whenever you must let go of the braid, the braided ends should be pinned together. Seams where new strips are added to the braid should be spaced so that no two joinings ever occur in the same place or the braid will be bulky and bumpy. Braids may be formed of any number of strips, usually from three to eight (see color plate A for rug).

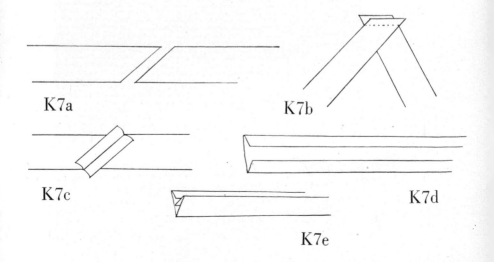

K7a

K7b

K7c

K7d

K7e

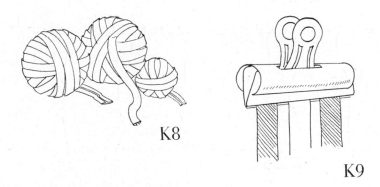

K8

K9

Three-Strand Braiding: Number strips from left to right. Bring the last strip, No. 3, over the center strip, No. 2, and under the first strip, No. 1 (K 10a). Renumber the strips and repeat (K 10b and c).

Multiple Braiding: Merely the weaving over and under of a few extra strips. Number your strips from left to right. Begin with the last strip and weave it over and under from right to left; then take the second last (the strip at the extreme right) and again weave over and under from right to left. Repeat this method always taking the strip at the extreme right. It is helpful to renumber the strips each time you repeat the process as shown (K 11). To end the last braid, cut each strand in the braid to a point; whip edges in and braid the ends together.

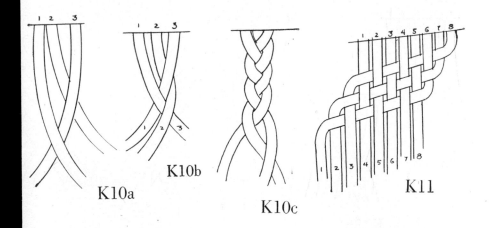

K10a

K10b

K10c

K11

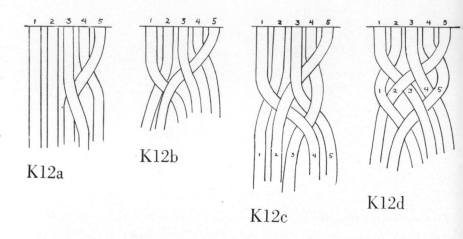

Fancy Five-Strand Braiding: Number strips from left to right. Bring last strip, No. 5, over No. 4 and under No. 3 (K 12a). Bring No. 1 over No. 2 and under No. 5 (K 12b). Renumber strips and repeat these two steps (K 12c and d).

Heavy Five-Strand Braiding: Number strips from left to right. Bring last strip, No. 5, over Nos. 4 and 3 (K 13a); bring first strip No. 1 over Nos. 2 and 5 (K 13b). Renumber strips and repeat these two steps (K 13c, d and e).

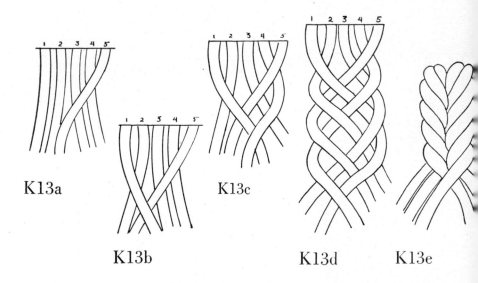

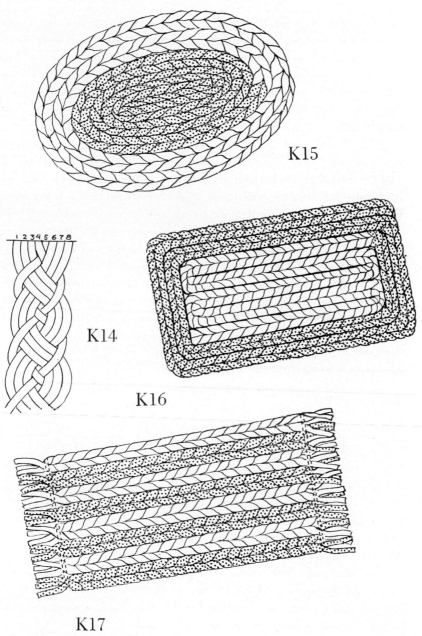

K15

1 2 3 4 5 6 7 8

K14

K16

K17

Fancy Eight-Strand Braiding: Number strips from left to right. Bring No. 4 over No. 5 under Nos. 6, 7 and 8. Bring No. 5 over Nos. 3, 2 and 1. Grasp Nos. 6, 7 and 8 as one unit and bring under Nos. 1, 2 and 3 as one unit. Bring No. 4 over Nos. 1, 2 and 3 and No. 5 under Nos. 6, 7 and 8. Bring No. 5 over No. 4 at center. Repeat these last two steps, continuing to braid first the three-strand units and then the single-strand units (K 14).

After several yards have been braided, start sewing with a strong needle or baste braids together with bias tape. To make the center of a round rug, coil the braid spirally and sew it firmly on the wrong side. Take a stitch first in the coiled part, then in the braid that is being added. The way to keep the rug flat is to work with it on the table and allow enough fullness at the curves. Oval rugs are made just like the round rugs except that instead of beginning with a coil, you make a strip about ⅓ as long as you wish the oval to be. The strip is made by measuring off the length you want, doubling the braid, like a hair pin, and sewing the braids together side by side. Then, sew the braid around and around this basic strand to form an oval (K 15). Oblong and square rugs can be made by continuing to double the braid like a hair pin, working back and forth and with a braid sewed around the entire piece (K 16). Or, by joining separate strips with the ends unravelled to form a fringe (K 17). Press all rugs with a damp cloth and hot iron.

Crocheted rugs

Crocheted rugs, like hooked rugs, can be made of wool or cotton yarn or fabric strips. Prepare and dye materials in same manner as for hooked rugs (pg 348). The width of strips will vary with type of material and how fine or coarse you wish the rug to be. A finer, firmer and more attractive texture is achieved with narrow, bias-cut strips, as they have more elasticity for crocheting. Materials of a knit type are particularly good for crocheted rugs. The size hook depends upon the size of the yarn or strips, and the stitch used is the single crochet (G 3a). It is advisable to fold the strips as explained for the braided rug, but if a shaggy effect is desired, the raw edges need not be turned in.

In crocheting an oval rug, as in the braided rug, the foundation chain is made ⅓ as long as you plan to make your rug. Work in single crochet (G 3) along both sides of foundation chain, making a single crochet in each chain. Work in single crochet throughout rug and always pick up both strands of the stitch. Place markers at center of sides and ends to guide you in distributing extra stitches as you find them necessary. No fast rule can be made for enlarging; but when you find you have to reach with your hook for the next loop, it is time to add a stitch. Never add at the same point as in the previous row, and mark where each stitch is added so as to make both sides even.

Many attractive designs and a variety of stitches (Chapter 7) can be used for the rugs crocheted of cotton or wool yarn.

Instructions for Crocheted Duck Rug (K 18b):

Materials Required:
Cotton Yarn—1600 yds. Med. Blue, 100 yds. each of white, black, and
    yellow.
1 Steel Crochet Hook Size G or 1 Bone Crochet Hook Size 6 (standard).
Rug measures about 22″ x 32″.
Gauge. 3 sts = 1 inch; 4 rows = 1 inch.

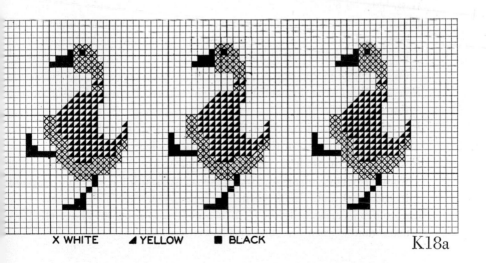

X WHITE   ◢ YELLOW   ■ BLACK   K18a

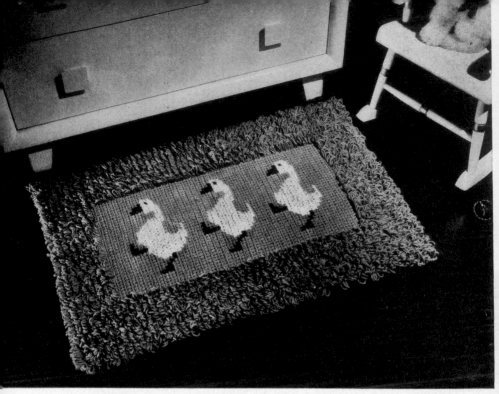

K18b

The rug is made with double strands of yarn.

With blue, ch 69 (G 2) and work 68 sc (G 3a and b) on ch, ch 1, turn.

Row 2: 1 loop st in each st (loop st: wind yarn over index finger, insert hook in st, draw yarn through, pulling yarn from under finger, drop loop from finger letting fall to right side of work and complete sc (With gauge G 25a and b), ch 1, turn.

Row 3: Work 1 sc in each loop st, ch 1, turn. Repeat these 2 rows 7 times.

Row 18: 1 loop st in each of the first 16 sc, 1 sc in each of the next 36 sc, 1 loop st in each of the remaining 16 sc, ch 1, turn.

Row 19: 1 sc in each st, ch 1, turn. Repeat last 2 rows 39 times, then work 8 rows of loop sts and 8 rows of sc, alternating rows to correspond to the other end. Break yarn.

Embroider in cross stitches (C 37a and b) according to chart (K 18a) using double yarn (K 18b) and block (pg 352).

Needlepoint rugs

Any one of the variety of needlepoint stitches as well as the charts shown in Chapter 10, can be worked on coarse canvas to make an attractive and priceless rug (K 19). These motifs were taken directly from the needlepoint hassock (Color Plate J).

Loop-Stitch, Knotted or Tufted Pile Rug: This type of rug resembles but uses more yarn than the simple needlepoint stitches. Cut yarn in short lengths approximately 3 inches long; double it and with the left hand, lay the loop on top against one of the double horizontal threads

K19

of canvas. With a large crochet hook draw the loop under the double threads of the canvas towards you (K 20a). Catch up the loose ends of the wool and draw them together through the loop. Pull the ends tightly so that the loop closes on the ends very close to the canvas (K 20b). Repeat this stitch in each mesh of canvas, keeping the knots in the same direction throughout the whole rug. The latch-hook needle facilitates the making of this loop stitch rug (K 20c).

Loop Stitch Rug on Burlap: For a rug with a shorter pile, a similar method using a blunt-end tapestry needle instead of a hook can be used. This stitch can be made with or without a metal gauge. If a gauge is used, split a tongue-depressor in half lengthwise or use a narrow piece of metal ½ to ¾ inch wide. Begin at lower left-hand corner of canvas, burlap or any closely woven fabric. Draw yarn through double horizontal threads of the canvas or fabric. With left forefinger or thumb hold yarn below stitch; to right skip 2 or 3 strands of foundation fabric and insert needle to left, bringing needle out in front of last stitch. Loop formed is usually ½ to 1 inch in length (K 21a). To right skip 2 or 3 strands of foundation fabric and insert needle to left, bringing needle out in front of last stitch. Draw yarn tight to fasten knot (K 21b). Continue in this manner, forming a loop in each mesh or at even intervals across row. The loops can be cut as you progress, or all loops cut when the rug is completed. An interesting effect is achieved by cutting the design and leaving the background uncut. 363

K21a

K21b

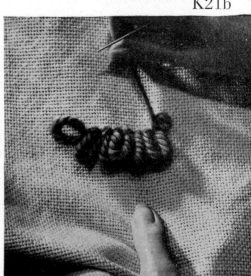

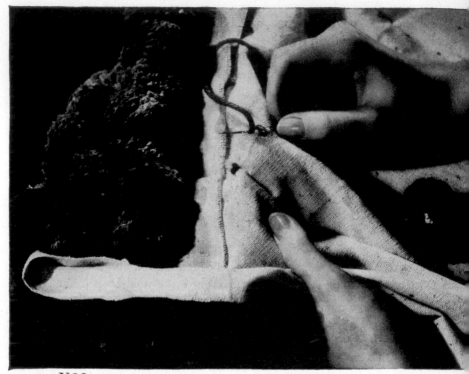

K22

Pompon Rugs: These rugs are merely many pompons made of one color or several colors arranged to form a design. A pompon is made in the usual manner by winding yarn 20 times or more around a gauge, approximately 1 inch in width. The loops are then cut and trimmed into a round pompon (N 14a, b, c). Place the knot of the pompon on the foundation and with a darning needle and carpet thread, sew pompon to foundation with 2 cross stitches (C 37), one over the other, on wrong side. Be sure to catch the pompon securely. Fasten thread. Attach next pompon approximately ½ inch from last pompon (K 22). When all the pompons have been sewn to the foundation and close enough to hide the foundation itself, turn hem under on wrong side. Finish in same manner as for a hooked rug (K 6).

Stitched Fringe Rugs: Make a winder 3 inches wide with a ¼-inch slit in the center. Wind the yarn around winder; place on sewing machine and stitch down through slit (K 23). Cut strip on one side with sharp scissors to form fringe, place on a strong, closely woven material foundation and sew fringe-strips close enough to cover backing. If intricate designs and greater accuracy are desired, it is advisable to use the machine-guide for this type of rug. The machine-attachment shown in the photograph cuts as you sew (K 23).

K23

Woven Rugs: For rugs woven on a four-harness loom, use the tie-up of the twill drafts (L 9a). If a 15 or 18-inch dent reed is used, skip every other dent as you thread your warp threads. Use carpet warp or heavy twine for warp threads; and felt or rag strips, or rug yarn for weft threads (Color Plate L).

CHAPTER 12

WEAVING

WEAVING

→》》 WEAVING is the interlacing of lengthwise threads, called the warp threads, among crosswise threads, called the woof, weft or filling threads. The most simple and fundamental weaving process is darning. In darning, the woof (crosswise) thread is run back and forth, over and under the warp (lengthwise) threads, to replace the lost fabric of a hole. This basic principle is followed in all types of weaving, whether it is done on huck, on a small wooden frame with nails as guiding posts, or on a large eight-harness loom with almost countless heddles.

In selecting a loom for weaving in its broader sense, if the weaver is content with simple types of weaving and lacks time and inclination to delve deeply into it, a two-harness loom is recommended. On this loom many modern and primitive techniques can be worked out most successfully, and the color and texture effects of the cloth are limited only by the ability and interest of the weaver. Overshot patterns, however, are not possible on less than a four-harness loom. This loom will do all that a two-harness loom is capable of, plus overshot, twill weaves, summer and winter weaves, and many other techniques. Many of the four-harness looms are constructed with space for the addition of an extra set of four harnesses to make an eight harness loom.

Instructions for Bag and Scarf (Color Plate L, pg 372).

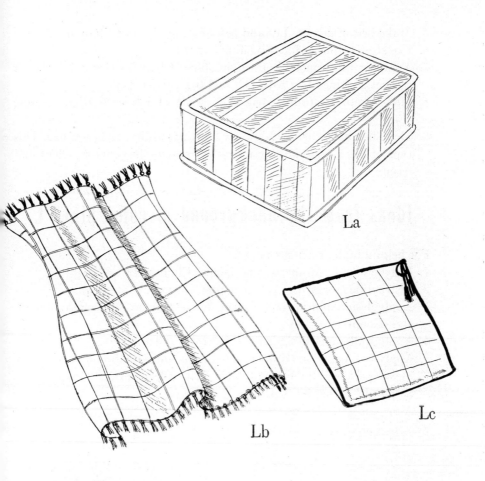

La

Lb

Lc

Design your own from color plate L

With a bit of ingenuity you can design from a woven bag and scarf.

1. Cut out two square pieces and one gusset piece and make a box-pillow (La and Chapter 13).

2. Use straight woven piece for carriage throw (Lb and N 16).

3. Use straight woven piece for pillow (Lc and Chapter 13).

4. Use original woven piece of scarf for place mat and napkin (Ld).

5. Make belt of gusset (Le) and belt of strap (Lg and Chapter 2).
6. Use straight pieces for travelling bag (Lf).
7. Applying the principle of stitch gauge (Chapters 6 and 7), knit or crochet a striped bag with belt and bag carrier (Lh).
8. Make simple half-moon bag of pieces A and B with zipper closing (Li).
9. Make bag in leather or fabric for knitting, utility, or beach bag. This type of bag is especially practical when made in water-repellent material.

Ideas from the background of color plate L

For helpful hints, turn the pages.
1. Instructions for draperies and lamps (Chapter 13).
2. Instructions for woven rug (Chapter 11 and Chapter 12).
3. Apply design in drapery for crocheted bedspread, tablecloth, afghan, etc. (Chapter 7).
4. Apply wall paper designs for ski sweater (Chapter 6).
5. Apply wall paper and drapery designs for simple embroidery (Chapter 3), cutwork embroidery (Chapter 4), textile painting (Chapter 14), patchwork (Chapter 5).

Ld

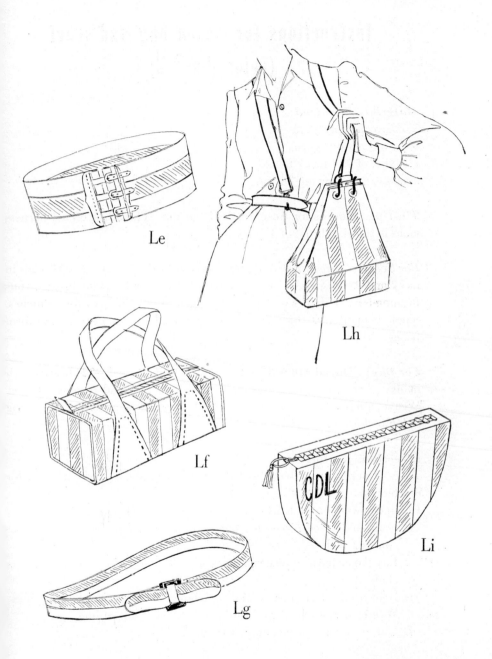

Le

Lh

Lf

CDL

Li

Lg

Instructions for woven bag and scarf
(color plate L)

Materials Required:
5 oz. green 3-ply yarn
8 oz. navy 3-ply yarn
1¼ yds. of 72″ navy felt
2 spools navy sewing cotton

Tie-Up: Same as for Rose Motif (Page 392). Threading on a 4-harness loom is the simple 1-2-3-4 (L 9a).

For Scarf: Thread 198 warp threads on a 15-dent reed—* 22 threads in navy and 22 threads in green. Repeat from * for the 198 threads, thus forming 5 navy stripes and 4 green stripes. Weave in navy for 45 inches. Single hemstitch (C 65) across each end in groups of 4 strands to form fringe.

For Bag: Thread 418 warp threads on a 15-dent reed—22 threads each in navy and green, thus forming 10 navy stripes and 9 green stripes. Weave in navy for 41 inches. Hemstitch (C 65) at each end. Press, using a damp cloth and moderate iron.

Directions for Bag:
Note: Buckram may be substituted for interlining, to make it easier for machine sewing.
In hand sewing, use a leather-needle with a 3-sided point.
1. Scale and trace pieces for bag (Lj) on heavy paper—each square equals 1 inch.
2. Lay paper pattern pieces on woven material, and trace with tailor's chalk.
3. Remove pattern pieces and machine stitch on the chalk lines. Wherever lines meet, machine stitch on each side of line.
4. Cut on outside of machine-stitching.

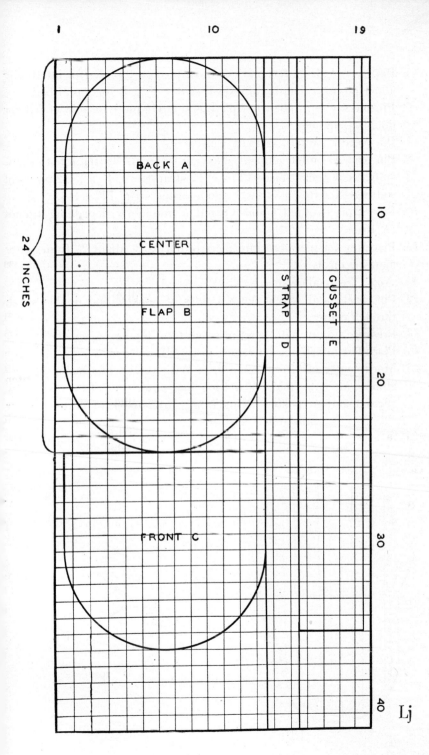

BACK A

CENTER

FLAP B

STRAP D

GUSSET E

FRONT C

24 INCHES

Lj

373

5. Pin piece A–B on felt and cut three pieces—2 pieces for interlining and 1 piece for bag lining. Mark center of A–B for top of bag.
6. Pin piece C on folded felt piece and cut 1 piece on fold of felt for double thickness.
7. Pin piece E on felt, and cut 2 pieces.
8. Pin piece D on felt and cut, allowing ½″ more width on both sides.
9. In felt, cut pocket-piece 12″ x 7″; 2 strap-loops, 4″ x 1″; 2 pieces of welting—1 strip 36″ x 1½″, and a second strip, 72″ x 1½″.
10. Place 2 pieces of felt A and B together, and join with padding stitches (A 16).
11. Place pocket-piece on third piece of felt A–B, about 2″ from center marking on A.
   Note: Seam allowance 1″.
12. Pin, baste and stitch along 3 sides of pocket, and double stitch through center.
13. Press welting in half, lengthwise, to form piping.
14. Place felt interlining on woven piece AB, and pin.
15. Mark center of 72″ welting strip. With woven side facing up, beginning at center mark of welting and center edge of flap, with raw edges together, baste welting from center mark of flap to center

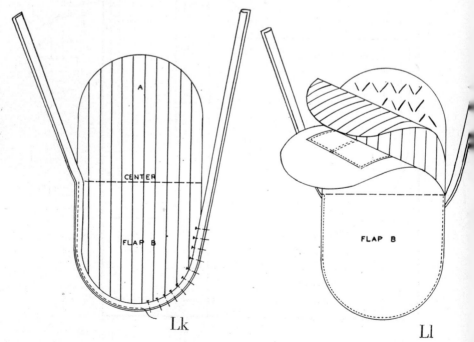

Lk   Ll

marking of flap on each side (Lk).

16. With woven side up, baste felt lining to bag, placing pocket to right side of woven fabric. Stitch through 6 thicknesses, following basting line to complete flap only (Ll). The back will be stitched to gusset later.
17. Turn right side out.
18. Pin welting that was left free on finished flap to backpiece A from top to center bottom, in similar manner as explained in Step 15 and slip stitch. Join seam welting at center bottom.
19. Baste woven piece of gusset to one felt gusset.
20. With woven fabrics facing, stitch gusset to back-piece A (Ln).
21. Place folded felt piece C on right side of woven piece C. Stitch across top at fold of felt piece C (Ln). Turn felt to wrong side of woven piece, so that stitching of the seam is hidden behind woven piece.
22. Allowing 1½″ from top of each end, apply welting to woven piece only (Lo) as explained for flap in Step 15. Conceal ends of welting in lining.
23. Stitch felt front piece to gusset.
24. Turn bag inside out. Stitch lining of back gusset and front gusset together.

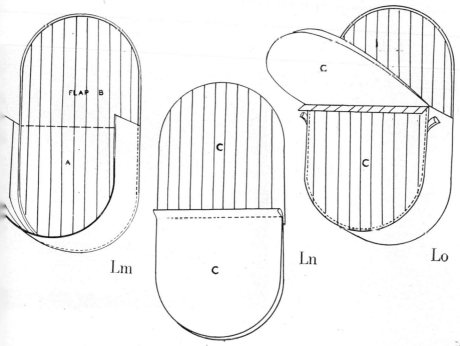

Lm

Ln

Lo

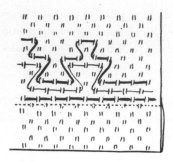

L1a

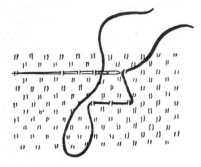

L1b

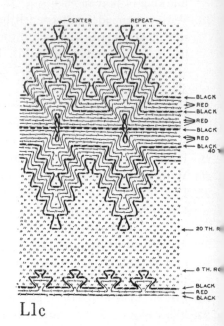

L1c

L1d

25. To form strap, place woven piece in center of felt piece. Fold felt sides over woven fabric and top-stitch close to raw edges of felt. Fold corners to form a triangular finish at each end.
26. For loops—(make 2): Fold edges to center to form ½″ band and stitch on each edge. Allowing ½″ at each end, fold loop around strap 2 inches from end and tack to gusset of bag.

Weaving on huck

Weaving on Huck: One of the simplest types of weaving. In this old art, the raised thread of the huck is considered the warp thread. This towel design was brought from Transylvania years ago (L 1d).

To Weave on Huck: Use huck toweling by the yard or a regulation huck towel in any width desired, No. 5 or 8 perle cotton or six-strand cotton and a small rather blunt-pointed needle.

To Place the Border: Cut away or rip out hem of towel, if toweling is used, turn hem on other side as the wrong side of toweling is used to weave the design. Place narrow border along top of hem (L 1a and b).

To Weave Design: Use 3, 4 or 6 strands of six-strand cotton or whole strand of No. 5 or 8 perle cotton in the needle at one time depending on weight of huck toweling; the finer it is, the thinner or less strands of cotton should be used. Follow chart (L 1c) for color and design counting the threads carefully. Take a strand of thread long enough to reach across towel from edge to edge of design (about 2 yards) without joining. Start weaving in center of towel with center of design; pull thread halfway through (other half of thread remains loose for other half of design) carry thread along through the two loose threads of the huck as shown in L 1b being careful not to go through material to wrong side. Repeat border to edge and end the thread by returning it through last 3 stitches, cut off. Turn chart (L 1c) upside down and work across in opposite direction to other edge ending in same way—be careful not to pull thread too tightly or design will pucker.

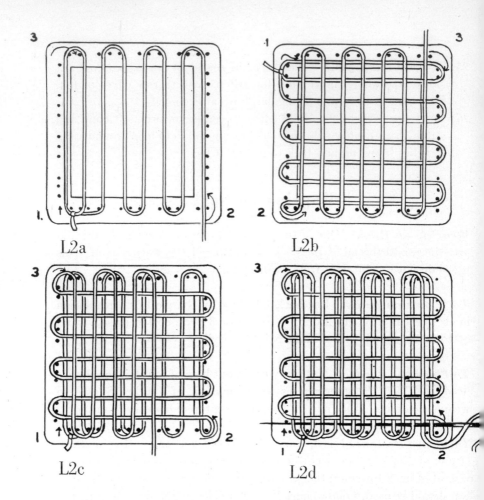

L2a

L2b

L2c

L2d

Weaving on a loom can be expensive or productive as your skill and perseverance allow. It is absorbing and requires time and patience to become familiar with its terms and the proper handling of the warp and woof threads to master its technique. All types of table and floor looms are available and the operation of each loom requires a special study. A simple hand-loom on which to learn to weave is the weave-it. It is a small wooden frame manufactured in three sizes, 2, 4 and 5-inch squares, with groups of small pegs on all four sides. A long steel needle is used in weaving. The simplest stitch made on this frame is most popular and makes of the finished square, a perfect fabric for cross stitching (L 2e).

To Make a Woven Square: Hold the frame with side marked with arrow No. 1 in front of you, the arrow pointing away from you. Holding end of yarn toward you at arrow, draw yarn between pins to far side of frame in direction indicated by arrow. Pass yarn to right around first two pins and return to side nearest you, drawing yarn out between second and third pins at right of the arrow. Tie securely with end of yarn close to pins. * Pass yarn to right around next two pins and draw to far side, bringing it out between first and second pins in group directly across. Pass yarn to right around two pins and back to near side, out between first and second pins in next group. Repeat from * until you have reached curved arrow No. 2 (L 2a).

Turn frame so that curved arrow No. 2 points directly away from you. Pass yarn around first two pins and go to far side, bringing yarn out between first and second pins in group directly across; * pass yarn to right around next two pins and back to near side between first and second pins in next group. Pass yarn to right around next two pins. Repeat from * until you reach curved arrow No. 3 (L 2b).

Turn frame again so that curved arrow No. 3 points toward you. Pass yarn through first and second pins to near side coming out between first and second pins. * Pass yarn to right around next two pins and go back to far side, bringing yarn out at open space; pass yarn to right around next two pins and back to near side coming out at open space. Pass yarn to right around next two pins. Repeat from * until filled (L 2c).

To Measure Correct Amount of Yarn Needed for Weaving: Wind yarn loosely 4½ times around frame on outside of pins and break yarn. Unwind yarn from outside of pins and thread needle. Starting at 2 between first and second pins, pass needle over outside loop, * under the next strand, over the next. Repeat from * across frame (L 2d) and draw yarn completely through. Go around two pins and come back over outside loop, under next, over next. Repeat across frame, bringing needle out at open space (L 2d). Repeat weaving in this manner across frame, ending with the last row of weaving *next to pins.* Turn corner and tie yarn into first loop around pins. Remove completed square from pins by pushing up from underneath (L 2e).

L3

Abbreviations
W . . . . weave
U . . . . under
O . . . . over

L2e

To Make Perfect Squares: Straighten out the square by pushing the yarn back against the pins on all sides before removing from frame.

To Sew the Squares Together: Match the corners and loops exactly. It is advisable to match the starting and ending knots and hold two squares together. Thread blunt-end needle with yarn and join loops with an overcast stitch (L 3) drawing the thread rather tightly. Conceal the ends by threading them back into the seam for an inch. Sew squares into strips, then sew strips together to form the desired article. Press flat on both sides with a damp cloth and moderate iron.

Variations may be made in the squares by using different weights of yarns; winding with one color and weaving with another; winding with two strands of a lightweight yarn and weaving with a double strand etc., also by weaving in an uneven manner to form fancy effects. The small and medium frames are used for fine work as afghans, wearing apparel, bags, toys etc. while the large frame is usually used for rugs.

Diagonal Weave (L 4):
Row 1—Weave across frame
Row 2—U3; W7; U3; W7; U3; W8
Row 3—W6; U3; W7; U3; W7; U3; W2

380

Row 4—W4; U3; W7; U3; W7; U3; W4
Row 5—W2; U3; W7; U3; W7; U3; W6
Row 6—W8; U3; W7; U3; W7; U3
Row 7—same as row 6
Row 8—same as row 5
Row 9—same as row 4
Row 10—same as row 3
Row 11—same as row 2
Row 12—same as row 2
Row 13—same as row 3
Row 14—same as row 4
Row 15—same as row 5
Row 16—weave across frame.

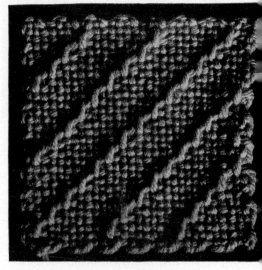

L4

Hour Glass (L 5):
Row 1—Weave across frame.
Row 2—W2; (U3, O1) 6 times; U3; W2
Row 3—W4; (U3, O1) 5 times; U3; W4
Row 4—W6; (U3, O1) 4 times; U3; W6
Row 5—W8; (U3, O1) 3 times; U3; W8
Row 6—W10; (U3, O1) twice; U3; W10
Row 7—W12; U3; O1; U3; W12
Row 8—W14; U3; W14
Row 9—same as row 8
Row 10—same as row 7
Row 11—same as row 6
Row 12—same as row 5
Row 13—same as row 4
Row 14—same as row 3
Row 15—same as row 2
Row 16—same as row 1

L5

L6

Zig Zag (L 6):

Row 1—Weave plain across frame

Row 2—W2; (U3, O1) 6 times; U3; W2

Row 3—W4; (U3, O1) 5 times; U3; W4

Row 4—W6; (U3, O1) 4 times; U3; W6

Row 5—W8; (U3, O1) 3 times; U3; W8

Row 6—W10; (U3, O1) twice; U3; W10

Row 7—W12; U3; O1; U3; W12.   *Row 8*—W14; U3; W14

Row 9—Weave across frame

Row 10—W2; U3; W21; U3; W2

Row 11—U3; O1; U3; W17; U3; O1; U3

Row 12—W2; U3; O1; U3; W13; U3; O1; U3; W2

Row 13—(U3, O1) twice; U3; W9; (U3, O1) twice; U3

Row 14—W2; (U3, O1) twice; U3; W5; (U3, O1) twice; U3; W2

Row 15—(U3, O1) 7 times; U3.   *Row 16*—Weave across frame.

Weaving

Before beginning to weave it is necessary to familiarize oneself with the names of the various parts of a loom; the process of preparing the loom for weaving; and its own lexicon. The following glossary lists a few of the terms:

Back Beam or Slabstock. . . .the beam at the back of the loom which corresponds to the front or breast beam.

Breast Beam. . . .the front beam over which the cloth passes on its way to the cloth beam.

Cloth Beam....the roll in the front of the loom on which the finished cloth is wound.

Warp Beam....the roll at the back of the loom on which the warp is wound.

Beater....the frame that holds the reed and which is used to beat the weft or cross thread.

Bobbin....the spool or tube on which the weft thread is wound.

Dent....the space between the vertical bars of the reed through which the warp is sleyed or drawn.

Reed....the part of the beater which holds the threads an equal distance apart and determines the fineness or coarseness of the cloth.

Reed Hook....a hook to draw the threads through the dents in the reed.

Frame....a metal or wooden frame on which the heddles are placed.

Harness....the frame on which the heddles are hung. Looms are generally classified by the number of harnesses they have.

Heddles....the strings, flat steel, or wires hung in the harness to hold the warp threads in place to make a shed.

Heddle Hook....the hook used to draw the warp threads through the eye or opening in the middle of the heddle.

Lams....the horizontal bars or levers extending between the harnesses and treadles, to which they are attached by cords or chains. Lams permit the harnesses to be pulled directly down from the center although the pedal to which the lams are attached may be far to the right or left of the center.

Levers....the bars on table looms which pull up the harnesses to make the shed.

Shed....the opening in the warp threads between which the shuttle with the weft thread is passed.

Shuttle....an implement on which the weft thread is wound, and which carries the weft thread back and forth through the shed. There are four kinds of shuttles.

Stick or Poke Shuttle....a flat stick on which weft or woof threads are wound.

Blanket Shuttle....a wide shuttle on which heavy weft threads are wound.

Boat or Throw Shuttle....a boat-shaped shuttle which has a bobbin.

Fly Shuttle....similar to a boat-shuttle that is worked by pulling a cord. It is usually automatic when used commercially.

Raddle or Spreader....a device for spreading the warp threads evenly as they are wound onto the beam. It is used when the loom is warped from the back to the front.

Treadles....the pedals at the bottom of the loom, operated by foot, which raise or lower the harnesses to make a shed.

Warp....the threads running lengthwise on the loom.

Weft, Woof or Filling....the thread running crosswise on the loom and which is interwoven with the warp to make the cloth.

Warp End....the term used for the warp thread when counting the number needed to make the warp.

Binder....the weft thread used to hold a pattern weft thread in place.

Cross....the crossing in the threads of either or both ends of the warp. The cross holds the warp threads in place and prevents tangling.

Beaming....the process of putting the warp on the beam.

Warping....the process of putting the warp thread onto the warp beam of the loom.

Threading or Entering....the process of bringing the warp threads through the reed and the heddles.

Sleying or Reeding....the process of drawing the warp threads through the dents in the reed.

Dressing....the complete process of sleying, entering and beaming to prepare the loom for weaving.

Battening....the process of beating the weft threads together.

Tension....the stretch or tautness of the threads during the process of weaving.

Draft....directions for weaving, usually shown on graph paper to indicate the correct threading through the heddles.

Heading....the term applied to the beginning and ending of the finished cloth.

Selvedge....the sides of the finished cloth.

Tabby....a plain weave.

Web....the finished woven fabric.

Repeat....term applied to a unit of the pattern, either in the warp or weft, which is repeated as many times as is necessary to complete the whole design.

Tie-Up....applies only to looms that have lams attached, therefore it never applies to a hand loom.

In pattern work, a tabby thread should follow a pattern thread, particularly if many warp threads have been skipped.

Always read drafts from right to left.

When commencing a pattern in two-harness weaving, always make certain that the last thread on the right side of the loom is *up*. If it is not in this position, cut a strand of weft-thread and bring shuttle from left side of loom. This will place the last thread in an up-position for the pattern-row.

Please note that wherever possible the same tie-up chart has been used to simplify the reading of the drafts.

Preparatory Steps: Before weaving can begin, some preparatory steps, beginning with the preparation of the warp and continuing through the winding of the shuttles, must be taken. The following plan is advisable:

1. Preparation of the warp, or determining the number of warp threads needed to weave a web or piece of material of a desired width and length.
2. Threading and sleying, or threading the warp ends through the heddles and threading the draft.
3. Tying the warp ends; or the tying of the warp ends onto the cloth beam rod.
4. Warping the beam or winding the warp onto the cloth beam.
5. Preparing the shuttles or filling the shuttles.
6. Testing the loom or trying the treadle of a foot loom and the lever of a hand loom. It is important that the weaver remember that the action of the foot-power loom is directly opposite to that of the hand-operated loom.
7. Weaving: The method of weaving varies with the individual weaver and is judged by the evenness of the selvedges and the uniformity of the beating.

Never weave a knot into a fabric. When a weft thread gives out, splice it with the new strand. When adding a new color or a new type of weft thread, follow a similar procedure. With heavy thread, separate it into several strands and splice so that a lump does not show. With two strands, bring one strand to the surface of the cloth about one inch from the selvedge, wrap the second strand around the end warp and put back into the same shed, overlapping the cut strand by about two or three warp threads.

8. Finishing ends of web and removal from loom *or* preparing and hemstitching (C 65) the ends of web before removing from loom. If a knotted fringe is desired, prepare, tie and trim the fringe (Chapter 14).

Weaving a unit of a pattern is that part which covers all the changes and forms in itself a complete design. For example, see charts for swatches of four-harness weaving. To thread a web the desired width the unit is repeated the number of times required to thread the loom the desired number of inches. In plain two-harness weaving, the complete unit consists of two threads only.

Two Harness Weaving

To Weave a Plain Web (L 7a, b, c): First place the warp threads on a loom and thread them through the reed and then the heddles. Tighten them and through the manipulation of the harnesses, a space is opened. This space is known as a shed. A shuttle carrying the woof or weft thread passes through this shed; the harnesses are changed and the thread is beaten back into position. Repeat this procedure until the desired piece of cloth is made.

Plain Weave (L 7b and c): If the same size threads are used for warp and weft, and the beating is correctly and evenly done, the web woven is called a 50/50 tabby weave. In a tabby weave there are the same number of warp and weft threads to the square inch. This plain weave is the basis of much pattern weaving and its technique should be thoroughly understood before attempting to create other patterns. A beginner should study intently the processes that occur when the harnesses are raised and lowered in alternating sequence; and when the shuttle which carries the weft thread is passed back and forth through the shed.

To Weave a Simple Weave on a Two-Harness Loom (L 7a): Thread all heddles on harness 1 with dark thread, and all heddles on harness 2 with light thread.

To Weave or Treadle on a Hand Loom: Operate lever 1 which lifts all the dark warp threads that have been threaded through the heddles on harness 1. The dark weft thread passes through the shed and lies on top and covers the light warp threads. Then operate lever 2 which lifts all the light warp threads that have been threaded through the heddles on harness 2. This time, the light weft thread passes through the shed, lies on top of and covers the dark warp threads. Repeat this procedure until the desired piece of cloth is woven.

To Weave or Treadle on a Foot Loom: Depress treadle 1 which draws down all the dark threads that have been threaded through the heddles on harness 1. The dark weft thread passes through the shed and lies on top of the dark warp threads. Then depress treadle 2 which lowers all the light threads that have been threaded through the heddles on harness 2. This time, the light weft thread passes through the shed and lies on top of the light warp thread. Repeat this procedure until the desired piece of cloth is woven.

Note that the hand loom and foot loom are worked in reverse. In hand loom treadling, the harnesses are raised by the action of the levers or hand treadles, while in foot-loom treadling, the harnesses are lowered by the action of the pedals or foot treadles. A variety of interesting patterns can be made on the two harness loom by merely applying the technique of tabby weaving.

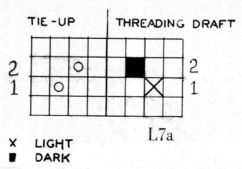

L7a

X   LIGHT
■   DARK

Leno or Imitation Gauze Weave (L 8a, b, c, d, e): The tie-up and threading is the same as for plain weaving (L 8a). Leno weave resembles hemstitching. It is easy to twist the warp threads if a double-hooked afghan needle is used to guide shuttle through twisted strands (L 8b).

To Twist a Single Set of Warp Threads (L 8c): With last thread up, start at right-hand selvedge, and, * with a double-hooked afghan needle, bring second warp thread up, over and under first warp thread—twisting the threads as shown in L 8c. Repeat from * across loom. If a larger loom is used, repeat this twisting of threads across a small section of the loom, doing a section at a time. With same color thread, or a contrasting thread (L 8b), push shuttle through twisted threads as you pull out the afghan needle. This same procedure is followed for the twisting of two threads (L 8d), and for three threads (L 8e).

Four-Harness Weaving: The interested weaver, who has mastered the two-harness loom and wishes to advance from the simple types to the more intricate patterns, attempts the four-harness loom. The four-harness loom will do all that is done by the two-harness loom, plus twills, overshot, summer and winter weaves and many other techniques. Of all techniques made on a 4-harness loom, the twill is the most popular.

L7b   L7c

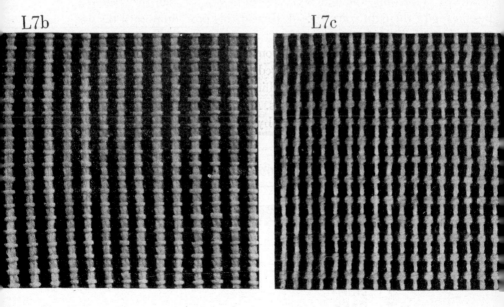

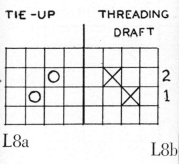

L8a

L8b

Twill (L 9a, b, c, d): Basically a 50/50 fabric, in which there are an equal number of weft and warp threads to the square inch. The twill threadings and variations on these threadings are countless. The slightest variation in threading or treadling produces a different result. There are plain weaves (L 9b), plain right (L 9c) and plain left twills, single, double and triple-point twills, zig-zag twills, herringbone twills (L 9d), and many more. Unlike the plain weaves woven on 1–3, 2–4 opposites, the twills are woven with an overlapping of one or more binder threads from the first

L8c

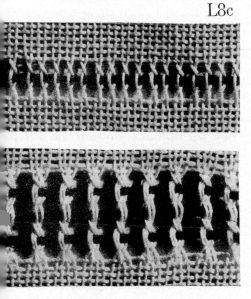

L8e

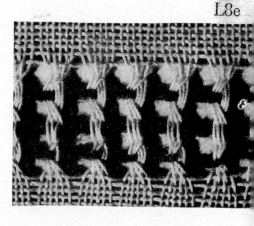

L8d

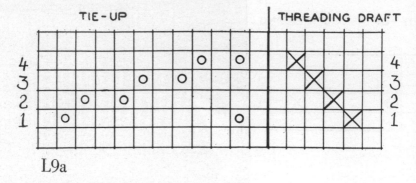

TIE-UP THREADING DRAFT

L9a

shot into the second, from the second into the third and so on. No matter how many harnesses are used, the same theory of an overlapping or binder thread holds true. However, each additional harness adds one more change and allows greater variation in pattern. Aside from the tabby-weave threading of 1–3, 2–4, there are four possible treadling combinations: 1–2, 2–3, 3–4 and 4–1.

To Weave a Simple Four Harness Twill on a Foot Loom: Pass the first shot *over* all warp threads threaded on harnesses 1–2 and *under* all on 3–4. Pass the second shot *over* all warp threads threaded on harnesses 2–3 and *under* all on 1–4. Pass the third shot *over* all warp threads threaded on harnesses 3–4 and *under* all on 1–2. Pass the fourth shot *over* all warp threads threaded on harnesses 4–1 and *under* all on 2–3. As explained above, the reverse would be true on a hand-loom. The continuation of the 1–2, 2–3, 3–4, 4–1 sequence produces a left-hand twill. If the sequence is reversed to 4–1, 3–4, 2–3, 1–2, a right-hand twill is produced. A sequence of 1–2, 2–3, 3–4, 4–1, 3–4, 2–3 will produce a zig-zag twill.

Overshot Weaving: In this weaving, it is advisable to have a weave which is the same number of threads per inch in both warp and weft; and the tabby and warp threads should be the same size. The fundamental motifs or design-units of any overshot pattern are called Rose, Star, Table, Cross, and Diamond. Patterns are seldom drafted on any single motif, and are usually combinations of two or more motifs. An understanding of the basic composition of each motif is necessary.

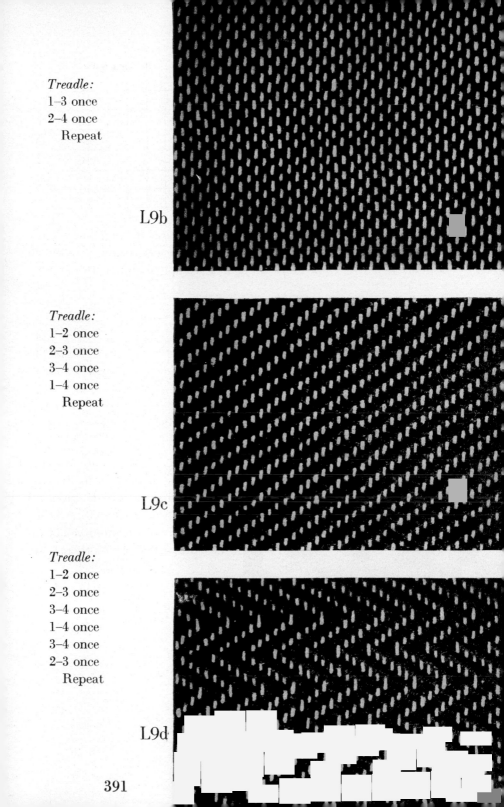

Treadle:
1–3 once
2–4 once
　Repeat

L9b

Treadle:
1–2 once
2–3 once
3–4 once
1–4 once
　Repeat

L9c

Treadle:
1–2 once
2–3 once
3–4 once
1–4 once
3–4 once
2–3 once
　Repeat

L9d

391

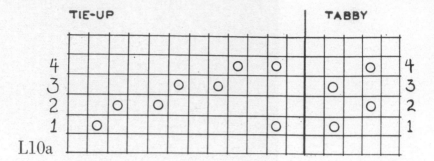

L10a

To Weave the Rose (10a, b, c): 1. Thread A to B the required number of times for width desired. 2. Thread B to C once only on last repeat to balance pattern. 3. Thread A to C for one complete unit (L 10b).

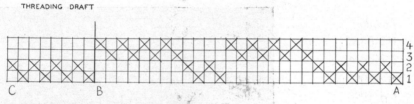

THREADING DRAFT

C   B   A

L10c

L10b

L10d

Star (L 10a, b, d): Thread and tie-up in same manner as for the Rose unit. The two pattern designs are directly opposite in composition, therefore, a reverse of either would produce the pattern of the other (L10d).

Rose and Star (L 10a, b, c, d):
Treadle:
1–2 seven times
3–4 seven times
1–2 three times
3–4 seven times
    Repeat

392

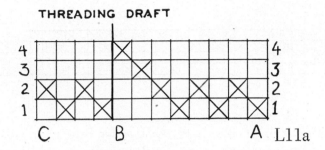

C   B   A   L11a

Table (L 11a, b, c): The tie-up (L 10a) is the same as for Rose unit, the threading (L 11a) is similar to the Rose and the Star described above, except there is greater variation in the arrangement of the threads. Thread same as for the Rose unit. Repeat the treadling for the larger units until the design has been squared. Always weave the Table unit square when it is part of a complete design.

L11b

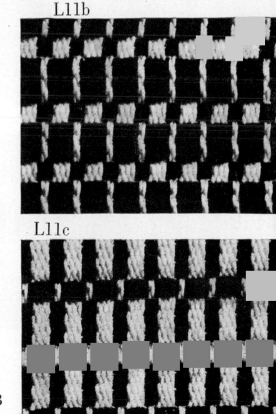

Treadle:
3–4 five times
1–2 three times
Repeat

L11c

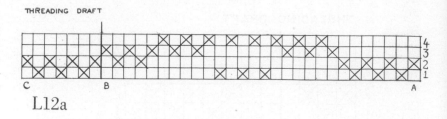

L12a

Cross: The tie-up (L 10a) is the same as for Rose unit. This design (L 12a) is on diagonals and undertones. It is woven on a twill and is used to connect larger pattern units. Thread in same manner as Rose unit.

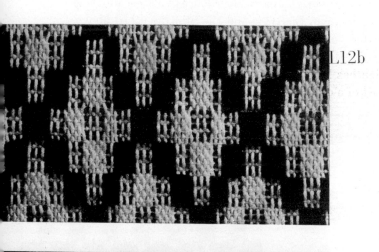

L12b

L12c

Treadle:
3–4 five times
1–4 five times
1–2 five times
2–3 five times
1–2 five times
1–4 five times
Repeat

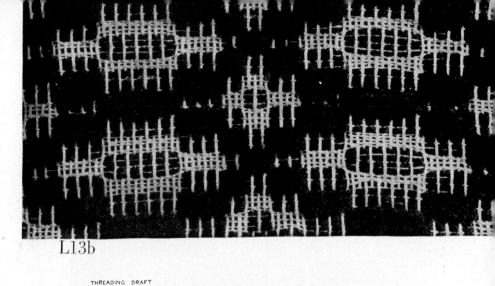

L13b

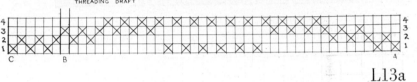

THREADING DRAFT

L13a

Diamond: (L 13a, b, c). The tie-up and threading is the same as for the Cross.

Treadle:

2–3 four times
1–2 four times
1–4 four times
3–4 four times
1–4 four times
1–2 four times

Repeat

L13c

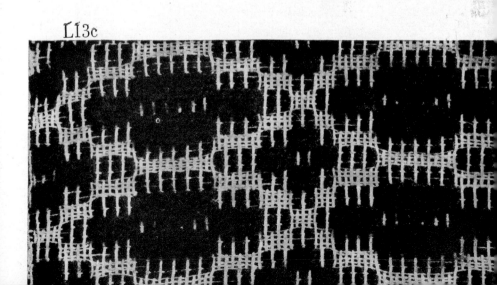

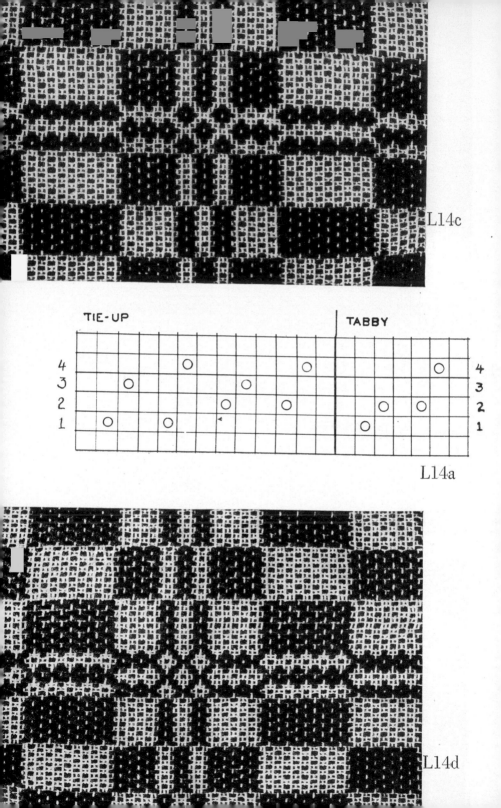

L14c

TABBY

4
3
2
1

4
3
2
1

L14a

L14d

Summer and Winter Weaves: One side of the web is dark and the other side light. The weave is firm, attractive and mostly geometric. In this weave there are no long skips of the weft thread. Its technique is not difficult, though the tie-up, as in double weaving, becomes more complex with each additional set of harnesses, as many treadles are required for the tie-up. Two harnesses are required to form each block of pattern and two are reserved for the binder or tabby threads.

Simple Summer and Winter Weave (L 14a, b, c, d): The threading draft is given in the condensed form as the shortened form is preferable and a time-saver. To avoid confusion, keep in mind that in this form each square represents four threads.

Treadle:

$\left.\begin{array}{l} 2\text{-}3 \\ 2\text{-}4 \end{array}\right\}$ eight times

$\left.\begin{array}{l} 1\text{-}3 \\ 1\text{-}4 \end{array}\right\}$ eight times

$\left.\begin{array}{l} 2\text{-}3 \\ 2\text{-}4 \end{array}\right\}$ eight times

1–2 once

2–3 once

3–4 once

1–4 once

3 4 once

2–3 once

1–2 once

    Repeat

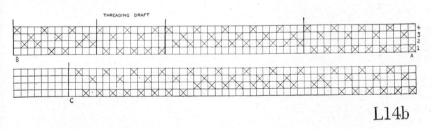

THREADING DRAFT

L14b

As is readily understood, more changes in pattern design are possible as more harnesses are added. The three, five, six and eight harness looms are used by the more experienced weaver, especially by one who has mastered the other two looms.

CHAPTER 13

SEWING FOR THE HOME

SEWING FOR THE HOME

→≫ EVERY woman desires to give expression to her own personality, to give utterance to innate and inimitable ideas, often with a small out-lay of money. Did you ever try to decorate a room with just "left-overs"? It's fun and a real test of your creative ability.

Take the lamp that needs a new shade—there are always hems of some old curtain that have not been exposed to the strong rays of the sun—the hems would make lovely ruffles for that wire frame.

Why discard that out-dated lace bedspread or evening dress when it can be cut to advantage for curtains, or sections of it combined with fabric for pillows, a dressing table skirt, or even a table cloth?

If you make your own clothes, what do you do with the scraps? They make attractive appliqué bedspreads or slipcovers—and they need not be of the ordinary patchwork variety. Cut according to the design of the print of the fabric, or in strips and appliqué the pieces onto muslin, tinted or untinted.

The windows of your room are too high and narrow—and you have an old piece of needlepoint for the piano bench you no longer use. That needlepoint piece would make a delightful valance—and the valance will add breadth to the window.

There is no end to what one can do with a few odd pieces of material and a few leisure moments.

*Instructions for Slipcovers (**Color Plate M, pg 417**).*

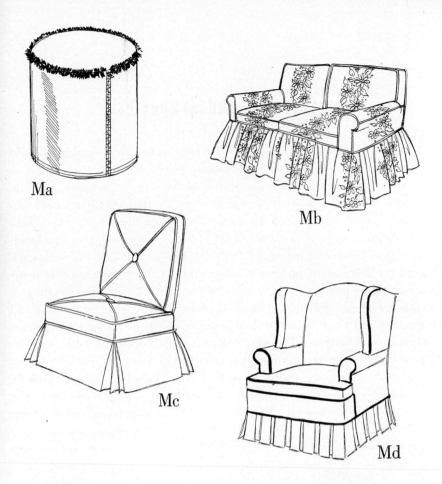

Ma

Mb

Mc

Md

Design your own from color plate M

With a bit of ingenuity, you can design from slipcovers.

1. Apply principle for making slipcovers to hassock (Ma).
2. Apply principle for making a slipcover with a ruffle (Chapter 1) for love seat (Mb).
3. Use slipcover with triple pleat for chair (Mc).
4. Make slipcover with box pleats (A 59) for wing chair (Md).
5. Use stripes of uneven widths for crocheted (Chapter 7) or knit (Chapter 6) afghan.

Curtains and draperies

Measurements for Curtains and Draperies: First consideration in planning curtains is to know the actual measurements of the window to be decorated (M 1). Measure width of window from jamb to jamb, length from fixtures to floor and the length from fixtures to sill. To length always add desired allowance for casing, heading, turning hem and shrinkage. *For glass curtains,* add 1½ to 2 inches for casing and heading; ¼ to ½ inch for turning; 1 to 2½ inches for hem and 1 inch for each yard for shrinkage if material is not preshrunk. In sheer fabrics the hems are made double, therefore, allow 4 inches for a 2-inch hem, heading or casing. *For draperies,* add at least 1 inch for rod; 2 inches for heading and top hem and 4 to 6 inches for floor hem; as well as 1 inch for each yard for shrinkage of material. The width allowance for curtain and draperies depends upon the type of fabric. It is usually 1½ times the width for heavy fabrics and twice the width for sheer fabrics. Glass curtains are usually sill length or floor length but they should never drape on the floor even though the corresponding draperies may be draped from 6 to 12 inches on the floor. Tie-backs may or may not be used. *Ruffles for glass curtains* vary in width from 3 to 6 inches. *Valances,* as you know, are used for decoration and to conceal the fixtures on which curtains are hung. They may be plain or draped and there is no definite ruling as to how deep valances should be. However, it is estimated that the deepest portion of a shaped valance should never be more than ⅙ the length of the curtain.

Cutting and Lining: If curtains and draperies are to hang well, cut all lengths on a drawn crosswise thread. Always draw a crosswise (woof) thread and cut along this line. Remove all selvedges, as selvedges have a tendency to draw, especially after hanging. Use a tape measure for measuring curtain and drapery lengths. Often, when a yardstick is used the fabric is stretched.

Lay the tape measure on the fabric in line with the edge that is being measured. Pull the material gently but effectively, stretching it diagonally from corner to corner; then alternate the pulling. Cut on a large, smooth surface. When one curtain or drapery length has been cut, lay this on a smooth surface or floor; with right sides facing, lay next piece over the first, matching the pattern and cut on the thread of the fabric. If piecing is necessary, be sure to conceal at the tieback line, behind the heading, or under a valance or tuck; or wherever piecing can become a decorative note.

It is not necessary to line draperies but it is advisable to protect the fabric and to add to the draping quality and elegance of the drapery itself. Cut the lining material four or five inches narrower and one to two inches shorter than the drapery fabric, depending on the size of the drapery hem. Stitch a two-inch hem with a narrow turn-under in the bottom of the lining piece. Stitch a bottom hem in the drapery fabric. With the drapery piece wrong side up, press a 1½-inch hem down either side. Use a gauge and do not pin. If you are planning to use a pinch-pleated heading with buckram, the buckram goes in now.

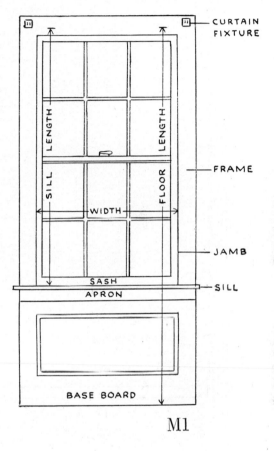

M1

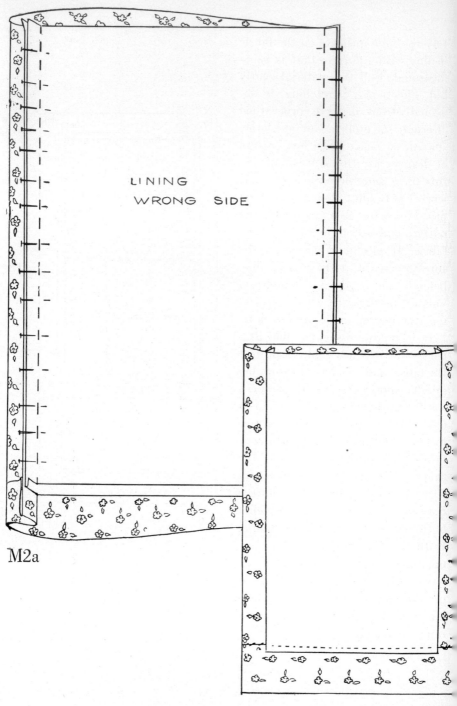

LINING

WRONG SIDE

M2a

M2b

With pressed side-hems opened out, lay the drapery piece right side up on a flat surface. With right sides together, lay the lining piece on top of the drapery piece. Arrange lining along one side of drapery so that side and top edges meet exactly. With pins at right angles, pin side edges together (M 2a). Now, slide lining over and pin opposite side edge. The drapery piece, being wider, will bag when pinned to lining this way. Stitch both side edges where pinned, about ½ inch from edge. Turn drapery and lining right side out and smooth out, pressing again the previously pressed-in side hems (M 2b). Turn the drapery towards the lining side so that the drapery and lining lie flat. If a buckram heading has been used, turn the lining in one inch and stitch to drapery material. If a pleating tape or "drawstring-buckram" is being used, turn in both drapery and lining one inch and stitch tape according to the instructions that come with it. Stitch bottom hem as shown in M 2b or M 2c.

To Line a Heading: Cut a strip of buckram ½ inch shorter than the finished width of the drapery; lay this strip one inch from top and between the hem-folds on each side. Fold the one inch down over buckram. Pin; baste to the buckram, not through to the right side of the drapery, and stitch.

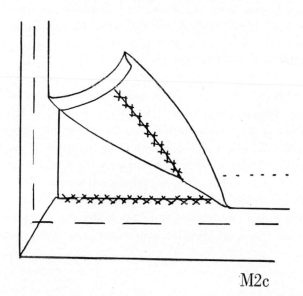

M2c

To Hem Unlined Draperies: Press side hems. Place stiffening one inch from top and between the hem-folds on each side. Turn edge over stiffening about one inch and stitch along this edge and along opposite edge of stiffening. Turn hems and press (M 3). If pleating tape or "drawstring buckram" is used, follow the instructions that come with it.

Placing Weights: Weights should be placed in the lower edge of all draperies. First turn hem and crease. Baste yardage weights along this line, using long diagonal basting stitches. In glass curtains, small yardage weights are placed back of the two thicknesses and held in place by a long running stitch through the fold of the hem (M 4).

Pleats: In curtains and draperies pleats are one of the means of controlling the fulness which is to hang in graceful folds. They are made in uneven groups depending upon the extra fulness allowed for in the cutting. To make the pleats, determine how much space on the rod the curtain is to cover. The width of the curtain minus the covered space including the turn of the rod, gives the amount to be taken up in pleats. Usually the first pleat is placed at the turn of the rod and the second pleat, usually 1½ to 3 inches from center edge. Determine on the type and the group arrangement of the pleats. Using pins, measure the exact position and width of pleats, fold, and following the grain of the material, stitch down to one inch below stiffened heading. For detail of pleats, shirring, ruffles, etc., see Chapter 1.

Valances: These tend to lower the ceiling, therefore it is advisable to cut a pattern of heavy paper or muslin the exact length of the board on which the valance is to be mounted plus the return allowance on each side. Try various widths to decide which gives the window and room the best appearance. Valances should be made over a stiff foundation as buckram, lined and interlined. Cut stiffening the exact size of finished valance; cut interlining and fabric one inch larger on all sides; then cut lining ¼ inch larger on all sides than the stiffening. Pin interlining to fabric, allowing 1 inch on all sides; stitch and press. Place stiffening on

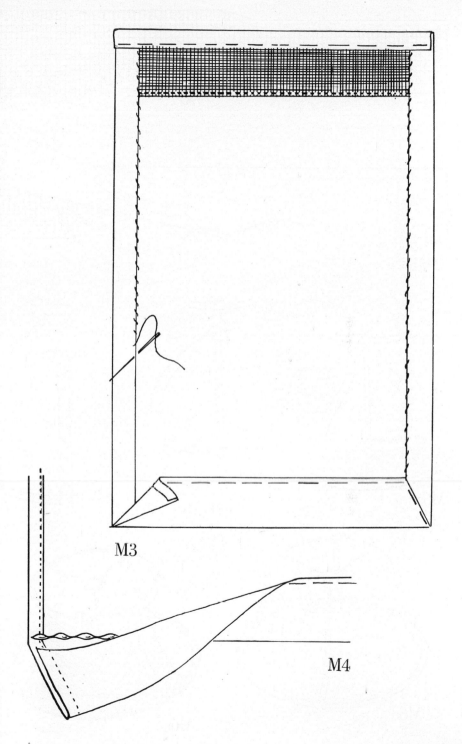

M3

M4

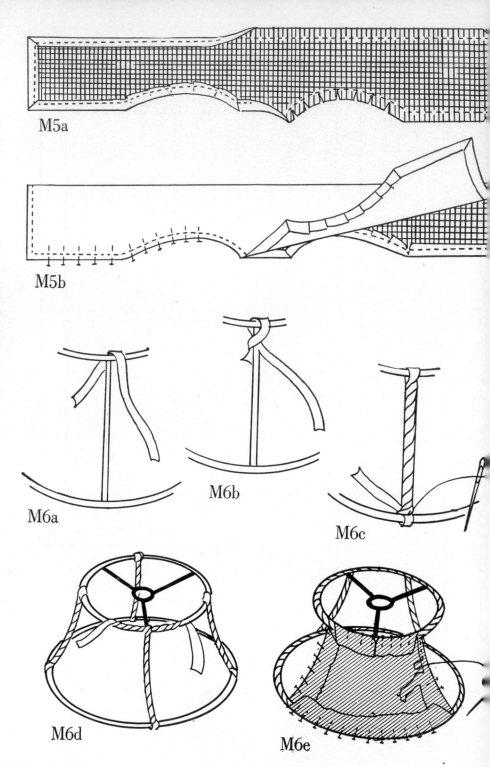

M5a

M5b

M6a

M6b

M6c

M6d

M6e

interlining and fold back edge over stiffening. Clip notched edges on outside curves and edges at inside curves (M 5a). Catch edges to stiffening. Fold under edges of lining and baste. Pin to back of valance and stitch together (M 5b). For drape, cascade and circular valances, it is best to experiment by trying different widths. The tie backs, of course, can be worked out in many interesting styles and should match the curtains themselves.

Lampshades

Lampshades: With a bit of ingenuity and a little material, attractive lampshades can be designed if the following rules are followed.

Method 1, Step 1: Tape all spokes with matching silk or rayon seam binding, or make your own tape by cutting material 2½ times the length of the spoke and ½ inch wide. Cover the upright spokes first. Lay tape over the upper rim (M 6a); hold end back of spoke, securing end as you wind. Always wind slantwise, overlapping half of tape (M 6b); tie over lower rim and stitch securely (M 6c). Never make a slip knot. Tape upper and lower rims in the same way, securing ends as you pass them (M 6d).

Step 2: First line half, quarter, or each section of shade from opposite spokes, depending upon the size and the shape of the shade itself. The fabric can be cut straight or on the true bias. But, be sure the *center* of each section is either straight or true bias. Shades, not of the usual cylindrical design, should be covered in sections to prevent the tendency of the material to stand away from the frame. With the material inside frame, work from the outside. Fasten material with pins at each spoke. Cut material to within 1½ inches beyond rims. Pull material as taut as possible, adjusting pins wherever necessary. Slash at center top crosspiece of frame. Start sewing; be sure to keep stitching on the outside of spokes and of upper and lower rims. Cut material close to stitching and frame (M 6e). For second section, lay edge of material along spoke of finished section wrong side up, and stitch along the stitching of first section, on inside of shade, covering the original stitching as you sew. Trim this seam close to stitching along spoke. Fold material over next

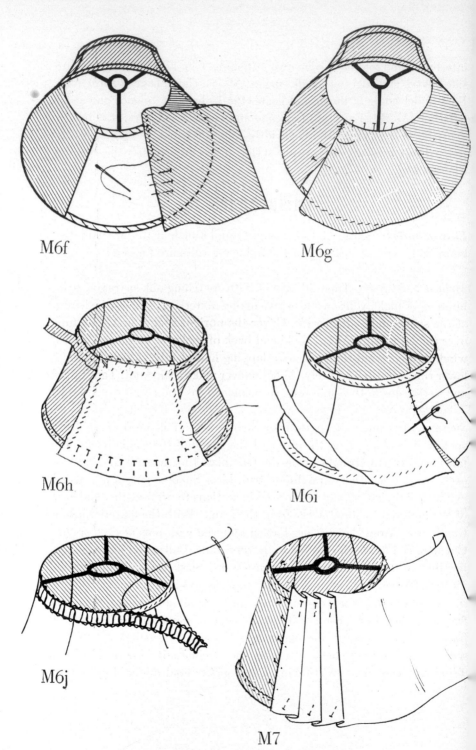

M6f

M6g

M6h

M6i

M6j

M7

section. Always pull material as taut as possible. Pin and continue in same manner as for first section. Remaining sections between first and last section are worked in same manner. For last section, stitch first edge along spoke same as second section (M 6f) and fold material over last section pinning along top and bottom rims; keep material taut. Turn under last edge allowing just enough extra to turn under and slip stitch to first spoke covered (M 6g). Slash sections at each of four corners, pull material under and over top and lower rims and stitch in usual manner.

Step 3: To cover, place material on true bias or straight over center of first section on outside of shade. Pin in place. Pull material taut, manipulating it while pinning over lining-stitching, and slashing wherever necessary. Sew down with very small, neat overcast stitches. Cut material close to stitching along spokes only (M 6h). Work in same manner for each remaining section as was done for lining (M 6i).

Step 4: Turn top and bottom edges of cover over previous stitching and stitch again in opposite directions so there is an even finish along the rims. After the final stitching, the superfluous material is cut away around top and bottom rims. In cutting away excess material, cut as close as possible without cutting into your stitches. Be certain that there are no threads or rough edges underneath or outside that will show through when lamp is lighted.

Step 5: You are now ready to apply the trimming. Use good taste in selecting types and colors to harmonize with the decorative scheme of your room. Pin the trimming over edges of shade, top and bottom, placing pins where pin-holes will not show. Now apply with a slip stitch, using a curved needle (M 6j). With each stitch, catch together only a few threads of cover, being careful that your stitches are concealed.

Pleated Lampshades:

Method 1a: Use only simple cylindrical frames and soft, flimsy materials. Material required is always $2\frac{1}{2}$ times the circumference of the bottom rim.

Step 1: Line in the same manner as described in first and second steps of Method 1.

Step 2: Pin pleats desired size across one half of the top rim. Pulling material as taut as possible and manipulating material to form graceful

M8

pleats at bottom to correspond with narrower pleats at top, pin each pleat as it forms itself (M 7). Form pleats for second half in same manner. Merely overlap first and last pleats to form seam. Do not stitch. Stitch along top and bottom rims and continue as explained in the fourth and fifth steps of Method 1.

Gathered Shade: Work in same manner, except edges are gathered instead of pleated (M 8).

Method 2: This method is less professional than the first and is used only for *small cylindrical wire frames and paper shades.*

Step 1: Tape wire frame as explained in the first step of Method 1.

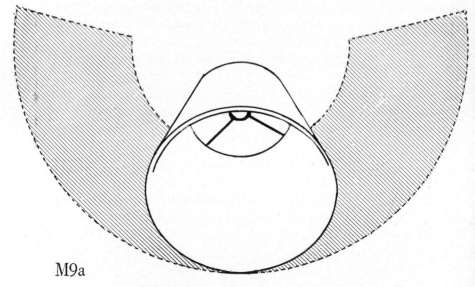

M9a

Step 2: Cut a pattern for frame by rolling frame on paper and marking the outline of the "complete roll" (M 9a). Cut material from this pattern, allowing ½-inch seams on all edges. Work from outside. Commence at center and pin material to top rim. Holding material as taut as possible and manipulating it, pin also to bottom rim. Slip stitch ends together, whip material to frame and cut off excess material. Cover the seam if desired, using either trimming or a bias-fold of the material itself. To make the bias-fold, cut a true bias band about an inch wide and a little longer than the side seam. Fold the outer edges to meet in center of fold, and fold again. Pin in place over the seam. Use a curved needle, holding it horizontal to rims, and slip stitch fold or trimming to material (M 9b). Be sure stitches do not show.

Step 3: To line shade, cut a lining piece in the same manner as for the cover itself. Place lining piece over shade on right side, slip stitch ends together, and whip to shade at bottom. Cut off excess material and turn to wrong side. Turn under raw edge at top and slip stitch to top rim. Trim with rope or braid as desired (M 9b).

Method 3: How to make a *pleated shade for a simple frame:*

Step 1: Cut a straight strip of material deep enough to cover shade and 2½ times the lower circumference of frame. Stitch to crinoline or mount on stiff drawing paper using wallpaper paste. Merely fold back ¼-inch hem at top and bottom, and press flat or bind top and bottom with tape or bias trim, stitching firmly. Lay on a flat surface and mark on wrong side at even intervals, ½ inch, 1 inch or 2 inches depending on the size of frame. Fold back and forth on a ruler on these markings, pressing a

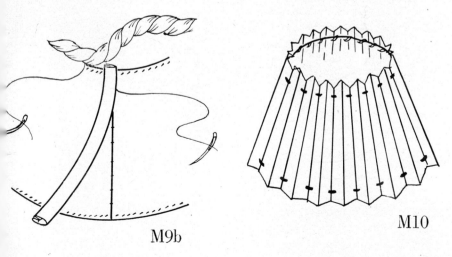

M9b

M10

413

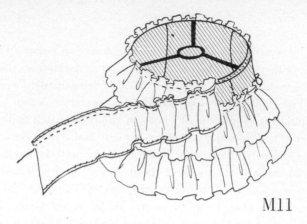

M11

few pleats at a time with a moderate iron. Thread a cord through all the pleats about 1 inch from the upper edge and a second cord, if desired, through all the pleats about ½ inch from lower edge. Unfold on cords, place over wire frame, overlap first and last pleat and paste together. Tack at even intervals around upper and lower rims, stitching over cord on inside of pleats. This same method can be used, substituting parchment or stiff paper specially treated for the making of lampshades (M 10).

Lampshade with Ruffles:
Step 1: Cover shade as explained in first four steps of Method 1.
Step 2: For width of ruffles, divide the depth of lampshade into number of ruffles desired and add 1⅔ inches for hems at top and bottom so that ruffles overlap slightly. Example: 7 inch shade with 3 ruffles would be

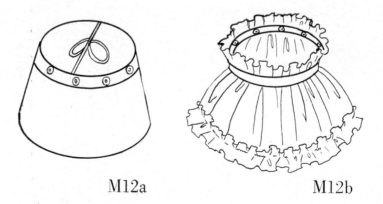

M12a   M12b

$2\frac{1}{3}$ inches, add $1\frac{2}{3}$ inches which makes ruffles 4 inches wide when cut. Or a 9 inch shade with four ruffles would be $2\frac{1}{4}$ inches, add $1\frac{2}{3}$ inches which makes ruffles $3\frac{11}{12}$ or 4 inches. Length of ruffles is to be twice the circumference of top rim or twice the circumference of the point to which it is to be sewed. Make a small rolled hem at top and bottom. Make a running stitch $\frac{1}{2}$ inch from top edge to gather. Gather to fit shade and catch-stitch (A 9) ruffle along the running stitches to top rim (M 11). Make a second ruffle in the same manner. Be sure to cut the material twice the circumference of the center of the frame. Catch-stitch to center of frame, just under the bottom edge of the first ruffle. Make a third ruffle in the same manner cutting the material twice the circumference of the lower rim. Catch-stitch just under the bottom edge of the second ruffle. Make as many more as desired, attaching in the same manner and on last one tack the bottom edge at irregular and widely scattered intervals to lower rim. For easy laundering snap-fasteners may be attached as shown in M 12a and b.

Bedspreads

Bedspreads are made in one large section which hangs straight on the sides and falls in easy folds at the corners or "fitted" on top with interesting side treatments, as ruffles, godets, flounces, etc. In the "fitted"

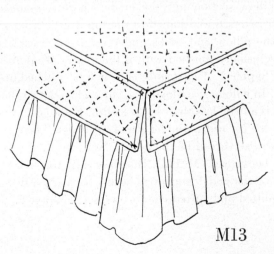

M13

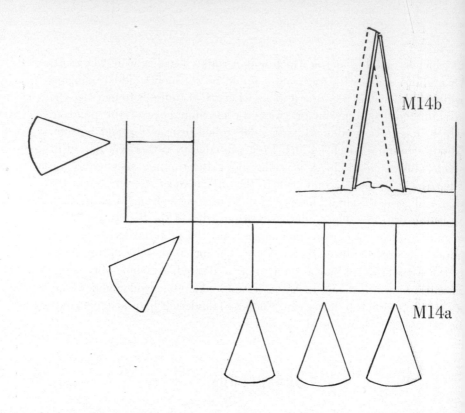

spread, the top is cut the same size as the top of the mattress and the
sides and end (bottom only), the length and depth desired, depending
upon the decorative note, whether pleated, ruffled, etc (M 13). In all
spreads, the pillow section may be made separate, made part of the
spread itself or reversed and joined to the top. In the last case, it comes
from behind the pillow and tucks under the front. In a fitted spread,
the corners are usually finished with a tailored or reenforced corner as
explained in Chapter 2. *A dust ruffle* can then be stitched about ½ inch
from the edge. In a flounce with godets, cut each godet so that the width
at the bottom is a little less than ½ its length. First, cut a wedge-shaped
pattern of the correct width and length of the godet. Then, cut the godet
with the lengthwise thread of the fabric. Now, insert the godets in the
slashes of the bedspread (M 14a). Reenforce the top line at the point.
Clip the ends of the godet and press seams back (M 14b). Then finish
flounce. For quilted and tufted comforters, see Chapter 5.

416

Slipcovers

If "form-fitting" and attractive slipcovers are to be made, great consideration must be given to the taking of measurements and the cutting of the pattern in muslin. Always take measurements from the floor. If a permanent cover or one with a flounce is desired, take the measurements from the floor, then deduct from the measurements of back, sides and front sections, the necessary allowance or the amount to be shortened. Always allow a generous amount for hems and seams. The following measurements should be taken (M 15a):

Back at center: From top A to floor B.

Length of Front-Back: From top A to seat C (add 2½ to 3 inches at C for "tuck-in").

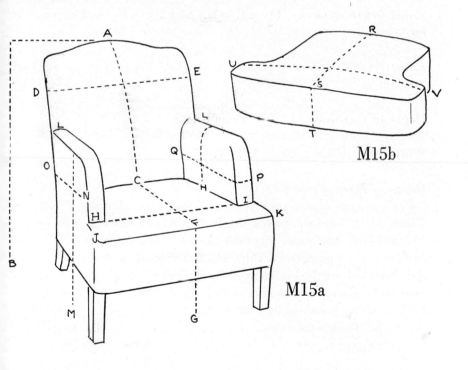

M15b

M15a

Width of Front-Back: At widest part from D to E.

Length of Seat: From C to F. (Add 3 to 4 inches at end for "tuck-in" and seam.)

Width of Seat: From H to I. (Add 2½ to 3 inches at each end for "tuck-in".)

Front: From F to G.

Width across Front: From J to K.

Length of Side (arm to floor): From L to M.

Width of Side (front to back): From N to O.

Front Depth of Arm: From L to H. (Add 2½ inches to 3 inches at H for "tuck-in".)

Front Width of Arm: From P to Q. (Add 2½ to 3 inches at Q for "tuck-in".)

Depth of Cushion (M 15b): From R to S.

Width of Cushion: From U to V.

Depth of Box: From S to T.

Block out on muslin each section of the chair, allowing a generous 1 inch on all sides for seams (M 16a). Always cut each piece on the lengthwise of the fabric. Pin each piece to the chair as it is cut. Cut cushion in same manner (M 16b). The box or band can be cut in 1 piece, if desired. This method is followed for all chairs. The wing chair requires more sections and an allowance must be made between the wing and the back, tapering from one inch at the top to 3 inches at the seat. Run a pencil line through the center of each section of the muslin. Place a pin

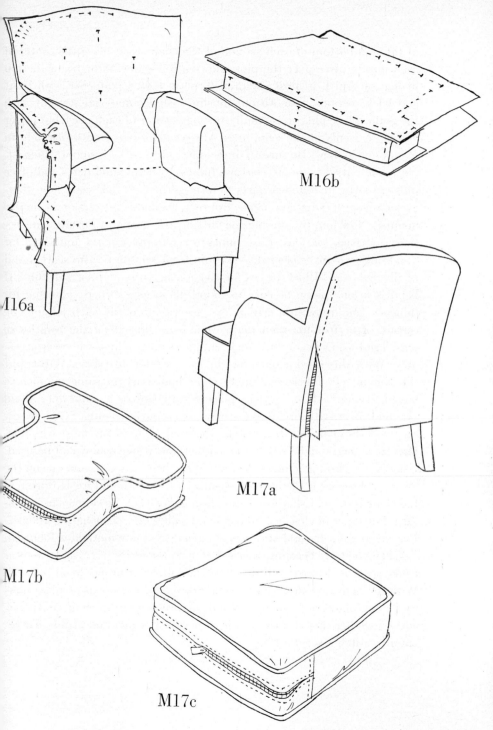

M16b

M16a

M17a

M17b

M17c

at top and bottom of each section of the chair, then place the center of each muslin piece over the pins allowing for seams. Now begin the pin fitting job which is most essential to perfect fit. Commence with front and back sections. Smooth out muslin, keeping material straight with the grain. Place pins occasionally through center of each piece but closer and more evenly at the seam lines. Always place pins lengthwise to form seam line (M 16a). Be sure to draw material to make a smooth snug fit. Next, pin outside side pieces. Ease fulness over rounded parts and place pins crosswise at rounded parts to form gathers. Notch seam-line wherever necessary. Next, pin inside arm sections and front section in similar manner. Now join by pinning the outside arm section to inside arm sections and back sections. Ease fulness over rounder parts and allow for "tuck-ins" wherever needed. Next join front section to arm section and finally join seat. Block pieces for cushion in same manner (M 16b). If band is in one piece, be sure to round all square corners, allowing for fulness. Examine with a critical eye, each section and each joining. Be certain of perfect fit; then mark each seam line along the lengthwise pins. Trim seams evenly to 1 inch, clipping and notching wherever necessary. With this muslin pattern, cut each section in fabric. With right side facing, pin fabric section to chair and mark in same manner as muslin sections. Baste sections placing seam line over seam line. Again examine cover critically, make any necessary adjustments. Stitch necessary gathers or darts, then stitch. The welt seam is the most common. However, the bound French, the corded and fringe seams can be used. Usually one closing on one side seam of the back (M 17a) and one on the lower back seam of the cushion is sufficient (M 17b and c). However, if the chair is an odd shape, several closings for each piece may be necessary. For types of closings, flounces and ruffles etc., see Chapter 1 and 2. For covers for sofas and all types of chairs, the same method is followed.

When you have become experienced in making slip covers and a welt or fringe seam is desired, you may use the following professional method. With the right side of the fabric facing the chair, pin seams of all sections to fit; cut, allowing ½ inch for seams and remove from chair. With raw edges together, insert welt or fringe between seams and stitch. To reenforce, stitch a second time.

Pillows: For pillow with mitred corner (M 18a and color plate C) cut 2 squares desired size—1 for front and 1 for back of pillow. Cut 8 border pieces desired width. Join 4 pieces mitering corners to form first square frame. Repeat for second frame. With right sides of borders facing, stitch outer edges of frames together. Turn inside out. With right sides of squares facing, insert border between squares and with raw edges

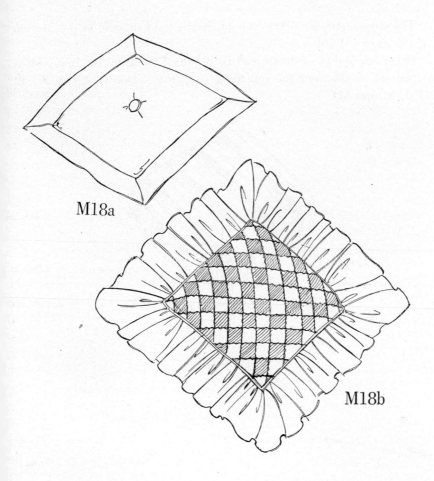

M18a

M18b

together, stitch along three sides plus one-quarter of the length of the fourth side. Leaving back square free, continue to stitch long the border and the remainder of the fourth side of front piece. Turn inside out, insert pillow form and slip stitch along opening. Place one button on each side in center of square and stitch through pillow to form tufted effect.

The ruffled pillow (M 18b) is made in the same manner as the pillow sham (Ek) in Chapter 5. The back may be made in one piece as explained for M 18a.

The striped pillow (M 18c) is made in the same manner as the cushion of the chair (M 16b).

Great originality of design can be obtained by using the many ideas explained in this and the foregoing chapters (Color Plates A, C, E, H, J, K, and M).

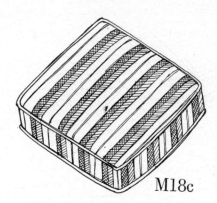

M18c

CHAPTER 14

MISCELLANEOUS

MISCELLANEOUS

⇢⟫ IN THIS chapter, you will find the necessary and the decorative, hints and suggestions that apply to all the phases of needlework explained in the foregoing chapters.

Needlework is a game with very simple rules, rules that may and may not be followed by the player when designing. For example, when the embroidered fruit wreath (Color Plate N) was made, the stitch gauge and the tension of the machine were known, yet continually changed, as was the direction of the running stitch, to give expression and animation to the fruit and leaves in the wreath.

In this chapter too, the duplicate stitch is described as a means of reenforcing worn or thin spots, and yet its primary purpose as explained in Chapter 6 is to decorate or embroider designs on knitwear. The slipper, too, describing textile painting is a combination of sewing, trapunto quilting and embroidery.

The designing of needlework apparently defies all rules, and yet is an application of the basic rules. The finished piece of needlework is always a presentation of the needlewoman's understanding of her subject, of her love and admiration of the hand arts.

Instructions for Machine Embroidered Picture (Color Plate N, pg 429)

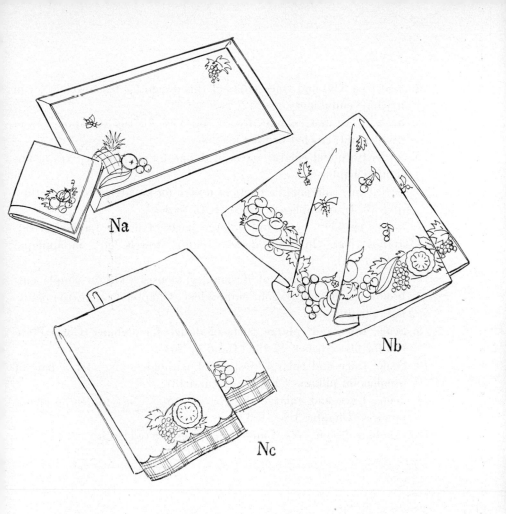

Na

Nb

Nc

Design your own from color plate N

With a bit of ingenuity, you can design from a machine embroidered picture.

1. Scale (pg 339) and trace parts of this design for place mat and napkin (Na) in machine embroidery.

2. Scale (pg 339) and trace parts of design for scarfs (Nb) in simple embroidery (Chapter 3), gold embroidery (Chapter 4) or textile painting (Chapter 14).

3. Scale (pg 339) and trace parts of this design for tea towels (Nc) in machine embroidery.
4. Scale, trace and enlarge design (pg 339) for rug (Chapter 11) in needlepoint, crochet or hooking (Nd).
5. Scale, trace and enlarge parts of design for potholders (Ne) in appliqué (Chapter 5).
6. Scale, trace and enlarge parts of design for sweaters (Nf) in outline stitch (C 4), or duplicate stitch (F 1a to d).
7. Scale (pg 339), trace and enlarge parts of design for bedspread, aprons (Ng), children's dresses, cloths, towels, etc., in appliqué (Chapter 5).
8. Scale and trace parts of design for blouses (Nh) in simple embroidery (Chapter 3), gold embroidery (Chapter 4) or textile painting (Chapter 14).
9. Scale, trace and enlarge parts of design for afghans (Color Plate G), for filet crochet (G 13, 14 and pg 264).
10. Scale, trace and enlarge designs of potholders (Ne) for a pair of needlepoint pillows (Chapters 10 and 13).
11. Scale, trace and enlarge designs of apron (Ng) for embroidered pictures (Chapter 3).
12. Combine designs (Ne, f and g) for embroidered cloth.

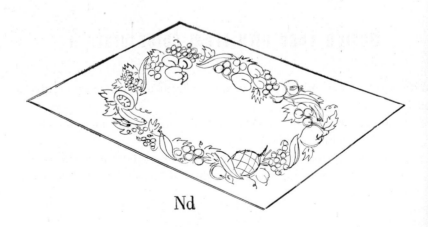

Nd

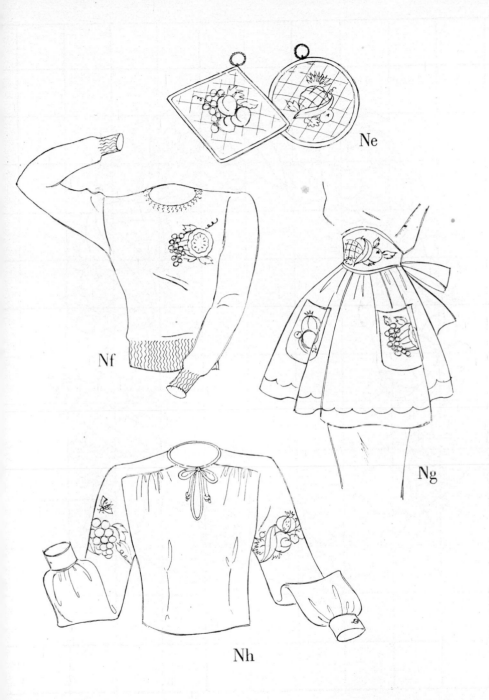

Ne

Nf

Ng

Nh

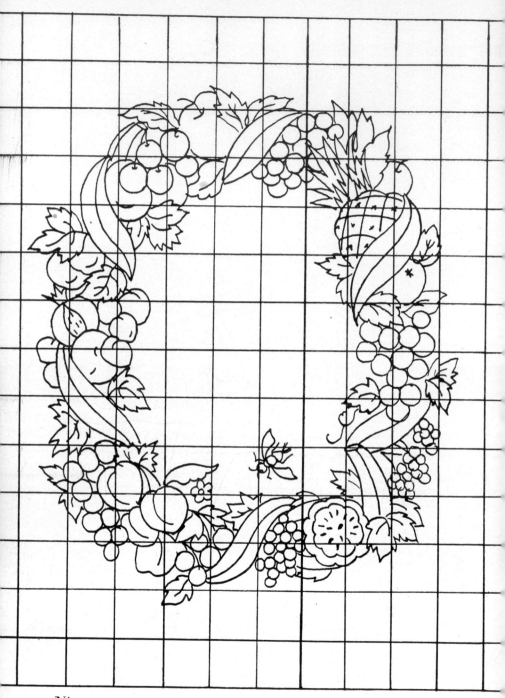

Ni

nstructions for machine-embroidered picture frame (color plate N)

Materials Required:

2 pieces of linen—1 black, 1 white, 14½″ x 18″
1 piece each of carbon and tracing paper
1 spool each of sewing cotton No. 70 in shades of green, purple, blue,
   pink, red, yellow, black, brown, orange, etc.
1 embroidery hoop and 1 white crayon pencil.

1. Scale to size design of wreath Ni—each square represents one inch.
   To scale design to size: On plain white or tracing paper measure off
   oblong 12″ x 14″. Divide this oblong into 168 1-inch squares (the
   same number shown in Ni) and copy, line for line, the part of the
   design shown in each square.
2. Press both pieces of linen, removing all creases.

Nj

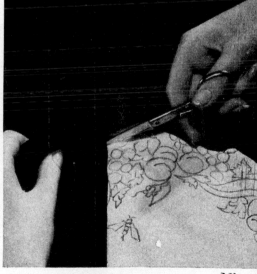

Nk

3. With right side up place white linen on smooth surface; lay carbon paper, face down on white linen. Lay tracing paper, face up on carbon paper, centering design. With sharply pointed pencil trace design (Nj).
4. With wrong side of black linen facing right side of white linen, baste together along outer edge of design so that part of the design is covered by black linen (Color Plate N and Nk).
5. With white pencil, draw concealed lines of design on black linen.
6. With the larger ring of the hoop facing the wrong side of the white linen, place small ring in position on right side of design (Nl).
7. Now work each part of design separately as shown in Nl.
8. Adjusting the machine to a fairly small stitch gauge and with tension suitable to the fabric with which you are working, outline a section to be embroidered in one color (Nl). Be sure to work from the inside edge to the outside edge of the design.
9. Following the contour of the particular part of the design which has been outlined, stitch in straight or curved lines (Nm). Practice is essential to produce a needlepainted machine embroidered design.

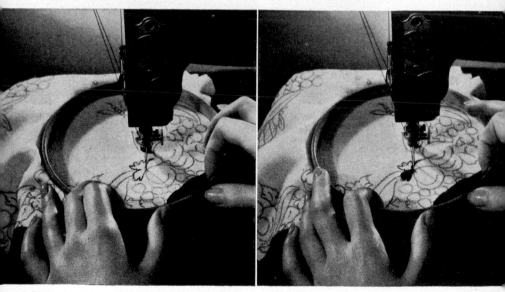

Nl.   Nm

10. When needle painting this design, the greater the variety of shades of one color used in each leaf or fruit, the more outstanding the finished piece will be.

Darning and tears

For successful mending, it is essential to use thread as nearly as possible the same color and weight of the warp or lengthwise thread of the fabric. Whenever possible, pull threads from the seams or hems and weave in and out following closely the design of the fabric. Closely woven fabrics require darning tightly, using as small a needle as the ravelling will allow and weave in and out very closely. If it is loosely woven, do not draw your threads too tightly.

Darning: Weaving on a small scale. It is essentially a practical application of the running stitches. Always darn on the right side of fabric and never make a knot as there is no strain on the fabric. Be sure to start and end the running stitches far enough beyond the hole so that the mend will not pull out. Never draw the thread tight. Leave a small loop at each turning to prevent puckers when the article is washed.

Straight Tear: Fit edges of tear together. Leave an end 6 inches or more and begin at least ¼ inch above tear. Sew back and forth across this space, across opening and continue below tear for at least ½ inch (N 1). To finish, catch thread through stitches of last row and clip. Thread needle with the thread left hanging at the beginning and catch it through stitches of the first row and clip.

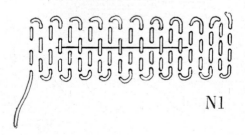

N1

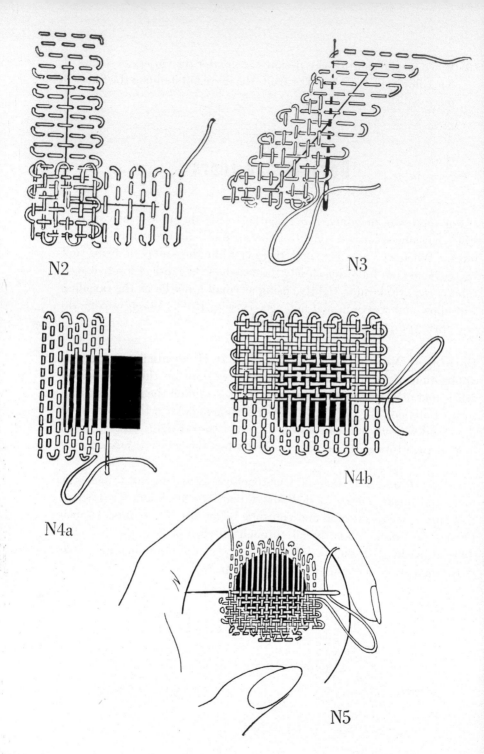

N2

N3

N4a

N4b

N5

Three-Cornered Tear: The stitches run at right angles to the opening. First, darn the lengthwise tear completely, then the crosswise tear, thus the stitches at the corners overlap and reenforce the tear at its weakest point (N 2).

Diagonal Tear: Darn in the direction of the tear; then darn at right angles to the first group of stitches to reenforce it (N 3).

Darning a Hole: First cut hole into a square or oblong and darn as shown in N 4a and b. Be sure to weave stitches in and out very closely over hole. For perfect darning it is advisable to follow the design of the fabric, picking up and laying down threads irregularly in accordance with the pattern of the material. In darning a hole in a stocking, be sure to work on bias to keep strain from rest of stocking (N 5).

Darning Knitwear: To reweave a thin spot, work in duplicate stitch (F 1a to d). To repair a "snag," pull out "drawn thread" and graft stitches together (F 20a and b).

Weaving a Small Hole in Knitwear: Do not cut away worn threads. Using a blunt-end needle, on wrong side secure yarn by weaving it in and out for several rows above hole, then weave thread across hole and for several loops or stitches on each side, thus replacing each broken thread. Work in duplicate stitch (N 6a) over first complete vertical row on right side of hole. Continue to work in duplicate stitch forming simple chain stitches over reenforced space. For run pick up stitches with a crochet hook (N 6b). Secure threads on wrong side and trim.

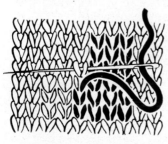

N6a

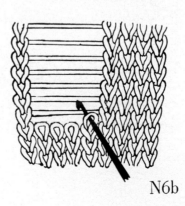

N6b

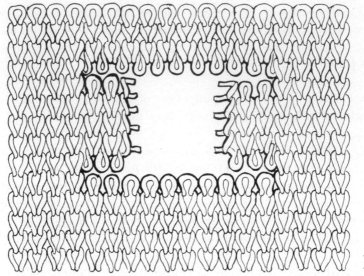

N7a

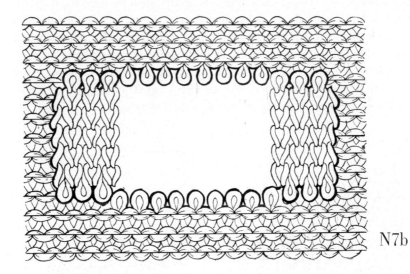

N7b

434

Weaving a Large Hole in Knitwear: Disengage stitches by unraveling all broken stitches to produce a square or rectangular space on the corners of which two or four loops are disengaged (N 7a). Turn stitches back on wrong side and blind hem (N 7b). Using a fine thread, pick up as in weaving, the horizontal stitches and one extra stitch on each side of the hole (N 7c). Fasten yarn on right side of hole, insert needle from wrong side of the work into the first disengaged loop under the two threads which come from the same stitch. Insert the needle in the same loop between the two diagonal threads and bring it out through the next stitch. Continue across row in this manner (N 7d). Be sure to keep newly formed stitches the same size as those in the article itself. Work back, reversing the method. Continue in this manner until the loops at the opposite end of the hole have been covered.

Machine Darning or Weaving: This is very simple and produces best results when the darning foot attachment is used to prevent work from rising with the needle. There are other attachments as a special darner made to fit the heel or toe of a stocking for hosiery repairs, and a flat darner for linens, towelling and dress fabrics. The same principle used in hand darning is applied in darning a straight tear, a three-cornered tear and a diagonal tear.

Darning to Reenforce: Cut a piece of fabric a little larger than worn portion. Baste to wrong side. Cover entire worn portion as for darning, weaving through both thicknesses of material.

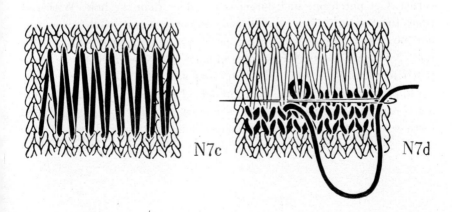

N7c   N7d

Patching

When the hole is large, it is best to patch. Always cut the hole into a square or rectangle, following the grain of the fabric. From a facing or underside of the hem, cut a patch ½ to 1½ inches larger on all sides than the hole. New washable materials should be washed to prevent shrinking after they are made. In print fabrics, be sure to match the figures and stripes accurately.

Simple Patch: From the wrong side, baste the raw edges of the hole over the patch. Then from right side, darn back and forth on each of the four sides, as for straight tear (N 1), thus crossing the stitches at corners for reenforcement. Catch-stitch (A 9) raw edges of patch to fabric on wrong side, taking care that the stitches do not show on right side.

Hemmed Patch: This is used for coarse, heavy fabrics. Cut a square or rectangular hole. Cut patch 1¼ inches larger on all sides than the hole. Clip about ¼ inch at each corner and turn raw edges under. From wrong side, baste patch in position over the hole (N 8a). From right side, hem the turned-under edges of the hole to the patch. Remove basting. Again on wrong side, hem the turned-under edges of the patch to the garment (N 8b).

Tailored Patch: The most satisfactory patch for a woolen or tweed material. Cut a square or rectangular hole. Clip about ¼ inch in at each corner. Cut patch one inch larger on all sides than the hole. With raw edges together lay patch on right side of garment and stitch across top, not too close to edge (N 9a). Turn patch to the wrong side through the hole (N 9b) and fold back raw edges of hole (N 9c). Seam each side of the patch to each of the remaining three sides of the hole. Using a damp cloth, press each seam open. On right side of garment with a fine matching thread and fine needle, draw each seam together using a back and forth weaving stitch. Again press, using a damp cloth on right side. Catch stitch (A 9) seams on wrong side if desired (N 9d).

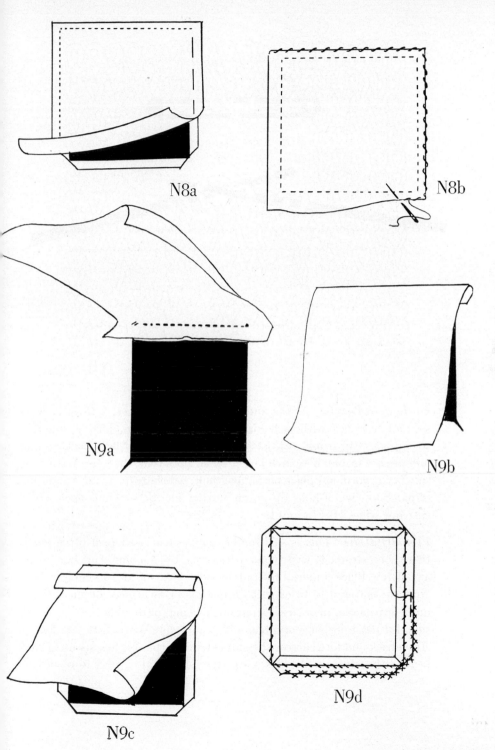

N8a

N8b

N9a

N9b

N9c

N9d

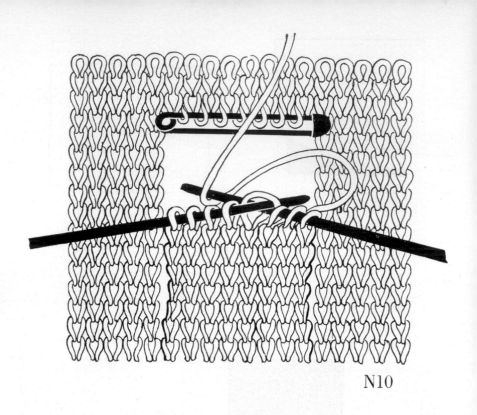

N10

Underarm Patch: At the underarm four seams meet. Cut away worn part into a square with each corner meeting at a seam. Turn garment to wrong side. Rip seams at least ½ inch. Turn edges of hole back ½ inch and press. Cut patch ½ inch larger on all sides than the hole. With right side facing garment, place patch over hole. Allowing for seam, baste edge of patch to edge of hole. Stitch on basting line. Press seams open. Overcast raw edges (B 21a and b).

Fitted Patch: This is satisfactory only when used in a place where there is no strain. It is stronger when done by machine. Cut hole as for any patch. Place material for patch under hole and draw shape of hole. Now cut material to fit exactly in the hole. Cut a piece of cheesecloth, mesh or paper an inch larger than the hole and baste over hole on wrong side. Fit patch in place and baste it to garment. With right side facing, stitch back and forth across the slit, extending the stitches about ¼ inch beyond the edges on all sides. Cross the stitches at corners to reenforce.

Remove the paper or net when patch is completed. If desired, merely trim edges of cheesecloth and do not cut away.

Knit Patch: Prepare as for weaving a large hole. Pick up stitches at bottom and knit a piece, matching the gauge and design of the garment itself to fit hole (N 10). Weave (F 20a and b) the stitches of the patch to the stitches at top of hole. Join sides of patch to sides of hole using a back and forth weaving stitch.

Mending Net or Lace: Weave horizontal threads as for ordinary darning; going back at least 3 meshes on each side to strengthen the edges (N 11a). Weave diagonally from upper right-hand corner to lower left-hand corner, going around the horizontal threads (N 11b). Weave diagonally from the upper left-hand corner to the lower right-hand corner in the same manner (N 11c).

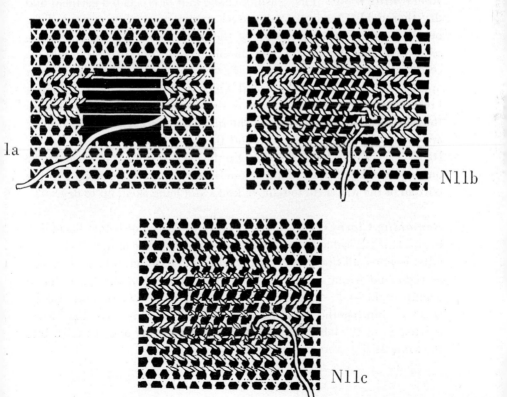

1a

N11b

N11c

439

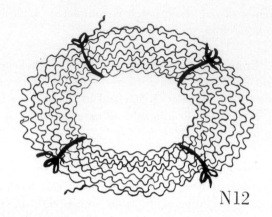

N12

Reclaiming Wool: First wash the hand knit or crocheted garment and dry thoroughly. Never try to unravel a sweater which is matted. Take out all seams, removing all ends of the sewing wool. Taking each piece separately, find the last stitch of the binding off. Pull it "free" and proceed to unravel the piece. When the stitches catch, gently ease them apart. Wind into skeins the strand which is being unraveled, around a bread board or large box, taking care that the end is visible. Tie securely the starting and finishing ends of the raveled piece. At 4 equal distances apart, tie contrasting thread around the strands of wool on the board. Remove wool from board (N 12). Dip the raveled skein into warm water until thoroughly soaked. Squeeze out excess water. Tie a weight to the bottom of the wet skein to remove kinks and hang skein up to dry.

Remaking Clothes: Wash or dry clean the garment before beginning to rip. It is advisable to cut the garment apart at the seams, if size permits. Remove all threads. Press material; mark straight of goods as well as right and wrong side of each section. Even when the fabric has a definite right and wrong side, it is possible to reverse it and still be effective. Pin together corresponding parts. This is to save time when cutting. Now the fabric is ready for the pattern. Lay and cut the fabric the same as if it were new material (Preface, pg 44).

Two Ways to Make Pompons: 1. Secure long strands of yarn between heavy pins. At regular intervals, wrap thread at least twice around strands and tie securely. Cut yarn between these threads (N 13). Roll between the palms of your hands and trim into a ball. 2. This method is more effective and takes more time. Cut out two discs the desired size and then cut a hole at least ¼ inch in center. Thread a blunt-end needle with two strands of yarn and cover the two discs (N 14a). When entire circumference of the cards is covered, slip the scissors between the two discs and cut all threads at the outside edge. Draw a thread between the two cards and wind several times very tightly around threads (N 14b). Fasten off with a firm knot, leaving ends long enough to attach ball to article. Snip the cards and remove. Trim ball (N 14c).

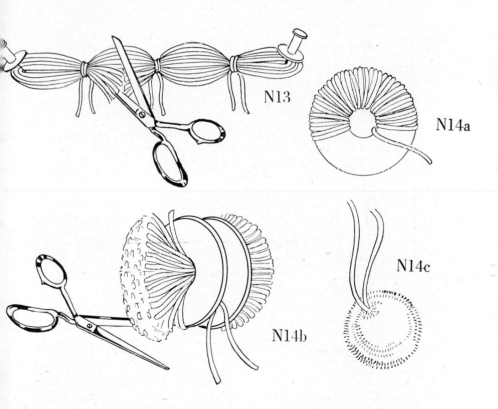

N13

N14a

N14b

N14c

Tassels: Cut a cardboard the desired length of tassel. Wrap thread around cardboard. Tie a thread around top strands, leaving ends for joining (N 15a). Cut bottom strands. Wrap thread several times about ¼ inch from top, tie and conceal ends in tassel (N 15b).

Fringe: Cut lengths of thread slightly more than twice the required length of the fringe. Take two or more strands, fold in half and with a crochet hook, draw the loop end through the foundation (N 16a). Then draw ends through the loop and pull tight (N 16b).

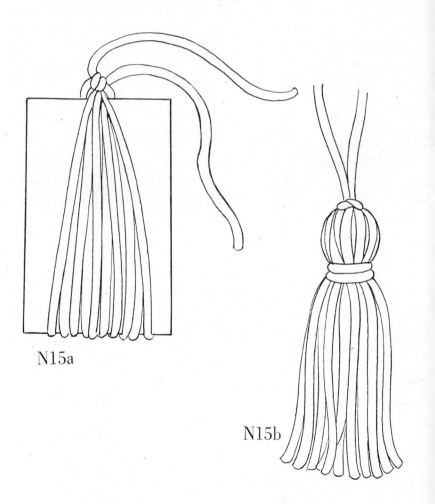

N15a

N15b

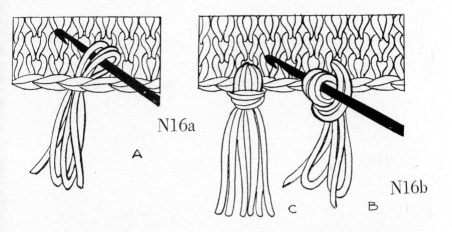

N16a

A

N16b

C   B

Cords: A simple way to make a cord is as follows: Calculate the length of the cord desired, then take three times this length of thread. An average cord is usually made of six strands of cotton or two strands of yarn. Tie a knot at each end. Insert a pencil in each loop. Twist pencils in opposite directions until the cord shows a tendency to curl (N 17). Hold the center and place the two pencils together. Allow the cord to twist of its own accord. Tie knotted ends together.

Monks Cord: Calculate the length of cord desired, then take nine times this length of thread. An average cord is made of at least two strands.

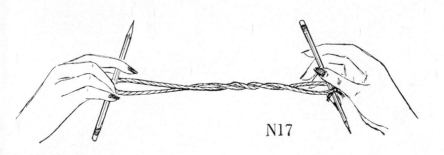

N17

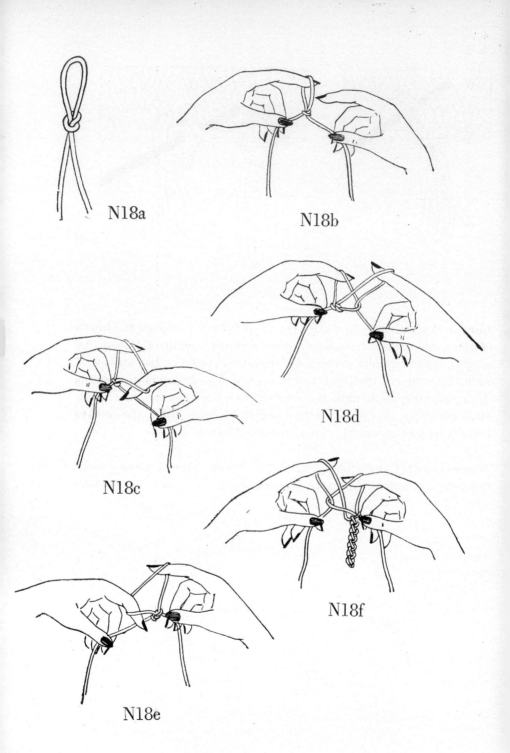

N18a

N18b

N18c

N18d

N18e

N18f

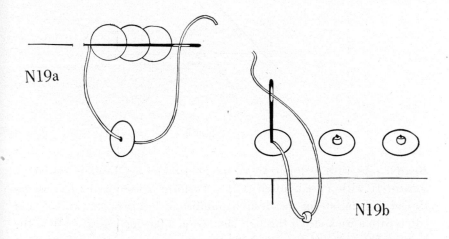

N19a

N19b

Fold in half and make a slip knot in center (N 18a). Slip this loop over forefinger of left hand (N 18b), holding knot between thumb and second finger. Note that the string that pulls easily is in the left hand and the string that does not pull is in the right hand. * Through this loop on left hand, draw a loop through the right strand with right forefinger (N 18c and d). Change knot to thumb and second finger of right hand and pull left strand tight. Through this loop on right hand, draw a loop through left strand with left forefinger (N 18e). Change knot to thumb and second finger of left hand and pull right strand tight. Repeat from *, alternating from side to side (N 18f). Pull strands through last loop and conceal in cord.

Sequins: To sew on single sequins, use a back-stitch (C 9) and sew on one at a time with right side up (N 19a). To sew on a sequin with bead center; bring needle up from the wrong side through the center of the sequin, thread it through head, then pass needle through center of sequin to wrong side again (N 19b). Carry thread along wrong side and bring it up through the center of the next sequin.

Nail Heads: Apply one at a time with several blows of a hammer and the aid of a small pressure gadget.

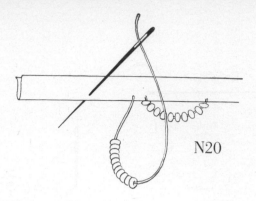

N20

Beads: As with sequins, in simple beading each bead is sewed on separately with a back-stitch (C 9). To form a festooned edge, secure thread in hem, string the desired number of beads on the thread and catch with a back-stitch through hem again, allowing less space than the length of the beaded thread (N 20).

A Simple Way to Copy a Design: Place tracing paper or tissue paper over original design and trace all lines. Baste this tracing onto right side of material. Through both the tracing paper and the material, make very small tacking stitches following the outline of the design, then pull or cut away tracing paper. This type of "tacked design" is especially effective for velvet and any materials with a rough nap.

Decorate with Ribbons: There is an art in the handling of ribbon which can be acquired by everyone. Here are a few geometric designs that are simple to apply (N 21e).

To Apply the First Design on a Crib Cover: 1. Determine the position of ribbon on cover and measure off as shown in N 21a. 2. Using the ⅝ inch wide ribbon, arrange the first ribbon, right side up as shown in N 21b; note where you start at one corner. Arrange the corner motifs by folding ribbon (N 21a to d); pin in place as you work. Continue around and back to the starting corner. N 21b shows how ribbon ends meet. Baste. 3. Using matching thread, catch long edges of ribbon to cover with tiny stitches. 4. Beginning at adjacent corner, arrange second ribbon over the first, slipping raw beginning end of second ribbon *under* the first ribbon as shown in N 21c. Continue around, always

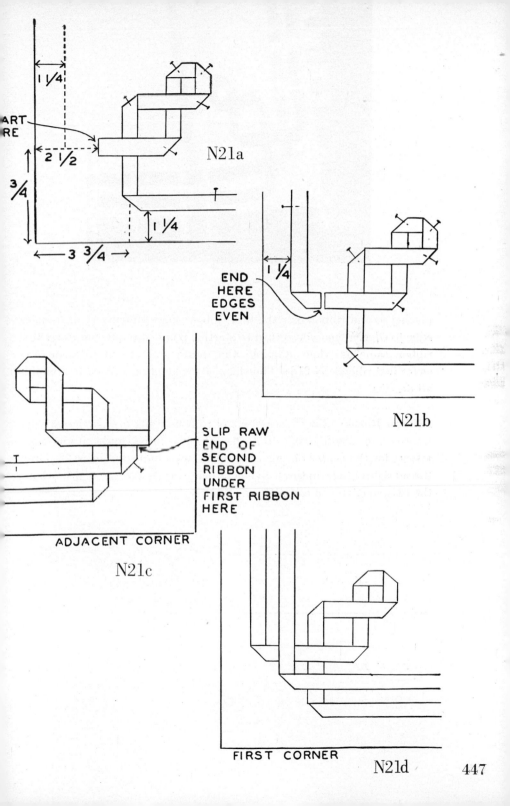

1 1/4

START
HERE

2 1/2

3/4

N21a

1 1/4

← 3 3/4 →

END
HERE
EDGES
EVEN

1 1/4

N21b

SLIP RAW
END OF
SECOND
RIBBON
UNDER
FIRST RIBBON
HERE

ADJACENT CORNER

N21c

FIRST CORNER

N21d

447

N21e

placing second ribbon *over* the first ribbon; space ribbons ½ inch apart, edge to edge. When you return to starting point, slip raw end *under* first ribbon same as when starting. Pin, baste and attach in same way as for first ribbon (N 21d). This detailed explanation will aid in applying all designs.

Ribbon Roses: Tiny roses made of ribbon or silk are particularly attractive and easy to make. If of silk, cut a bias piece, double it and make a twist for the center on one end, then sew as indicated in N 22. Draw thread tightly to form three, five or as many petals as desired, sew around the twisted center to complete the rose (N 22).

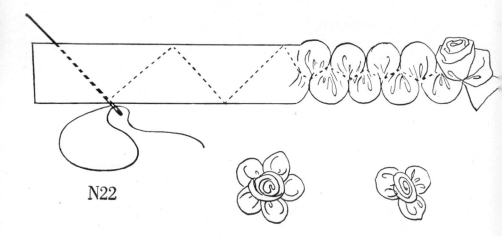

N22

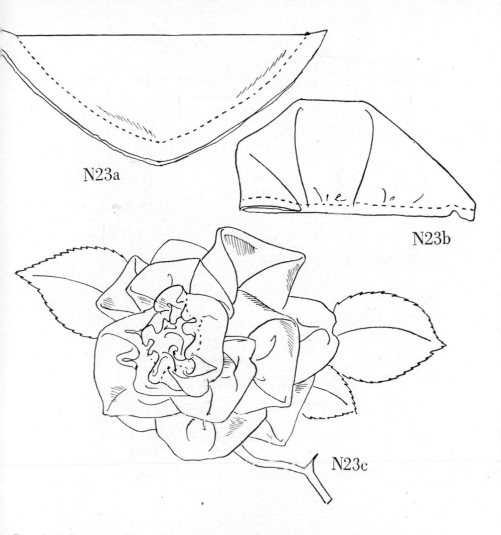

N23a

N23b

N23c

Petaled Roses: Cut a bias piece, double and sew along bottom in curve (N 23a) and gather. The "cupping" of the petal is gauged by the curve of the gathering at the bottom. A second and larger petal is made by folding a straight piece at right angles at the corner (N 23b) and finishing as explained for first petal. Use first petals for the center of the rose and the large petals for the outside (N 23c). Conceal the base of the rose or cover it with a piece of ribbon. These roses are most effective when used close together to hide the thick stem.

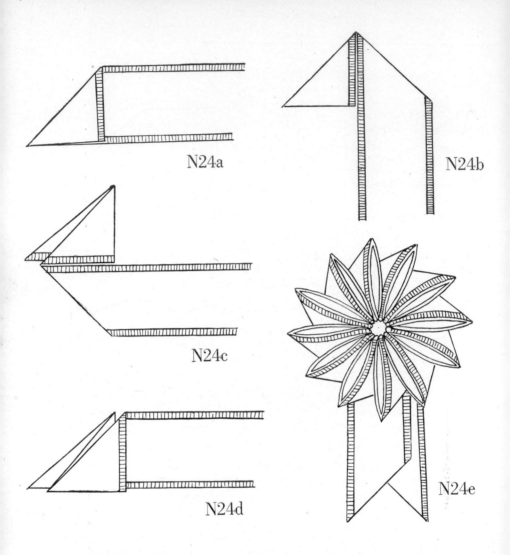

N24a

N24b

N24c

N24d

N24e

Ribbon Cocarde: Fold upper left end of ribbon at right angle to length of ribbon (N 24a). Fold length of ribbon to right angle, meeting first folded piece (N 24b). Fold this triangle in half, with free edges at right-hand side. Fold length of ribbon at right angle to lower edge (N 24c). Continue to fold (N 24d), forming triangles until desired size. If streamers are desired, form cocarde allowing about 5 inches at each end (N 24e).

Textile painting

Materials Required:
Textile colors
Extendor
Stencil brush
Stencil cutter, sharp knife or razor blade (in holder)
Stencil paper
White blotting paper
Scotch decorators tape

Directions
A. Wash cloth.
   1. If it is a washable material which you will want to wash after use, wash in warm soapy water to remove all sizing.
   2. Rinse thoroughly and press.
B. Cut the stencil.
   If it is a one-color stencil:
1. Draw or trace design on tracing paper allowing a 2-inch margin on all sides of design, cut at right angles to form a square or oblong piece.
2. Place tracing-paper design on stencil paper and trace design with hard pencil. (This transfers design to stencil paper, leaving an indented impression.) Be sure to place right angle markings on stencil to form a rectangular or square stencil same size as tracing paper design.
3. Cut the stencil along the depressed lines with a stencil cutter, sharp knife or razor blade (N 25a).
If it is a design of more than one color.
1. Follow Step 1 above, indicating which spaces are to be painted in different colors.
   Note: It is advisable to cut a separate stencil for each color.
2. Place carbon paper on second sheet of tracing paper and trace all parts of the design that are to be one color. Use the same size tracing paper for each color traced, keeping continuity of original design.
3. Place tracings together and hold to the light to be sure various parts of design fall into proper place.

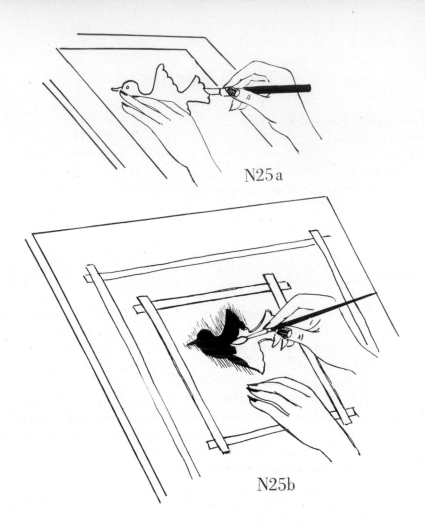

N25 a

N25b

4. Following Step 2 of one-color stencil, make a separate stencil for each color. Be sure to keep each stencil the same size.
5. Same as Step 3 of one-color stencil.

Note: When doing letters, it is necessary to break letters (as shown by dotted lines in N 27 and N 28) and make stencil in two parts to prevent' encircled areas from dropping out. Figure this out carefully before cutting stencil. Make edges of break overlap slightly (⅛ inch) to be sure of getting a continuous line.

C. Mix the colors.

1. Stir colors and extendor before using.
2. Mix desired color.
3. To bring color to proper consistency for stencilling, add extendor. It makes the color go farther and makes it easier to work with. It should be about the consistency of thick cream.
   a. To make color lighter, add extendor until desired hue is obtained.
   b. If a very light tint is desired, start with extendor and add color—it saves color.
   c. To make a color darker, add black (a little goes a long way).

D. Apply the colors.

1. Always use a white blotter under fabric.
2. Stretch the cloth smoothly and fasten to a drawing board or heavy cardboard with tape or thumb tacks.
3. Place the stencil in position and fasten with tape or thumb tacks.
   a. If you are using several stencils for different colors, put two pieces of tape or pins at right angles where the upper left corner of each stencil paper falls.
   b. If you are using several colors, some of which overlap, use lightest color first and end with darkest.
4. Work the color into the brush, then stroke across a cloth or paper to remove excess color. Remember—all you need is a very little color on your brush.
5. Allow your brush to hit the stencil about ½″ from the opening and sweep across the opening toward the center. Use a firm stroke. Repeat the stroke until you have the desired color (N 25b).
6. If the color begins to thicken, add a little penetrator or thinner.

E. Dry thoroughly.

Allow finished work to dry for 24 hours.

F. "Set" with hot iron.

1. After the colors dry, place a dry cloth over the design, face up, and press with a hot iron (350° F.) for at least 3 minutes. For rayon use 220° for a longer period.
2. Turn material over and press the back in the same way.
3. Then steam press if desired.

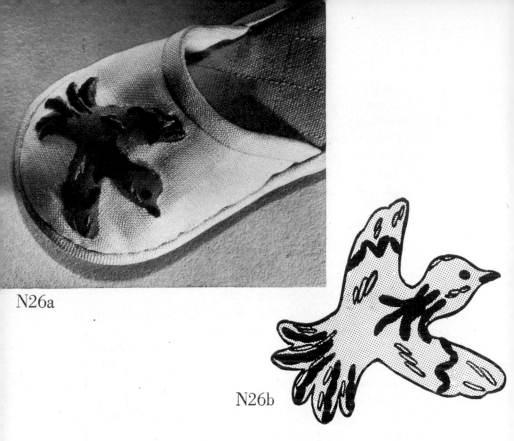

N26a

N26b

Textile Painted Scuffs: 1. Cut top of slipper from a pattern or old slipper. 2. Cut stencil of pigeon (N 26a and b). 3. With textile paints apply pigeon design to linen (instructions, pg 451). 4. Baste cheese cloth to wrong side of linen and pack with cotton batting as explained for trapunto quilting (E 8c). 5. Give animation to the pigeon with outline stitch (C 4).

Application and Use of Graph and Line Charts:
A. *Any graph chart can be used:* For cross stitch (Color Plate G, charts Gn and o); for Assisi embroidery (D 21); for knitting (Color Plate F, chart Fj and F 76); especially Fair-Isle designs (F 38c and F 39d) and duplicate stitch (F 1a to d); for crocheting (Color Plate G, charts Gn and Go); for needlepoint (Color Plate J, charts Jj to n and J 14 to 24); for crocheted rugs (K 18a and b) and needlepoint rugs (K 19); for weaving (L 10b to L 14b).

N27

N27

a b c d e f g

h i j k l m

n o p q r s t

u v w x y z

N28

457

For example:

1. Use chart of prancing ducks from crocheted rug (K 18a) to embroider one, two or three ducks on child's sweater in duplicate stitch (F 1a to d).
2. Use chart of butterflies of crocheted afghan (Color Plate G) for tea cloth using embroidery cotton on linen.
3. Use charts of alphabet and figures of needlepoint hassock (Color Plate J) to cross stitch (C 37) names, monograms and designs on children's dresses, bibs, sweaters, mittens, pinafores, crib covers, etc.

Note: In monogramming or embroidering names, if letters different in size are preferred scale each letter to size (pg 339) individually and use as desired (N 29).

B. *Any line chart can be used:* For simple embroidery (Color Plate C; charts Cg and Ch); for advanced embroidery (Color Plate D; chart Dj); for appliqué, quilting and tufting (Color Plate E, charts Ek to Em); for hooking rugs (Color Plate K, chart Kj); for machine-embroidery (Color Plate N, charts Ni); for textile painting (Charts N 26 to N 29)

For example:

1. Scale to size (p 339) and use chart of embroidered pictures (Cg) for hooked rug (Color Plate K).
2. Scale and use chart for quilted spread (Ek) for embroidered cloth in stem stitch (C 4).
3. Use alphabet from textile painting (Charts N 27 and 28) for monogramming in satin stitch (C 39 to 43).

C. Apply any cross stitch chart for a line chart, and vice-versa.

For example:

1. Take cross stitch chart for duck (Jn) and outline design (N 30) for simple embroidery—do not follow the straight lines of the graph.
2. Trace line chart of pigeon (N 26b) on graph paper and fill squares between the double lines with crosses (N 31).

N29

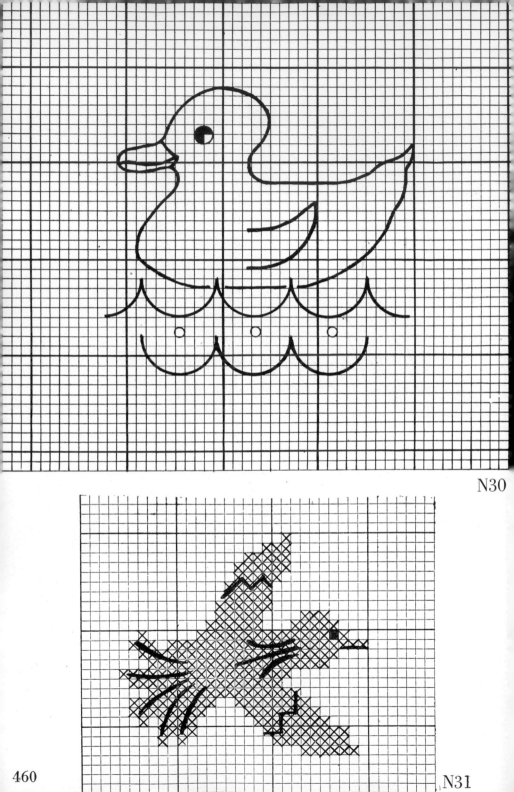

FOR YOUR OWN CHART DESIGNS

It's fun to design your own motifs and easy when you can scale the motifs to the desired size. Select the size graph paper that has the same number of stitches per inch as your knit or crocheted piece or that has the same number of squares per inch as your canvas, and block out your own creation.

1. These tiny squares are most suitable for petit point and weaving motifs.

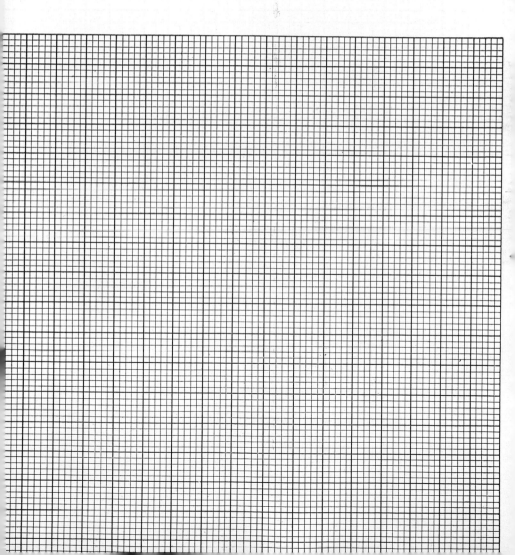

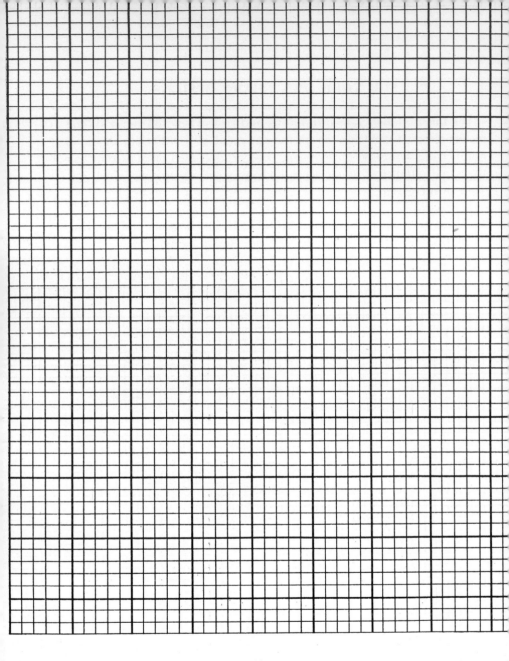

2. Use this size for your gros point, Florentine or cross stitch designs.

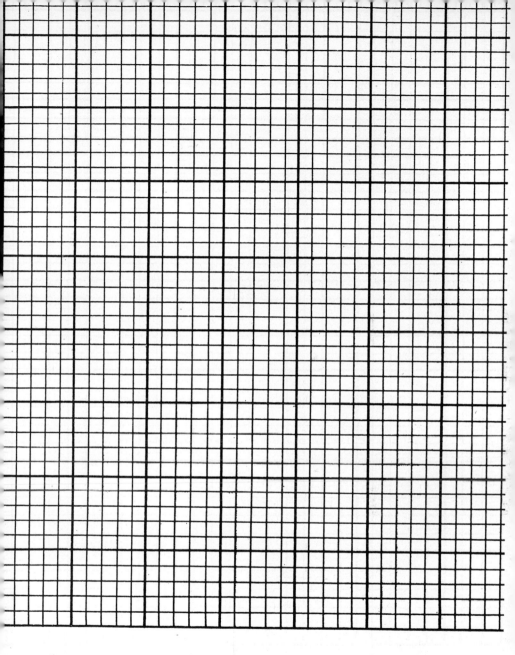

3. Block out Fair Isle and afghan motifs here—check your stitch gauge.

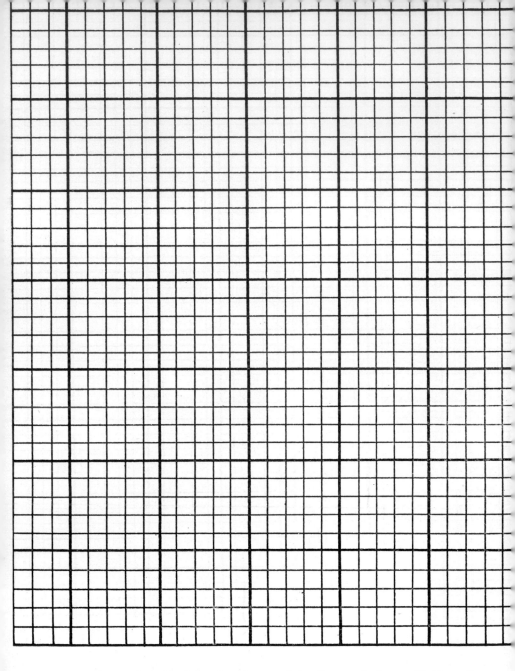

4. Cross stitch, Assisi embroidery and duplicate stitch are effective when
   scaled to this size.

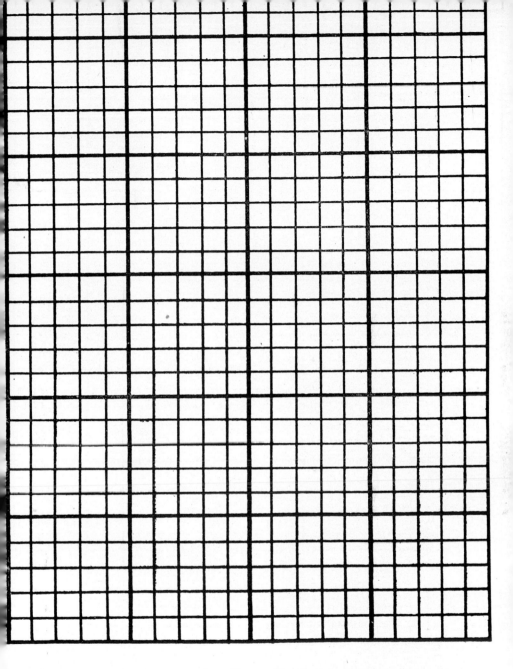

5. Start your rug design (crocheted or needlepoint) here, then rule paper
   to this size for the entire rug.

INDEX

with embroidery, 134–137, 454

477